Exploring
Ethics

Selected Readings

 Christian Schools International
Grand Rapids, Michigan

CHRISTIAN SCHOOLS INTERNATIONAL
3350 East Paris Ave., S.E.
Grand Rapids, Michigan 49512

© 1992 CHRISTIAN SCHOOLS INTERNATIONAL
Printed in the United States of America

10 9 8 7 6 5 4 3

ISBN 0-87463-880-1

The development of *Exploring Ethics: Selected Readings* was made possible with grants from Christian Schools International Foundation and Canadian Christian Education Foundation, Inc. Cover design by Judy Zylstra.

Table of Contents

Foreword

How should a person live his or her life? More specifically, what norms for ethical behavior should a Christian follow? What is morality? How should we make moral decisions? And what implications does a Christian system of ethics have on major issues in society today? These are questions that many Christians have wrestled with, and this book includes some of the answers that have been suggested.

The readings in this collection are divided into three main parts. The first section defines ethics, creating a context for the rest of the book. The second section raises the issue of decision making—how to make moral choices. The third section considers some significant issues being debated in our world. The pieces in this section deal with work, human sexuality, the environment, wealth and poverty, racism, medical ethics, and peacemaking.

Some of the readings in this book were originally written as articles; others appeared in full-length books. The readings were selected to give a broad cross section of views on these important and challenging topics. Each reading is introduced by a short section introducing the author. After each reading is a list of questions to help you review the author's main ideas and to consider and evaluate the author's point of view.

The selection of readings was made by the editorial staff at Christian Schools International; Hazel Timmer was the general editor for the project.

It is our hope that the readings in this book will help you come to a better understanding of morality and will help you make a commitment to follow Christ in every part of your life.

1
Defining Morality

The Three Parts
of Morality

C.S. Lewis

*C.S. Lewis was one of the most influential Christian writers
and thinkers of this century. His book* Mere Christianity *is
a defense of the essentials of the Christian faith. This selection is taken from that book. Here Lewis shows how moral
rules are necessary for living. He points out three areas with
which morality is concerned: relations between individuals,
things inside the individual, and relations between humans
and God.*

There is a story about a schoolboy who was asked what he
thought God was like. He replied that, as far as he could make
out, God was "The sort of person who is always snooping
round to see if anyone is enjoying himself and then trying to
stop it." And I am afraid that is the sort of idea that the word
Morality raises in a good many people's minds: something
that interferes, something that stops you having a good time.
In reality, moral rules are directions for running the human
machine. Every moral rule is there to prevent a breakdown, or
a strain, or a friction, in the running of that machine. That is
why these rules at first seem to be constantly interfering with
our natural inclinations. When you are being taught how to
use any machine, the instructor keeps on saying, "No, don't do
it like that," because, of course, there are all sorts of things that
look all right and seem to you the natural way of treating the
machine, but do not really work.

Some people prefer to talk about moral "ideals" rather
than moral rules and about moral "idealism" rather than
moral obedience. Now it is, of course, quite true that moral
perfection is an "ideal" in the sense that we cannot achieve it.

In that sense every kind of perfection is, for us humans, an ideal; we cannot succeed in being perfect car drivers or perfect tennis players or in drawing perfectly straight lines. But there is another sense in which it is very misleading to call moral perfection an ideal. When a man says that a certain woman, or house, or ship, or garden is "his ideal" he does not mean (unless he is rather a fool) that everyone else ought to have the same ideal. In such matters we are entitled to have different tastes and, therefore, different ideals. But it is dangerous to describe a man who tries very hard to keep the moral law as a "man of high ideals," because this might lead you to think that moral perfection was a private taste of his own and that the rest of us were not called on to share it. This would be a disastrous mistake. Perfect behaviour may be as unattainable as perfect gear-changing when we drive; but it is a necessary ideal prescribed for all men by the very nature of the human machine just as perfect gear-changing is an ideal prescribed for all drivers by the very nature of cars. And it would be even more dangerous to think of oneself as a person "of high ideals" because one is trying to tell no lies at all (instead of only a few lies) or never to commit adultery (instead of committing it only seldom) or not to be a bully (instead of being only a moderate bully). It might lead you to become a prig and to think you were rather a special person who deserved to be congratulated on his "idealism." In reality you might just as well expect to be congratulated because, whenever you do a sum, you try to get it quite right. To be sure, perfect arithmetic is "an ideal"; you will certainly make some mistakes in some calculations. But there is nothing very fine about trying to be quite accurate at each step in each sum. It would be idiotic not to try; for every mistake is going to cause you trouble later on. In the same way every moral failure is going to cause trouble, probably to others and certainly to yourself. By talking about rules and obedience instead of "ideals" and "idealism" we help to remind ourselves of these facts.

Now let us go a step further. There are two ways in which the human machine goes wrong. One is when human individuals drift apart from one another, or else collide with one another and do one another damage, by cheating or bullying. The other is when things go wrong inside the individual—when the different parts of him (his different faculties and desires and so on) either drift apart or interfere with one another. You can get the idea plain if you think of us as a fleet of ships sailing in formation. The voyage will be a success only, in the first place, if the ships do not collide and get in one another's way; and, secondly, if each ship is seaworthy and has her engines in good order. As a matter of fact, you cannot have either of these two things without the other. If the ships keep on having collisions they will not remain seaworthy very long. On the other hand, if their steering gears are out of order they will not be able to avoid collisions. Or, if you like, think of humanity as a band playing a tune. To get a good result, you need two things. Each player's individual instrument must be in tune and also each must come in at the right moment so as to combine with all the others.

But there is one thing we have not yet taken into account. We have not asked where the fleet is trying to get to, or what piece of music the band is trying to play. The instruments might be all in tune and might all come in at the right moment, but even so the performance would not be a success if they had been engaged to provide dance music and actually played nothing but Dead Marches. And however well the fleet sailed, its voyage would be a failure if it were meant to reach New York and actually arrived at Calcutta.

Morality, then, seems to be concerned with three things. Firstly, with fair play and harmony between individuals. Secondly, with what might be called tidying up or harmonising the things inside each individual. Thirdly, with the general purpose of human life as a whole: what man was made for: what course the whole fleet ought to be on: what tune the conductor of the band wants it to play.

You may have noticed that modern people are nearly always thinking about the first thing and forgetting the other two. When people say in the newspapers that we are striving for Christian moral standards, they usually mean that we are

striving for kindness and fair play between nations, and classes, and individuals; that is, they are thinking only of the first
thing. When a man says about something he wants to do, "It
can't be wrong because it doesn't do anyone else any harm,"
he is thinking only of the first thing. He is thinking it does not
matter what his ship is like inside provided that he does not
run into the next ship. And it is quite natural, when we start
thinking about morality, to begin with the first thing, with
social relations. For one thing, the results of bad morality in
that sphere are so obvious and press on us every day: war and
poverty and graft and lies and shoddy work. And also, as long
as you stick to the first thing, there is very little disagreement
about morality. Almost all people at all times have agreed (in
theory) that human beings ought to be honest and kind and
helpful to one another. But though it is natural to begin with
all that, if our thinking about morality stops there, we might
just as well not have thought at all. Unless we go on to the second thing—the tidying up inside each human being—we are
only deceiving ourselves.

What is the good of telling the ships how to steer so as to
avoid collisions if, in fact, they are such crazy old tubs that
they cannot be steered at all? What is the good of drawing up,
on paper, rules for social behaviour, if we know that, in fact,
our greed, cowardice, ill temper, and self-conceit are going to
prevent us from keeping them? I do not mean for a moment
that we ought not to think, and think hard, about improve-
ments in our social and economic system. What I do mean is
that all that thinking will be mere moonshine unless we realise
that nothing but the courage and unselfishness of individuals
is ever going to make any system work properly. It is easy
enough to remove the particular kinds of graft or bullying that
go on under the present system: but as long as men are
twisters or bullies they will find some new way of carrying on
the old game under the new system. You cannot make men
good by law: and without good men you cannot have a good
society. That is why we must go on to think of the second
thing: of morality inside the individual.

But I do not think we can stop there either. We are now getting to the point at which different beliefs about the universe lead to different behaviour. And it would seem, at first sight, very sensible to stop before we got there, and just carry on with those parts of morality that all sensible people agree about. But can we? Remember that religion involves a series of statements about facts, which must be either true or false. If they are true, one set of conclusions will follow about the right sailing of the human fleet: if they are false, quite a different set. For example, let us go back to the man who says that a thing cannot be wrong unless it hurts some other human being. He quite understands that he must not damage the other ships in the convoy, but he honestly thinks that what he does to his own ship is simply his own business. But does it not make a great difference whether his ship is his own property or not? Does it not make a great difference whether I am, so to speak, the landlord of my own mind and body, or only a tenant, responsible to the real landlord? If somebody else made me, for his own purposes, then I shall have a lot of duties which I should not have if I simply belonged to myself.

Again, Christianity asserts that every individual human being is going to live for ever, and this must be either true or false. Now there are a good many things which would not be worth bothering about if I were going to live only seventy years, but which I had better bother about very seriously if I am going to live for ever. Perhaps my bad temper or my jealousy are gradually getting worse—so gradually that the increase in seventy years will not be very noticeable. But it might be absolute hell in a million years: in fact, if Christianity is true, Hell is the precisely correct technical term for what it would be. And immortality makes this other difference, which, by the by, has a connection with the difference between totalitarianism and democracy. If individuals live only seventy years, then a state, or a nation, or a civilisation, which may last for a thousand years, is more important than an individual. But if Christianity is true, then the individual is not only more important but incomparably more important, for he is everlasting and the life of a state or a civilisation, compared with his, is only a moment.

It seems, then, that if we are to think about morality, we must think of all three departments: relations between man and man: things inside each man: and relations between man and the power that made him. We can all co-operate in the first one. Disagreements begin with the second and become serious with the third. It is in dealing with the third that the main differences between Christian and non-Christian morality come out.

Questions

1. What are the three parts of morality? What analogies does Lewis use to describe how they work together? Do those analogies help you to gain a clearer understanding of morality? What other analogies might he have used?

2. Why is it important to consider the subject of morality in an individual's life?

3. After reading this essay, how would you respond when you hear someone say, "It can't be wrong because it doesn't do anyone else any harm"?

Commands for Fiddlers

Lewis B. Smedes

Lewis B. Smedes is a theologian who has written many books answering tough ethical questions. This selection is from his book Mere Morality, *in which he discusses the essential elements of morality for all humanity. In this selection Smedes lays out four reasons why the Ten Commandments are specifically designed to be absolute moral rules for all of God's creatures and creation.*

He is a little man in a long green coat and a cocked hat, standing with one leg on a steep roof, playing the fiddle. He is all of us, trying to make some meaningful music out of our lives but lacking a level place to stand on. "We are all fiddlers on the roof, trying to scratch out a pleasant little tune without falling down and breaking our necks." And how do we keep our balance? "I'll tell you," sings Tevye in the opening song of the musical inspired by Chagall's painting, "in one word, I'll tell you, tradition! Because of our tradition, everybody knows who he is and what God expects him to do."

To know in advance what God expects us to do—before a new wind threatens to blow us off the roof, before a new crisis shakes our foundations—would be a great gift! Is it possible? Are there signals from God—directions, norms, rules, commandments ? . . .

Is there any help for us fiddlers as we try to scratch out our individual tunes without falling off the roof?

We are talking about God's will for the stubborn and haunting presence in our lives that we call moral, the sense that keeps us wondering whether we are in the *right* or the wrong with our own conscience or with some standard that outranks even conscience. To ask what God expects us to do is to ask how we can know whether we are doing the *right* thing. This question flits about the edges of our minds even after we have earned a dollar or two, felt beautiful feelings, and created exciting relationships.

It is a truism today that we are in a crisis of morals. The crisis is not simply that people are doing wrong things; that has been going on since the Fall in Eden. The crisis is the loss of a shared understanding of what is right. Worse, it is a crisis of doubt as to whether there even is a moral right or wrong at all. The most obvious and sensational evidence of the crisis is in sex and marriage, but it reaches almost every other arena of life as well. Can anyone know any more "who he is and what God expects him to do"?

The Jewish people of Anatevka knew what God expected of them because they knew their traditions. Christian believers today are not as certain that their ethnic or religious traditions serve as signposts to God's will. For some, this ambivalence may come from having neglected their own tradition. But they also recall how often Jesus opposed Jewish traditions. "Why don't your disciples follow the traditional rules?" the Pharisees asked him, certain that tradition told them what God expected of them. Jesus threw the challenge back. They had lost track of God's will: "You leave the commandments of God and hold fast the tradition of men" (Mark 7:8). Paul, though shaped by Jewish tradition, came to hate the rules and regulations of all traditions, and he cringed when Christian believers kowtowed to them: "Why do you submit to regulations . . . human precepts and doctrines?"—in other words, tradition— he demanded (Col. 2:20, 22).

But if the New Testament makes us wary of tradition as the way to know what God expects us to do, how do we know and where do we look for God's will? Does the answer come in the wind, which "blows where it wills, and you hear the sound of it, but you do not know where it comes from or where it is going" (John 3:8)? Does God speak to each of us privately through the intimations of the spirit, heart to heart, mind to mind, divine Word direct to human soul? Must each of us go it alone while waiting for the voice of the Lord?

No, says the sage of Ecclesiastes, it is neither tradition nor private revelation which tells you how to find out what God expects you to do. I will give you the answer in one word: "Let us hear the conclusion of the whole matter: Fear God, and keep his *commandments*; for this is the whole duty of man" (Eccl. 12:13). The direct word from the commanding Lord answers the challenge of keeping one's balance while playing the fiddle on the steep slopes of this risky life. "Then shall I not fall and break my neck, when I have respect unto all thy commandments" (Ps. 119:6). If Tevye had been a biblical Hebrew instead of a modern Russian Jew, he too would have said: the commandments, the Torah, the law of God! And Jesus would agree, for when a rich young ruler asked him what he should do, Jesus did not say "Consult your tradition," but "You know the commandments" (Mark 10:19; Luke 18:20).

To read through the first five books of the Old Testament is almost to be washed away in a cascade of commands covering an enormous variety of human situations which might arise within the ancient community of Israel. There are commandments for settling civil conflicts, regulating cultic customs, and guiding the moral lives of the people who were brought together in a covenant they made with the Lord God at the foot of Mt. Sinai. The religious and moral nucleus of these is the "decalogue," the Ten Commandments.

We are told that God wrote the Ten Commandments with his own finger on two tablets of stone at the top of the mountain. A cloud covering the mountain marked it as a holy place, which the people, encamped around it, were not to touch. God called Moses to the top of the mountain. He went up and came down several times; we cannot keep track of all his meetings with God at the summit. But each time Moses came down, he brought more commandments for the life of the covenant people. And each time the people covenanted to live by them: "All that the Lord has spoken we will do."

Among the many words Moses carried from God was the code of the covenant for the myriad of ordinary affairs in

Israelite life. Its wording resembled the legal codes of other peoples in the area—the Hittites and Assyrians, for example. There is perhaps one crucial difference in content. Property is of the essence in other Mesopotamian legal codes; almost every loss, including a human life, can be compensated by a property settlement. In God's code human beings are of the essence. They alone are God's image, and they cannot be replaced with material things. The difference can be seen in the fact that capital punishment is never required by Moses' law for a violation against property, though it is for the violation of human beings.

After Moses' rage against the people's impatient lapse into idolatry led him to shatter the first edition of the Ten Commandments, he went up into the mountain for the last time. There he stayed with God for forty days, eating no bread and drinking no water. During those days God gave him the foundational commandments, the ten words which became the sum and substance of all that God expects his children to do. Moses returned to the people, his face so radiant with the reflection of God's presence that the people could not look at him. And they accepted the words as the way of life for a people of God.

Thus, a God no one can see and a multitude of recently liberated slaves enter into a covenant, a treaty between a Superior and a subordinate in which the inferior swears to do all that the Superior expects him to do. It is in this covenant setting that we still may find the small capsule of commands which we recognize as the substance of moral duty, not for Israel alone, but for all who belong to the human family.

The decalogue is recorded with slight variations in Exodus 20 and Deuteronomy 5. Many scholars believe that both versions have their origin in a simpler, shorter form that might have gone something like this:

These are the words of Yahweh.
I am the Lord who brought you from Egypt.
You shall have no gods besides me.
You shall not make yourself a graven image.

You shall not take the name of Yahweh in vain.
Remember the Sabbath day.
Honor your father and mother.
You shall not kill.
You shall not commit adultery.
You shall not steal.
You shall not bear false witness.
You shall not covet.

There is much we do not know about the story of the decalogue. We do not know, for instance, exactly how it came to take the different forms we find in Deuteronomy 5 and Exodus 20. But we are certain that the covenant people originally received these commandments from Moses' hands at Mount Sinai. We know that they formed the heart of Hebrew life and worship ever after, the standard by which the life of the people was judged. The massive indictments that later prophets like Isaiah and Amos brought against the people centered on the failure to live up to what the decalogue required. And when Jesus came to fulfil the law, he fulfilled this law, the law of the Ten Commandments. When he set the law anew on its foundations of love, it was the decalogue that he restored to its place. All of Judaeo-Christian morality is lodged within a covenant made by the Savior God, who wills that we should be just to each other and love one another, and who gives his commandments to show us how.

Our task is to find out what the commandments for this ancient covenant tell us about the will of God today. If God gave us new commandments in each new situation, speaking directly to each of us, we would not have to consult the ancient words. As it is, we read his commandments as they were spoken to other people—people with customs and a language strange to ours, people who never wondered whether it is right or wrong before God to remove an irreversibly brain-damaged person from a respirator. So the question of this book will be: can the ancient commandments tell us, in our time and our place, what God expects us to do?

Before going on, I should specify some limits to the claims we can make for the commandments. For one thing, I do not mean that God speaks his moral will only through the "Thou shalt's" and "Thou shalt not's" of the Bible. The Bible has many styles and many methods for telling us what God expects us to do. Moreover, the Bible is not the only place that God speaks his will. The community of faith may discern the will of God in the silences and storms of its own life, and it may hear the voice of God in the cries of the hungry children of our world.

But I am going to the commandments because, of all the places where God's voice may be heard, they speak it most urgently and clearly. Where else does God confront people as urgently as in his undebatable "Thou shalt"? Where does he preempt people's freedom to do wrong as clearly as when he utters his "Thou shalt not"? Never mind, for the moment, that he spoke his "Thou shalt's" and "Thou shalt not's" long ago. The fact is that he did speak them, and biblical faith holds that in speaking them to others, he somehow spoke them to us. There they are in print, the commandments of God—not the only way, but the one way that no one can ignore. How can we take these clear commands into the confusing dilemmas of contemporary life and hear what God wants us to do there, at the borderline of ignorance, where the wisest and best of persons dare not claim to know what they ought to do?

Second, I do not mean to say that *all* the commandments in the Bible tell us what God wants us to do. Anyone with a shred of moral sensitivity will recognize that some commandments recorded in the Bible are not the voice of God telling us what we ought to do. God is not telling today's parents to have their rebel children executed (Deut. 21:18f.) or today's city fathers to kill someone caught in adultery (Deut. 22:22). And we have learned—insufferably late in time—that God is not still commanding slaves to obey their masters with all honor (1 Tim. 6:1). Many today are not sure whether the Lord commands women everywhere to subject themselves to their husbands (Eph. 5:24). But can anyone doubt that, in saying "Thou shalt not kill" to the Hebrew people, God said it to all people? . . .

Finally, I do not mean to suggest that all we need in order to know God's will is a book of commandments, indexed to help us find the one that applies. The divine commandments are not the blueprint for a morally ordered life, with specifications for every nook and cranny in it. We must not suppose that the Bible gives regulations to fit every situation, and that if a rule does not fit our situation, we can lop off the bothersome corners of reality to make the situation fit our rule. A morality guided by biblical commandments is not necessarily legalism. The commandments in the Bible give us more to go on than loving hunches and benevolent intuitions, but they do not offer a detailed and up-to-date road map.

. . . What sort of thing are these ancient commandments, that modern believers should listen to them as if God is still speaking through them? Let me propose some descriptions of the biblical commandments which, if true, qualify them to be commands for us.

1. *The commandments fit life's design.* . . . Is there a creative Mind who wills human life to develop and grow within certain patterns and toward a purposed goal? . . . I am not talking about a kind of fate, as if each of us is born with a moral script imprinted on our genes. I am asking about a personal will which an intelligent Creator has for rational creatures, a design to which he would have us adapt our choices but which we are free to ignore or deny if we choose. Is there a way in which we ought to walk? . . .

All I mean to say here is that if the ancient commandments are still commandments for us, there must be a stable, abiding order for life which they match.

2. *The commandments tell us all what God expects us to do.* When the Lord God commanded specific people in biblical times to do this or not to do that, he usually left no doubt about whom he was talking to or what he expected them to do. His word was direct, specific, and clear. The only question left over once the command was given was that of obedience: would the persons addressed do what they were commanded

to do? In this sense, the commands are not like abiding laws laid down for all time and all places.

If God's ancient commands tell all people everywhere what he expects them to do, those commands must somehow embody an abiding law of human life. If the "Thou shalt" aimed at a very specific person in past time is also directed to human beings of all time, it must have told that one person to do what everyone ought to do. Something about that person's life-situation and very being must have made God's commandment just the right thing for him to do, not just as an ancient Hebrew but as a human being. . . .

At least some of the biblical commandments, therefore, are both direct commands and abiding laws. Perhaps an example can show how a specific command can carry a universal law. A father tells his son: "Tom, bring the car home by 11:00 tonight." Here is a command meant only for Tom, about one car, and on one night. There is no abiding law here. But at breakfast the next day, Tom's father says: "Tom, tell me the truth about why you didn't come home until 1:00 this morning." This second command is also personal, directed to Tom, about one car and one morning. But this command invokes an abiding law. Tom ought to tell the truth because, in human communication, truthfulness is a law of life.

It seems clear that the Ten Commandments convey duties for everyone, though they were aimed at specific persons and were to be obeyed simply because it was the Lord God who commanded. "Thou shalt" can be translated "Everyone ought." What must be obeyed because of God's authority ought also to be obeyed because what he commands matches what we are and what we are meant to be. The commander is the Creator; what he expects all of us to do fits what he created us to be. This is what I mean by an abiding moral law of life.

But if some of the Bible's commands convey abiding laws, others certainly do not. God's dreadful word to Abraham does not carry an abiding law: "Take your son, your only son Isaac, whom you love, and go to the land of Moriah, and offer him there as a burnt offering upon one of the mountains" (Gen.

22:2). What God commanded Abraham to do at that moment is something any reasonable father would consider insane. No one is likely to believe that this command tells all fathers what to do with their sons. . . .

3. *The commandments tell us to do what we already know we should do.* When Moses announced God's moral expectations for the covenant community, he did not stun the crowd with novelties. No Israelite could have been the least bit surprised to hear that God was against stealing and lying. What Moses brought from Sinai endorsed a morality that was endemic to the human race, affirmed in conscience as much as it was violated in practice. People who know little and care less about what the Bible tells us to do tend nevertheless to know in spite of themselves what the Bible actually requires in the moral life. Paul assumed that, as far as morality was concerned, people who never heard of God's commands were somehow familiar with his will:

> When Gentiles who have not the law do by nature what the law requires, they are a law to themselves, even though they do not have the law. They show that what the law requires is written on their hearts, while their conscience also bears witness and their conflicting thoughts accuse or perhaps excuse them on that day when, according to my gospel, God judges the secrets of men by Christ Jesus (Rom. 2:14-16).

. . . Even if they did poorly, they *knew* better.

. . . If you do not experience God as Savior, you will not know that he gave his commandments as pointers to a truly human life within the love of Christ. But you *can* know the sheer moral content of the law. You *can* know that God says No to certain things, and you can know it because your own conscience says No to them. And when you do those things anyway, you can claim neither that God was unreasonable nor that you were ignorant.

4. *The commandments are the way of life in Christ.* Having insisted that the Bible's basic commandments are guidelines

for a basic human life-style, I must add that they are the commandments of the Lord of saving mercy. From the beginning at Sinai they were clearly identified as the will of the Redeemer for the survival of the redeemed community: "I am the Lord your God, who brought you out of the land of Egypt." The commandments came *after* liberation; they pointed to a life of freedom within the covenant. This is why the Psalmist is continually singing love songs to the law (cf. Ps. 119:97). But remember that the covenant community was the first seedling of the renewed human family tree.

If we remember that the commandments to his special covenant community were God's guides for the human community, we can understand Jesus' attitude toward them, and Paul's as well. Jesus, to be sure, was not a moralist; he was a Savior. He did not come like Moses with a set of commands; he came with grace and truth (John 1:17). But he was not an enemy of Moses nor of his commandments, though he vigorously opposed a religious system that twisted them into prescriptions for gaining status with the Creator. As to the commandments themselves, he assured his listeners that not one of them would ever become invalid. "Think not that I have come to abolish the law and the prophets," he said "I have come not to abolish them but to fulfil them" (Matt. 5:17).

Having affirmed the commandments, however, Jesus demonstrated that their purpose was to point the way to a loving community. First, he showed that traditional rules clustering around the divine commands were invalid if they kept people from the humanizing intent of the law. With his disciples on a Sabbath afternoon's walk, he casually violated a Jewish rule for the holy day. Feeling a little hungry, the Master and his men picked and ate some grain growing along the way. Why not? It was pleasant to eat and the company was splendid. The Pharisees leaped to the attack. There are rules, you know, and harvesting grain is against the rules. Jesus was well aware of the traditional rules, but he ignored them because they did not serve the loving purpose of the divine commandment. "The Sabbath is made for man, not man for the Sabbath"

(Mark 2:27). The commandments are signals of the life of constructive joy; they aim at our welfare and happiness.

The second thing Jesus saw in the law was this: the commandments depend on love. Love turns the negative "Don't's" into positive "Do's." Love turns the passive avoidance of evil into the active doing of good. Love translates the morality of "live and let live" into a morality of "love and help others live." Law without love tells us not to kill a stranger; law with love moves us to go out of our way to help a wounded enemy. . . .

The God of morality is the gracious Savior; the lawgiver of Sinai is the God who was in Christ reconciling the world to himself. He who leads us through the wilderness by his command is the Father who made us and wants us only to be true to our own being. He cares for us, loves us, and seeks us by means of his commands; and he thereby offers us the best way to keep our balance on the slippery shingles of human existence while we scratch out our little tunes. . . .

Encircled by grace, the commandments point to the life grace came to restore (Titus 2:11, 12). . . . The commandments are guides to grace-filled living, invitations to the good life within the grace of God. They are only guides, helping us find our way to the humanity we almost lost, the true human life opened to us again by grace. They cannot give us the steam to make it; only God's Spirit can do that. But a guide along the way helps us.

grace is the undeserved love of god. laws of 10 commandments reflect human needs.

Questions

1. According to the author, why should the Ten Commandments be considered moral absolute rules?
2. Why isn't tradition alone enough to keep people morally balanced?
3. Are some of the Ten Commandments more "absolute" than others?
4. Is it important that nonbelievers as well as believers can understand God's moral rules? Why?

Sin

Philip Yancey

Sin
→ Rebellion against gods will

*Philip Yancey is a popular Christian writer and magazine
editor. This selection is taken from* Christianity Today,
*which he serves as an editor-at-large. Here Yancey deals with
the issue of personal sin. After experiencing the grace of God
and realizing that the Ten Commandments are given for the
benefit of people, he is able to reflect on the fact of sin in
fruitful ways.*

*"All day long, and all the days of our life, we are sliding, slipping,
falling away—as if God were, to our present consciousness, a smooth
inclined plane on which there is no resting."*

—C. S. Lewis

"I ain't got to, but I can't help it."

—William Faulkner

Sin. The very word has a slithery, reptilian sound to it. For
me, the word summons up overtones from the past, when
heavy breathing Southern revivalists would stretch it out in
full two-syllable fury. "Siiiiii-yun," they would shout, and
raise their fists in defiance against the satanic force that lay in
wait for each of us, that lay in wait inside us.

I trembled as a child when I heard about sin and the hor-
rors of its punishment. Subconsciously, my images of God
were forming as I listened to those revivalists. God was no
Father to me, for I had no image of father to draw on—mine
died of polio just after my first birthday.

So God was more like the authority figures I knew, especially the tanklike German matron who inspired fear in the
hearts of any first-grader daring to whisper or throw spitballs

in her domain. Only, God was far larger and stricter, the strictest teacher imaginable.

Martin Luther grew up haunted by a stained-glass window from his boyhood church, a window depicting Christ as a stern king with a raised sword. The sword appeared to Luther exactly like a rod. To my child's mind also, God loomed as the great Enforcer who brought swift and terrible punishment to all who misbehaved. And it did not help that church members told me my earthly father, now in heaven, was looking down on me to help spy out my hidden sins.

Now, looking back, my early, oppressive encounters with the word *sin* almost seem to belong to someone who lived on another planet. I rarely come across the word these days in Christian books or magazines, rarely hear it railed against from the pulpit, never hear it on network television. Fear of sin, the dominant force of my childhood, and that of many others, has nearly disappeared from view.

. . . We thus find ourselves in the schizophrenic position of ignoring the most obvious fact about human behavior, the fact of sin. I suspect if a true prophet from God came in judgment against the sins of our modern culture, he would be greeted first with incredulous laughter, then scorn, then violent opposition (curiously, the exact same responses greeted most of the Old Testament prophets).

As I reflect on my own pilgrimage of faith, I find that it has mirrored the schizophrenia of the larger culture. Sometimes I am dominated by sin-consciousness, sometimes I rebel vigorously against it, but most often I avoid it completely. Yet always I have been plagued by a nagging, underlying sense that I must somehow come to terms with this word that shows up on so many pages of the Bible.

One person's sins

Sin as an abstract idea teaches very little. Sinners themselves teach much, and perhaps for that reason the Bible expresses in story form most of what it says about sin. And to learn about my own sin, I had to begin by tracing its progress in my life. I had to identify my sin—not just a stray sin here or there, but patterns of sin that keep breaking out. Here are a few sins from my long list:

• *Deceit.* I am ashamed to admit it, but I have struggled with a consistent pattern of deceit. Earlier, justifying my deceit as a creative way to oppose "the system," I would engage in such shenanigans as mailing all utility bill payments without postage stamps (causing the utility companies to pay postage, until the Postal Service wised up and stopped delivering such mail) and subscribing to record clubs in order to tape-record the records and send them back for a refund. Over time, plagued by a guilty conscience, I cut out such practices, but I still recognize a deep temptation to rely on deceit when I feel trapped.

• *Permanent discontent.* You may not find this one on any biblical list of sins, but this root attitude affects me in many sinful ways. Years of working as an editor gave me an editor's personality that is never satisfied. I always want to strike out words, rearrange sentences, crumple up whole first drafts. While such dyspepsia can serve a worthwhile purpose in editing, in life it does not. I find myself editing my wife's behavior, and my friends'. I constantly yearn for what I cannot have and cannot be. Mainly, I make myself nearly impervious to that spirit the Bible calls joy.

• *Hypocrisy.* All Christians fight this sin to some degree (there I go again, rationalizing), but writers perhaps more than most.

I write about leprosy patients in India, and about the extraordinary humility and sacrifice of missionaries I have visited there—but I write from the comfort of an air-conditioned office, with strains of classical music filling the room. How do I live with that disparity? How should I?

• *Greed.* Do you know of any ministry other than writing that has a one-to-one relationship between ministry and income? Each person I "reach" in a book means more money in my pocket. Need I detail the dangers of mixed motives that can result?

• *Egotism.* Again, a most embarrassing admission I would much prefer to leave off my list of sins. Like every other author and speaker, I begin with the rather audacious assumption that I have a viewpoint worth listening to. If I did not believe that, I would not go through the painful process of writing. The danger of pride rides with every thought, every sentence, every word.

You will note that my list of sins excludes many overt ones such as child abuse, drunkenness, and adultery. I am not tempted toward those sins, and that fact offers my first clue into the nature of sin. Sin strikes at the point of greatest vulnerability.

I spend my days secluded in an office, away from people, susceptible to an introvert's self-absorption. The sins of discontent, egotism, and greed are internal sins. They grow like mold in dark, moist corners of the mind and psyche, nourished by slight rejections, mild paranoia, and loneliness—the precise occupational hazards of every writer.

A brash public figure such as quarterback Jim McMahon or comedian Joan Rivers will face a different set of temptations. And those who depend for a living on the successful preening of their bodies will likely fall at different points; adultery constantly tempts them, as Hollywood divorce rates easily prove. Similarly, while a poor man may struggle mostly with envy, a rich man battles greed.

We who battle "internal sins" can easily think our sins somehow more respectable than more blatant sins such as adultery and drunkenness. The moment we entertain such thoughts, we fall into an even deeper hole. I have attended meetings of Alcoholics Anonymous and have never met a recovering alcoholic who denied his or her own sinfulness; but I have met many Christians who find it difficult to confess their own sins. I know such Christians well, for I am one.

Malcolm Muggeridge expressed the danger this way: "It is precisely when you consider the *best* in man that you see there is in each of us a hard core of pride or self-centeredness which corrupts our *best* achievements and blights our *best* experiences. It comes out in all sorts of ways—in the jealousy which spoils our friendships, in the vanity we feel when we have done something pretty good, in the easy conversion of love into lust, in the meanness which makes us depreciate the efforts of other people, in the distortion of our own judgment by our own self-interest, in our fondness for flattery and our resentment of blame, in our self-assertive profession of fine ideals which we never begin to practise."

We can quickly work up ire against the decay of our society—witness the furor over abortion and violence and pornography and other external sins—but unless we also come to terms with our own private sins, we will have missed the message of the gospel. If you ever doubt that, simply turn to the Sermon on the Mount, in which Jesus painted with one brush lust and adultery, hatred and murder.

A shift in outlook

In my childhood, thinking about sin terrified me. In adolescence, it repulsed me. Yet now I find myself thinking about sin often, and fruitfully. What caused the change in perspective?

I now recognize that the faith I learned in childhood fixated on sin, stopping short of grace. Only after I experienced firsthand the loving grace of God could I begin to think about sin healthily. I had a guide in learning about grace, a gentle old Scottish Presbyterian minister named George MacDonald. He died in 1858, but he left behind a collection of sermons that have taught me about grace (many, edited by Rolland Hein for a modern audience, are found in the books *Life Essential* and *Creation in Christ).*

MacDonald preached the gospel of grace so strongly that one of his sons protested, "It all seems too good to be true!" MacDonald replied, "Nay, it is just so good it must be true!" As I immersed myself in the writings of that godly man, many of the calluses that had grown thick against the harsh fundamentalism of my childhood began to soften and fall away. The first to fall was my image of God as a cruel and heartless teacher.

I had viewed God as a cranky old codger who concocted an arbitrary list of rules for the express purpose of making sure everyone would be punished for breaking one or two of them. The rules made no sense in themselves, I thought, especially the 613 Old Testament laws.

However, George MacDonald taught me another way of looking at law. It was not a new insight, and yet MacDonald's understanding penetrated me with gradual emotional force until it changed the whole way I viewed God and rules. The key is this: the rules were not given for God's sake—just so he would have an excuse for punishment—but rather they were given for our sakes. I suppose I had paid lip service to that truth, but emotionally I was still reacting to my childhood image of God as stern taskmaster.

Every parent knows the difference between rules designed primarily for the benefit of the parent (*Don't talk while I'm on the telephone! Clean up your room—your grandmother's coming!*) and those designed for the benefit of the child (*Wear a hat—it's below freezing! And don't skate on the pond yet!*). The law, even the Old Testament Law, primarily fell into the latter category. In Israel, God selected a race of people as "a kingdom of priests, a holy nation" to demonstrate his own holiness. Yet at the same time he, as creator and designer of the human race, knew that human society would work best without adultery, without murder, without lying, without idolatry.

I began to look at the Ten Commandments in this light. They emerged as the skeleton of a society designed primarily for the benefit of the people themselves. Each negative command could be turned around and stated positively. At its core, each protects something of great value to the human race. Consider a few examples:

• I, the Creator, am giving you myself. You will need no worthless images of wood or stone, for you can have me, the Lord of the Universe.

• I am giving you my name, and you can be called by my name. Treat it as your sacred possession, and do not defile its meaning by using it in vain.

• I have made human life sacred and eternal, stamping my likeness on every child born. Protect and value what I have created. Cause it to live, not die.

• I am giving you marriage, and the mystery of love and intimacy between one man and one woman. Preserve it against dilution through adultery.

I do not read Hebrew, but those who do tell me that the familiar English forms "Thou shalt not" and "Thou shalt" may be misleading. In English, the verb "shall" conveys both imperative ("You *shall* obey!") and future ("I shall come Tuesday"). The Hebrew in the Ten Commandments is closer to the future form. God is giving a description of what a holy people will look like.

The nation failed, of course, breaking the covenant. Then Jesus came with a new covenant based on forgiveness and grace. The apostle Paul, reflecting on that Old Testament history, called it a "schoolmaster to bring us to Christ." "But now," he wrote, "by dying to what once bound us, we have been released from the law so that we serve in the new way of the Spirit, and not in the old way of the written code" (Rom. 7:6, NIV).

A health expert

I once resisted any thought of God as an authority figure. But lately I have been thinking of other images, realizing that in many areas of life I gladly submit to authority. When I encounter a problem with my computer software, I frantically dial a toll-free number and then scrupulously follow the orders of the expert on the other end of the line. When I want to master a new sport, say, downhill skiing, I pay for expensive lessons. And when I am sick, I go to a doctor.

Perhaps that last image, of a doctor, is the most instructive in thinking about God and sin. What a doctor does for me physically—guides me toward health—God does for me spiritually. I am learning to view sins not as an arbitrary list of rules drawn up by a cranky Teacher, but rather as a list of dangerous carcinogens that must be avoided at all costs.

I once saw in a medical textbook side-by-side photographs of two sets of lungs. The lungs on the left were a brilliant, glossy pink, so shiny and smoothly textured they could have been taken from a newborn. In stark contrast, the lungs next to them looked as if they had been used to clean a chimney. Black sediment coated them, clogging all the delicate membranes designed to capture oxygen molecules. The photo caption explained that the lungs on the left had been removed during the autopsy of a Wyoming farmer; those on the right came from a resident of a factory town who had chain-smoked all his life.

I cannot comprehend how any doctor who has seen such lungs, side by side, could ever smoke again. And I remind myself of that image whenever I think about sin. What those impurities do to a person's lungs, sin does to the spiritual life. It retards growth, ravages health, chokes off the supply of new life.

I think back to the sins I have mentioned. What effect do they have on my own spiritual health?

• *Deceit.* What would happen if I ignored warning signs and consistently yielded to promptings toward deceit? No one—not my neighbors, not my wife—could fully trust me. I would become a sad and lonely recluse, isolated by my own duplicity.

• *Permanent discontent.* I have already said what this tendency produces: an instinctive resistance to joy. It also blocks out gratitude, the emotion doctors judge most nourishing to health.

• *Hypocrisy.* Think of the worst hypocrite you know. Do I want to end up like that? Could anyone suggest that a person is better off for hypocrisy, that personal growth is encouraged and not stunted by this sin?

• *Greed.* I know well what greed does to me. When I write, it changes the questions I ask from *Is this thought true? Does it have value?* to *Will it sell?*

• *Egotism.* I battle it even at this moment. Should I really risk exposure in an article about sin? Should I write about my "spiritual disciplines" instead? Or will the strokes I get for honesty outweigh the criticism from those who question my spiritual maturity? Unchecked egotism would ultimately make me a manipulative boor.

Each of my sins, those I have mentioned and those secret

ones I would not dare mention, represent a grave danger to my spiritual health. If I give in to any one of them as a consistent pattern, I will suffer grave loss. My spirit will shrivel and atrophy, like the lung tissue of the chain-smoker.

The more I see my sins in this light, the more I see beyond the harshness of God's punishments. I find myself gazing into the grieving eyes of a parent whose children are destroying themselves. He responds to our sins with punishment and forgiveness, which may seem opposites. But, paradoxically, both have exactly the same purpose: to break the stranglehold of sin and make wholeness possible. He offers healing; we choose the cancer. God allows sins to happen for punishment

I confess that it has taken me many years to learn to trust God. The kind of sins and the type of authority I encountered as a child proved untrustworthy. But through fits and starts of rebellion, apathy, and occasional obedience, I have learned that God himself can be trusted. I can trust him with my health, and I can trust him with my sins. He welcomes me. As Jesus said, applying the doctor image to himself, "It is not the healthy who need a doctor, but the sick. I have not come to call the righteous, but sinners to repentance."

At times, of course, I do not trust him. Sometime today, sometime tomorrow, I will recreate the original rebellion of Eden and act by my standards and my desires, and not God's. God cannot overlook such behavior; it must be accounted for, as it was with Adam and Eve. But in that reckoning he aims not to destroy but to heal. No surgeon who wills the health of a patient can effect it without some pain.

> *The wounded surgeon plies the steel*
> *That questions the distempered part;*
> *Beneath the bleeding hands we feel*
> *The sharp compassion of the healer's art*
> *Resolving the enigma of the fever chart.*
> —T. S. Eliot, *Four Quartets*

Questions

1. Describe Yancey's false view of God, which made thinking about sin terrifying to him as a youngster. How did his view of God change later?
2. Is the analogy of the diseased lung helpful to gain a clear picture of the destructive effects of sin on a person's spiritual health? Why or why not?
3. Yancey writes, "Sin strikes at the point of greatest vulnerability." What areas of your life are most vulnerable to sin?
4. How does Yancey's discussion of sin add to your understanding of morality?

5. When we look to Christ, why does the law have no value?
   - Christ lived and did what we cannot do.

Hardness and Freedom

Paul Brand and Philip Yancey

Paul Brand is a well-known Christian medical doctor, a surgeon. Philip Yancey is a professional writer. In these selections from their book Fearfully and Wonderfully Made *the authors describe the properties and functions of bone. They then liken these important aspects of the human skeleton to doctrine that gives strength and stability to the body of Christ.*

People are never born without bones, but some are born with defective bones in a condition called brittle bone disease. When this occurs, the victim's bone consists of deposits of calcium without the organic material welding them together—the grit without the glue. A fetus with this disorder may survive the pressures of birth, but with half its bones broken. Just diapering such a child may break his or her fragile legs; a fall could break dozens of bones.

At our Carville hospital a patient was given massive doses of steroids during treatment of her leprosy, and as a result her bones became soft. She could fracture her foot by walking too briskly. Whenever I examined the woman and checked her x-rays for fractures, I was reminded that the most important feature of bone is its hardness. That one property separates it from all other tissue in the body, and without hardness bone is virtually useless.

An analogous body as advanced and active as the Body of Christ's followers also needs a framework of hardness to give it shape, and I see the Church's doctrine as being just such a skeleton. Inside the Body lives a core of truth that never changes—the laws governing our relationships to God and to other people.

Do I hear a groan? Our age smiles kindly on musings about unity and diversity and the contributions of individual cells. But the drive which stirred church councils and framers of the Constitution has stalled. Bones are dusty, crumbling, dead, belonging in a musty museum display case. Other parts of the body are memorialized: the heart on Valentine's Day, the sexual parts and the muscles in magazines and fashion, the hands in sculptures. The skeleton is relegated to Halloween, a spooky remnant of the past, leeringly inhuman.

Today one can easily muster up sympathy and support for Jesus' ethics governing human behavior. But squeezed in between His statements on love and neighborliness are scores of harsh, uncompromising statements about our duties and responsibilities and about heaven and hell.

The modern world is still pictured as a courtroom scene, as described by the ancients, but not with God as Judge, setting the rules and arbitrating disputes. Rather, He stands indicted, and prosecutors are stalking across the stage jabbing their fingers at Him, demanding to know why He allows such a miserable world to continue and what right He has to make such grandiose claims about His Son. Don't all religions ultimately point to God? Isn't belief really an individual quest for ultimate meaning that each must find in his or her own way? What is this talk about "No man comes to the Father except by me" and "I am the way, the truth and the life"?

As I encounter the Body of Christ, I keep hitting against the hard tissue, the principles that do not change. Joining that Body involves . . . an acknowledgment that someone else, not I, has already determined the way I should live. In some areas of my life I gladly accept restrictive laws. For instance, traffic laws inhibit my freedom (what if I don't want to stop?), yet I accept the inconvenience. I assume some skilled engineer calculated the number of one-way streets and red lights, and even if I doubt his ability, I prefer traffic laws to auto anarchy. But something within me rebels against being told how to live morally.

I came across this property of hardness when I was first

taught about God. God is perfect, I was told, and cannot tolerate sin. His character requires Him to destroy sin whenever it is present, so I am branded an enemy of God. That fact, rooted in the first chapters of Genesis, is stressed throughout the Bible. God cannot ignore rebellion; His nature demands that justice be done, and nothing I can do will soften the inflexibility of that fact. I must meet Him on His terms, not my own.

Later, I learned how justice was accomplished. God obtained it on our behalf by becoming man and taking on Himself all the sin and rebellion we had stored up against Him. The debt of mankind was paid, but in a way that cost only God, not those of us who had piled it up. To the servant with a three-million-dollar debt Jesus announced, "It's forgiven; you owe nothing." And His message to the Prodigal Son: "The table is set; come join the party. The past may all be forgiven; all that counts is how you respond to what God has offered."

Even at its core, the hard, unchangeable part that does not flex, the gospel sounds almost like a fairy tale. "It's too good to be true," someone protested to George MacDonald. "No," he replied, "it's so good it has to be true." The way back to God is hard, but only because there is just one way.

Others more skilled in theology than I must describe and interpret specific doctrines for us. Today some within the church attack law and doctrine. Situation ethics suggest that right and wrong often depend on the need and mood of the moment. I merely submit this single aspect of God's law: it must be consistent, like bone. Trust demands it.

I think back to an encounter with trust I had many years ago. Before I trained for surgery, I worked in the general practice of my father-in-law, near London. One day a woman came in with a list of complaints that exactly described gastritis. After a brief examination I told her my diagnosis, but she looked up at me with large, fear-filled eyes.

I repeated to her soothingly, "Really, it's not a serious condition. Millions of people have it, and with medication and care, you'll be fine." The fear did not fade from her face. Lines of tension were jerking in her forehead and jaw. To my "You'll be fine," she flinched as if I had said, "Your disease is terminal."

She quizzed me on every point, and I assured her I would be doing further tests to verify my diagnosis. She repeated to me all her symptoms and kept asking, "Are you sure? Are you sure?" So I ordered a barium meal and extensive x-rays.

When the test results came back, all pointed conclusively to gastritis. I saw the woman on one last visit. She trembled slightly as I spoke to her, and I used my most comforting and authoritative doctor's tone. "It is perfectly clear—no doubt—that you have gastritis. I thought so from the first visit, and now these tests have confirmed it. The condition is chronic and will require you to change diet and medication, but it should settle down. There is absolutely no reason for alarm."

The woman stared into my eyes with a piercing gaze for at least a minute, as if she was trying to see into my soul. I managed to hold her gaze, fearing that if I looked away she would doubt me. Finally, she sighed deeply, and for the first time her face relaxed. She sucked her breath in sharply and said, "Well, thank you. I was sure I had cancer. I had to hear the diagnosis from somebody I could trust, and I think I can trust you."

She then told me a story about her mother, who had suffered a long, painful disease. "One tortuous night the family doctor made a house call while mother was groaning and pressing her hands to her stomach. She was feverish and obviously suffering. When the doctor arrived, mother said, 'Doctor, am I really going to get better? I feel so ill and have lost so much weight . . . I think I must be dying.'

"The doctor put his hand on my mother's shoulder, looked at her with a tender expression, and replied, 'I know how you feel. It hurts badly, doesn't it? But we can lick this one—it is simply gastritis. If you take this medicine for a little while longer, with these tranquilizers, we will have you on your feet in no time. You'll feel better before you know it. Don't worry. Just trust me.' My mother smiled and thanked him. I was overwhelmed by the doctor's kindness.

"In the hallway, out of her hearing, the doctor turned to me and said gravely, 'I'm afraid your mother will not last more than a day or two. She has an advanced case of cancer of the stomach. If we keep her tranquilized, she will probably pass away peacefully. If there's anyone you should notify—'

"I interrupted him in mid-sentence. 'But, doctor! You told her she was doing fine!'

" 'Oh, yes, it's much better that way,' he replied. 'She does not know, and so she won't worry. She'll probably die in her sleep.' He was right. My mother died that same night."

This woman, now a middle-aged patient herself, had first gone to that same family doctor with her stomach pains. He had put a hand on her shoulder and said gently, "Don't worry. It's only gastritis. Just take this medicine, and you'll be feeling fine very soon." And he smiled the same paternal smile he had shown her mother. She had fled from his office in tears and would never see him again.

When people complain to me about the rigid, unbending laws of God, I think of that woman. The family doctor had obliterated all possibility of helping her because of his flexible attitude to truth. Only one thing could relieve her anxiety and despair: trust in someone who believed in truth that could not be twisted and bent.

Occasions will come when to be untruthful is more convenient or less offensive. But a respect for truth cannot be worn and then casually removed like a jacket; it cannot be contracted and then relaxed like a muscle. Either it is rigid and dependable, like healthy bone, or it is useless.

He came to me as a patient in England: a brawny, burly Welshman who spoke lyrically and with a workman's vocabulary. "Mornin', doctor," he growled. As he removed his wool plaid jacket, I saw the reason for his coming. The upper part of his right arm was not pink skin, but grimy steel and leather—

an awkward, brace-like contraption covered with black coal dust. I removed the brace. This was no artificial limb; his forearm was intact, but the flesh between his elbow and shoulder was flaccid. A long section of bone appeared to be missing. But if a mining accident had crushed his upper arm, how had his forearm survived?

After I studied the miner's records and x-rayed his arm, the puzzle fell into place. Years before, a bone tumor in his upper arm had led to a serious fracture which splintered large sections of bone there. Under the bright lights of the operating room his doctor had deftly stolen an eight-inch pipe of living bone and sewed back the muscles and skin around the space. As the miner lay recovering, his boneless arm seemed perfectly normal. Who would know the interior landscape had changed?

Everyone would know, the first moment this miner used the muscles, still strong and intact, in his upper arm. Bones and muscles work on a triangle principle: the joint provides the fulcrum, and two bones work with a muscle. To pull the hand up, the biceps muscle, attached to the upper arm, pulls on the forearm. The arm bends at the elbow, and the triangle is complete. But one muscle and one forearm bone do not make a triangle; this coal miner lacked the third element, the bone of the upper arm.

Ever since his surgery years before, whenever the miner contracted his biceps muscle his entire upper arm shortened, like an earthworm spastically pulling in towards its middle. The fixed, resistant bone between his elbow and shoulder had become a soft, collapsible space, canceling out the triangle that should have transferred force to his forearm. His ingenious Welsh doctor had fitted the miner with a crude exoskeleton, a bulky contraption of leather and steel which positioned stiff rods between his elbow and shoulder. When his biceps contracted, because these steel rods prevented his upper arm from merely shortening, the forearm could pull upward. The steel frame outside his arm worked much the same as the now-missing bone had inside his arm.

I have surgically removed such upper arm bones, though

today we circumvent the awkwardness of an external skeleton by jamming a bone graft into the vacant space. A bone graft unites with the stumps above and below it, and gradually the arm will adjust to its new member. But this man's crude external brace had served him well for years, allowing him to work as a vigorous coal miner. He came to me asking for a new bone mainly because he was tired of having to buckle on his exoskeleton every day.

Because it is hard and sometimes subject to fracture, bone has acquired the reputation of a nuisance to human activity. Bone prohibits us from squeezing into small spaces and from sleeping comfortably on hard ground. And what prevents skiers from adding twenty meters onto the looping, graceful ski jump and what keeps the slalom course in the domain of a few experts? The old nemesis of broken bones. A person who breaks a leg skiing could wish for stronger bones. But stronger bones would be thicker and heavier, making skiing far more limited or impossible.

No, the 206 lengths of calcium our body is strapped to are not there to restrict us; they free us. In the same way that the Welsh miner's arm was able to move only when it contained a proper scaffolding, external or internal, almost all our movements are made possible because of bone—rigid, inflexible bone.

In the Body of Christ also the quality of hardness is not designed to burden us; rather, it should free us. Rules governing behavior work because, like bones, they are hard.

Moral law. The Ten Commandments. Obedience. Doing right. A "thou shalt not" negativism taints the words, and we tend to view them as opposites to freedom. As a young Christian, I cringed at such words. But later, especially after I became a father, I started thinking beyond my reflex reaction to the very nature of law. Are not laws essentially a description of reality by the One who created it? His rules governing human behavior—are they not guidelines meant to enable us to live the very best, most fulfilling life on earth?

I do not slip easily into such reasoning. Laws are too

encrusted with cultural barnacles that obscure their true essence. They can summon up in me deeply embedded memories of parental disapproval, and instead I crave another kind of freedom—freedom from law, not freedom by it.

I have discovered, however, that it is possible to see beyond the surface negativism of, for example, the Ten Commandments and to learn something of the true nature of laws. Rules soon seem as liberating in social activity as bones are in physical activity.

The first four of the Ten Commandments are rules governing a person's relationship to God Himself: Have no other gods before Me. Don't worship idols. Don't misuse My name. Remember the day set aside to worship Me. As I contemplate these once-forbidding commandments, more and more they sound like positive affirmations.

What if God had stated the same principles this way:

I love you so much that I will give you *Myself*. I am true reality, the only God you will ever need. In Me alone will you find wholeness.

I desire a wonderful thing: a direct, personal relationship between Myself and each of you. You don't need inferior representations of Me, such as dead wooden idols. You can have Me. Value that.

I love you so much that I have given you My name. You will be known as "God's people" on the earth. Value the privilege; don't misuse it by profaning your new name or by not living up to it.

I have given you a beautiful world to work in, play in, and enjoy. In your involvement, though, set aside a day to remember where the world came from. Your bodies need the rest; your spirits need the reminder.

The next six commandments govern personal relationships. The first is already stated positively: honor your father and mother, a command echoed by virtually every society on earth. The next five:

Human life is sacred. I gave it, and it has enormous worth. Cling to it. Respect it; it is the image of God. He who ignores this and commits the sacrilege of murder must be punished.

The deepest human relationship possible is marriage. I created it to solve the essential loneliness in the heart of every person. To spread what is meant for marriage alone among a variety of people will devalue and destroy that relationship. Save sex and intimacy for its rightful place within marriage.

I am entrusting you with property. You can own things, and you should use them responsibly. Ownership is a great privilege. For it to work, you must respect everyone else's right to ownership; stealing violates that right.

I am a God of truth. Relationships only succeed when they are governed by truth. A lie destroys contracts, promises, trust. You are worthy of trust: express it by not lying.

I have given you good things to enjoy: oxen, grains, gold, furniture, musical instruments. But people are always more important than things. Love people: use things. Do not use people for your love of things.

Stripped down, the commandments emerge as a basic skeleton of trust that links relationships between people and between people and God. God claims, as the Good Shepherd, that He has given law as the way to the best life. Our own rebellion, from the Garden of Eden onward, tempts us to believe He is the bad shepherd whose laws keep us from something good.

Yes, one might reply, the Ten Commandments can be twisted around to reveal a more positive side. But why didn't God state them that way? Why did He say, "You shall *not* murder. You shall *not* commit adultery. You shall *not* steal. . . ."?

I suggest two answers. First, a negative command is actually less limiting than a positive one. "You may eat from any tree of the garden except one" allows more freedom than "You must eat from every tree of the garden, starting with the one in the northwest corner and working along the outer edge of the orchard." "You shall not commit adultery" is more freeing than "You must have sex with your spouse twice a week between the hours of nine and eleven in the evening." "Do not covet" is more freeing than "I am hereby prescribing limits on ownership. Every man is entitled to one cow, one ox, three gold rings. . . ."

Second, people were not yet ready for an emphasis on the positive commands. The Ten Commandments represent a kindergarten phase of morality: the basic laws needed for a society to operate. When Jesus came to earth, He filled in the positive side.

Quoting the Old Testament, He summarized the entire law in two positive commands: "Love God with all your heart and with all your soul and with all your strength and with all your mind," and "Love your neighbor as you love yourself" (Luke 10:27). It is one thing not to covet my neighbor's property and not to steal from him. It is quite another to love him so that I care for his family as much as I care for mine. Morality took a quantum leap from prohibition to love. (Paul affirmed and developed this thought in Romans 13:8-10.)

Jesus' Sermon on the Mount puts the capstone on His attitude toward the law. There, He described the Ten Commandments as the bare minimum. They actually point to profound principles: modesty, respect, non-violence, sharing. Then Jesus submitted the ideal social ethic—a system governed by only one law, the law of love. He calls us toward that ideal. Why? So God can take a fatherly pride in how well His little experiment on earth is progressing? Of course not. These laws were not given for God's sake, but for ours. "The Sabbath was made for man, not man for the Sabbath," He said, and "You will know the truth, and the truth *will set you free*" (Mark 2:27; John 8:32). Jesus came to cleanse the violence, greed, lust, and hurtful competition from within us *for our sakes*. His desire is to have us become like God.

The Ten Commandments were the fetal development of bone, the first ossification from cartilage. The law of love is the fully developed, firm, liberating skeleton. It allows smooth movement within the Body of Christ, for it is hinged and jointed in the right places.

If you examine one law, like a random bone plucked from a pile, it may seem strangely shaped and illogical because laws, like bones, are designed for the complex, connected needs of a whole body. For example, as we have observed, the pelvis is a crazily shaped structure. It represents a compromise of converging needs: to walk, to protect abdominal organs, to sit, to support the back, and, in the woman's case, to bear children. Its shape exists to serve the body, not to dominate it. Similarly, God's laws governing us are a combination of conflicting human desires and needs, chosen to allow us to live life most fully and healthily. God, knowing our weaknesses and human frailties, designed the dogma of our faith and His laws to give strength and stability where we need them.

The law requiring sexual faithfulness in marriage to many people appears oddly and needlessly restrictive. Why not allow interchangeability, with men and women enjoying each other freely? We have the biological equipment for such practices. But sex transcends biology; it intertwines with romantic love, need for stable families, and many other factors. If we break one law, gaining the freedom of sexual experimentation, we lose the long-term benefits of intimacy that marriage is intended to provide. As my Welsh miner proved, removing one bone can ruin complex motion. . . .

A skeleton is never beautiful; its contributions are strength and function. I do not inspect my tibia and wish it to be longer or shorter or more jointed. I just gratefully use it for walking, thinking about where I want to go rather than worrying about whether my legs will bear my weight. I should respond that way to the basic fundamentals of the Christian faith and the laws governing human nature. They are merely the framework for relationships which work best when founded on set, predictable principles. Of course, we can break them: adultery, thievery, lying, idolatry, oppression of the poor have crept into every society in history. But the result is a fracture that can immobilize the entire body. Bones, intended to liberate us, only enslave us when broken.

Questions

1. How does church doctrine function like a human skeleton? Why is hardness an important property of both?
2. According to Brand, why did God give the Ten Commandments as negative statements?
3. Bones liberate the body by providing the potential for freedom and movement. How does doctrine do the same in Christ's body, the church?

Law and Morality

Frederick Buechner

Frederick Buechner is both a well-known author and a Pres-
byterian minister. His novel Godric *was nominated for the*
Pulitzer Prize in 1980. In these two selections from his book
Wishful Thinking: A Theological ABC *Buechner explains*
his view of law and morality. Both have more to do with
what is than with what ought to be.

There are basically two kinds: (1) law as the way things
ought to be, and (2) law as the way things are. An example of
the first is NO TRESPASSING. An example of the second is the
law of gravity.

God's Law has traditionally been spelled out in terms of
category No. 1, a compendium of do's and don'ts. These do's
and don'ts are the work of moralists and when obeyed serve
the useful purpose of keeping us from each other's throats.
They can't make us human but they can help keep us honest.

God's Law *in itself*, however, comes under category No. 2
and is the work of God. It has been stated in eight words: "He
who does not love remains in death" (1 John 3:14). Like it or
not, that's how it is. If you don't believe it, you can always put
it to the test just the way if you don't believe the law of gravity,
you can always step out a tenth-story window.

It is no secret that ideas about what is Right and what is
Wrong vary from time to time and place to place. King
Solomon would not be apt to see eye to eye with a Presbyterian missionary on the subject of monogamy. For that reason, a
popular argument runs, morality is all relative to the tastes of

the time and not to be taken any more seriously by the enlightened than tastes in food, dress, architecture, or anything else. At a certain level this is indisputably so. But there is another level.

In order to be healthy, there are certain rules you can break only at your peril. Eat sensibly, get enough sleep and exercise, avoid bottles marked poison, don't jump out of boats unless you can swim, etc.

In order to be happy, there are also certain rules you can break only at your peril. Be at peace with your neighbor, get rid of hatred and envy, tell the truth, avoid temptations to evil you're not strong enough to resist, don't murder, steal, etc.

Both sets of rules are as valid for a third-century Hottentot as for a twentieth-century Norwegian, for a Muslim as for a Jesus Freak, for Ralph Nader as for Pat Nixon.

Both sets of rules—the moral as well as the hygienic—describe not the way people feel life ought to be but the way they have found life is.

Questions

1. Describe the two kinds of laws as defined by Buechner.
2. Why has God's law traditionally been understood as a list of do's and don'ts? How does this view limit God's law?

2
Making Moral Choices

38 Who Saw Murder Didn't Call the Police

Martin Gansberg

Martin Gansberg has been an editor and reporter for the New York Times. *This account, first published in the* New York Times *in 1964 and reprinted numerous times, gives the details surrounding a tragic murder witnessed by dozens of people who refused to help the victim.*

For more than half an hour 38 respectable, law-abiding citizens in Queens watched a killer stalk and stab a woman in three separate attacks in Kew Gardens.

Twice their chatter and the sudden glow of their bedroom lights interrupted him and frightened him off. Each time he returned, sought her out, and stabbed her again. Not one person telephoned the police during the assault; one witness called after the woman was dead.

That was two weeks ago today.

Still shocked is Assistant Chief Inspector Frederick M. Lussen, in charge of the borough's detectives and a veteran of 25 years of homicide investigations. He can give a matter-of-fact recitation on many murders. But the Kew Gardens slaying baffles him—not because it is a murder, but because the "good people" failed to call the police.

"As we have reconstructed the crime," he said, "the assailant had three chances to kill this woman during a 35-minute period. He returned twice to complete the job. If we had been called when he first attacked, the woman might not be dead now."

This is what the police say happened beginning at 3:20 A.M. in the staid, middle-class, tree-lined Austin Street area:

Twenty-eight-year-old Catherine Genovese, who was called Kitty by almost everyone in the neighborhood was returning home from her job as manager of a bar in Hollis. She parked her red Fiat in a lot adjacent to the Kew Gardens Long Island Rail Road Station, facing Mowbray Place. Like many residents of the neighborhood, she had parked there day after day since her arrival from Connecticut a year ago, although the railroad frowns on the practice.

She turned off the lights of her car, locked the door, and started to walk the 100 feet to the entrance of her apartment at 82-70 Austin Street, which is in a Tudor building, with stores in the first floor and apartments on the second.

The entrance to the apartment is in the rear of the building because the front is rented to retail stores. At night the quiet neighborhood is shrouded in the slumbering darkness that marks most residential areas.

Miss Genovese noticed a man at the far end of the lot, near a seven-story apartment house at 82-40 Austin Street. She halted. Then, nervously, she headed up Austin Street toward Lefferts Boulevard, where there is a call box to the 102nd Police Precinct in nearby Richmond Hill.

She got as far as a street light in front of a bookstore before the man grabbed her. She screamed. Lights went on in the 10-story apartment house at 82-67 Austin Street, which faces the bookstore. Windows slid open and voices punctuated the early-morning stillness.

Miss Genovese screamed: "Oh, my God, he stabbed me! Please help me! Please help me!"

From one of the upper windows in the apartment house, a man called down: "Let that girl alone!"

The assailant looked up at him, shrugged and walked down Austin Street toward a white sedan parked a short distance away. Miss Genovese struggled to her feet.

Lights went out. The killer returned to Miss Genovese, now trying to make her way around the side of the building by the parking lot to get to her apartment. The assailant stabbed her again.

"I'm dying!" she shrieked. "I'm dying!"

Windows were opened again, and lights went on in many apartments. The assailant got into his car and drove away. Miss Genovese staggered to her feet. A city bus, O-10, the Lefferts Boulevard line to Kennedy International Airport, passed. It was 3:35 A.M.

The assailant returned. By then, Miss Genovese had crawled to the back of the building, where the freshly painted brown doors to the apartment house held out hope for safety. The killer tried the first door; she wasn't there. At the second door, 82-62 Austin Street, he saw her slumped on the floor at the foot of the stairs. He stabbed her a third time—fatally.

It was 3:50 by the time the police received their first call, from a man who was a neighbor of Miss Genovese. In two minutes they were at the scene. The neighbor, a 70-year-old woman, and another woman were the only persons on the street. Nobody else came forward.

The man explained that he had called the police after much deliberation. He had phoned a friend in Nassau County for advice and then he had crossed the roof of the building to the apartment of the elderly woman to get her to make the call.

"I didn't want to get involved," he sheepishly told the police.

Six days later, the police arrested Winston Moseley, a 29-year-old business-machine operator, and charged him with homicide. Moseley had no previous record. He is married, has two children and owns a home at 133-19 Sutter Avenue, South Ozone Park, Queens. On Wednesday, a court committed him to Kings County Hospital for psychiatric observation.

When questioned by the police, Moseley also said that he had slain Mrs. Annie May Johnson, 24, of 146-12 133d Avenue, Jamaica, on Feb. 29 and Barbara Kralik, 15, of 174-17 140th Avenue, Springfield Gardens, last July. In the Kralik case, the police are holding Alvin L. Mitchell, who is said to have confessed that slaying.

The police stressed how simple it would have been to have gotten in touch with them. "A phone call," said one of the detectives, "would have done it." The police may be reached by dialing "O" for operator or SPring 7-3100.

Today witnesses from the neighborhood, which is made up of one-family homes in the $35,000 to $60,000 range with the exception of the two apartment houses near the railroad station, find it difficult to explain why they didn't call the police.

A housewife, knowingly if quite casually, said, "We thought it was a lover's quarrel." A husband and wife both said, "Frankly, we were afraid." They seemed aware of the fact that events might have been different. A distraught woman, wiping her hands in her apron, said, "I didn't want my husband to get involved."

One couple, now willing to talk about that night, said they heard the first screams. The husband looked thoughtfully at the bookstore where the killer first grabbed Miss Genovese.

"We went to the window to see what was happening," he said, "but the light from our bedroom made it difficult to see the street." The wife, still apprehensive, added: "I put out the light and we were able to see better."

Asked why they hadn't called the police, she shrugged and replied: "I don't know."

A man peeked out from a slight opening in the doorway to his apartment and rattled off an account of the killer's second attack. Why hadn't he called the police at the time? "I was tired," he said without emotion. "I went back to bed."

It was 4:25 A.M. when the ambulance arrived to take the body of Miss Genovese. It drove off. "Then," a solemn police detective said, "the people came out."

Questions

1. What fact about this murder makes it so difficult to accept?
2. Do you think accounts such as this change the way most people react in similar situations? Would it change the way you would react?

Conformity: A Way Out

Martin Bolt

Martin Bolt teaches social and general psychology at Calvin College. This selection is taken from the book he co-authored with David G. Myers, The Human Connection: How People Change People. *Bolt draws from several* Candid Camera *episodes and psychological experiments to illustrate the great influence other people have on the choices we make.*

In one of the segments from the television program "Candid Camera," an unsuspecting person waits in an office building for an elevator. The elevator arrives, the doors open, and the passenger steps in. One by one others follow but then proceed to behave strangely: they all face the back. The victim peers quizzically at each, fidgets nervously, and then meekly conforms.

The Impact of Others

. . . Although we like to think of ourselves as independent, other people's influence is difficult to resist. It often shapes our thoughts, our actions, our choices. Some of the classical experiments in social psychology have verified its power. What others tell us to do or even how they act sometimes affects our behavior more than does our own perception of what is right.

Imagine you have volunteered to participate in an experiment on visual judgment. You and seven other participants are seated in front of two cards on which are lines of varying lengths. Your task is to judge which of three lines is closest in length to a fourth, which serves as the standard. It is clear to you that line B is the correct answer. But the first person to make a judgment looks carefully at the lines and says, "Line A." To your surprise, so does the second, the third and so on down the line. When your turn finally comes, what will you say? Will you agree with the majority, or will you exercise critical judgment and state what *you* believe is right?

Asked to predict their own reaction, most people say they will resist influence and report what they know is right. That's what Peter thought, too, before denying Jesus. However, the results of the study indicate otherwise. They demonstrate the powerful effects of an incorrect majority on subjects' responses. Only a quarter of the subjects were able to resist the false norm consistently.

Why do we conform to those around us? One reason is our need to gain others' approval, or to avoid their disapproval. For example, some of those who went along with the group in judging the line lengths did so to avoid appearing different or deviant. They feared being rejected.

Violating social expectations or constraints can be traumatic. Stanley Milgram offers a challenge to those who think it's easy. "Get on a bus," he says, "and sing out loud. Full-throated song now, no humming." While many think it can be readily done, not one in a hundred is able to do it. Or another of Milgram's challenges, one he himself tried, is to board the subway and ask a stranger for his seat. After several attempts in which the words lodged in his throat, Milgram finally choked out the request. Experiencing a moment of panic, he found the man actually giving up his seat. After taking his place, Milgram reported he had an overwhelming need to behave in a way that justified the request. He writes, "I actually felt as if I were going to perish." Only after he was off the train did the tension disappear.

All of us can recite examples from our own lives. Others' pressure, real or imagined, overwhelms us, and we act differently than we would if we were alone, even in ways that violate our Christian conscience. How difficult not to join in approval of that humorous story that disparages another ethnic group or the other sex. . . .

Ten years ago our home was situated in the middle of an old apple orchard. Today we have many close neighbors. While for me the expenditure necessary to maintain a watered and weed-free lawn is at best questionable, I'm sensitive to neighborhood pressure—usually implicit, occasionally explicit—to do something about the one weedhaven on the block. On occasion new students recount the difficulty they are having adjusting to college and particularly to living in the campus residence halls. They've found their lifestyle different from that of other students. And they are uneasy as they see themselves conforming when they know they should resist.

Rejection is painful. To obey God rather than people can be agonizing. We may believe that God's approval has first priority. We may even be convinced that we will withstand tempting influences. Still, the task of being in and not of this world is extraordinarily difficult. When the chips are down, when we have little time or opportunity to reflect on our choice of action, when God seems distant and the pressure is present, we flow with the crowd. With Peter we say by our actions that we "don't know the man."

Milgram's Studies of Obedience

To what degree can social pressure lead us to violate our moral standards? Is it possible that someone can induce us to engage in harmful, destructive acts? Milgram tried to answer this question in what have become the most famous studies in social psychology.

. . . Men from diverse backgrounds and occupations were recruited to participate in an experiment said to investigate the effects of punishment on learning. The participant was assigned the role of teacher. His task was to deliver an electric shock to the "student" whenever a mistake was made on a simple learning task. The switches on the shock generator ranged from a mild 15 volts to a supposedly dangerous 450 volts. The experimenter instructed the teacher to begin punishment of initial errors with the mild shock and to raise the voltage each time an additional error was made until the highest voltage was being administered. The "student" was an accomplice of the experimenter who, although he received no shock, had been carefully coached to act as though he did. When the student made many mistakes and loudly protested the shocks, the experimenter told the teacher to continue raising the voltage. How far did subjects go? When Milgram described the experiment to psychiatrists, college students and middle-class adults, virtually no one expected anyone to proceed to the end. The psychiatrists guessed one in a thousand. Contrary to expectation, almost two-thirds of the participants fully obeyed, delivering the greatest possible shock.

How could subjects bring themselves to continue shocking the victim? Were they evil people? No, they were not unusually hostile or vicious people. Many belonged to Christian churches and, when asked, firmly stated their moral opposition to injuring others.

Some participants were totally convinced of the wrongness of what they were doing. Yet they succumbed to social pressure. They were afraid that if they broke off they would appear arrogant, discourteous or impolite. One participant, obviously concerned over the welfare of the learner, said to the experimenter, "I don't mean to be rude, sir, but don't you think you should look in on him?" Even the minority who refused to comply in the Milgram study did not reprimand the experimenter for his evil instruction.

John Sabini and Maury Silver have noted the difficulty most of us have in resisting wrongdoing. To question another's behavior openly is crude, uncivil. Even when our rights are violated we are reluctant to object. Better to suffer through the annoying cigarette smoke than to confront the passenger in the seat beside you. And going to the library is less painful than reminding a suitemate to observe quiet hours. Intervening on behalf of another is even more difficult. Who wants to be a meddler? As I left the grocery store last Saturday morning an advocate of children's rights was distributing leaflets. Apparently an advertising campaign is even necessary to get people to report child abuse. Adolph Eichmann stated that the most potent factor in soothing his own conscience was that no one dissented against the Final Solution.

Were Milgram's subjects merely unwilling participants,

coerced against their better judgment to do evil? Hardly. To view them so is to overlook other important lessons of the study. More subtle forces were also at work.

The Need for Information

Conformity sometimes stems not from our wanting people to like or admire us, but rather from our need to understand ourselves and make sense out of the world. One line of thinking is this: Others, particularly those we respect, may know something we do not know; hence they may provide us with evidence about reality, even about ourselves. By believing and acting as others do, we may gain the benefit of their knowledge.

Another "Candid Camera" clipping provides an amusing example of this "informational" conformity. Three "Candid Camera" art critics (actually actors) assess the aesthetic merit of an abstract painting. Their enthusiastic evaluations are lengthy and involved, and even include identification of hypothetical objects in the painting. Outside observers are impressed. They agree with these experts. Suddenly one of the experts notices that they have the wrong painting. Quickly the critics reverse their opinion. And so do the onlookers.

This informational influence is different from conformity produced by blatant pressure. Here there is not simply a temporary behavior change in violation of our beliefs. Change is more pervasive, more lasting. The presence of others shapes our inner perspectives, our opinions. And because informational influence generates so little conflict, and may in fact even reduce tension, we are less conscious of it.

Milgram argues that in general people have a strong tendency to accept definitions of reality provided by legitimate authority. Thus in his study we should not view the relationship between the experimenter and subject as one in which a coercive figure merely forces actions from an unwilling subordinate. Rather a legitimate authority redefines the meaning of the situation and the subject accepts it. You are no longer delivering a painful shock; rather you are assisting in the lofty pursuit of scientific knowledge.

Not only do authorities shape our perception of reality. Muzafer Sherif's studies using the "autokinetic phenomenon" show how peers may define for us an ambiguous situation. The phenomenon is produced by projecting a still spot of light on the wall in a dark room. After a few moments, an illusion occurs: the light seems to move. How far does it move? Estimates vary greatly.

In Sherif's study several subjects were taken into a darkened room and asked to estimate how far the light moved. While initial judgments varied considerably, after a while their estimates converged. Influenced by each other, they typically developed a common false belief. But each was unaware that his interpretation of reality was being shaped by the people around him. Social influence extends far beyond our yielding against our better judgment. Others can shape the judgment itself.

Are we Christians as sensitive as we should be to informational conformity? To whom do we look for answers to basic questions? Where do our standards come from—from Scripture, the church or simply the society in which we live? Paul's counsel "Do not be conformed to this world" warns against subtle social influences that alter our perspective and commitment. The world's pervasive influence is recognized by Paul in his command "Be transformed" (Rom 12:2 RSV). Clearly he sees the problem of conformity to this world as extending beyond relatively insignificant beliefs and actions to the core of our being, to our perceptions of reality, our most central beliefs and values. Otherwise the familiar warning against conformity would not be followed with a call for transformation, for a change relating to the entire person.

John Alexander writes, "From our perspective we need only moderate change. Our way of life is only tilted a little to one side. . . . I suggest that Jesus came to tell us things that are not obvious and that he offered a worldview that is quite contrary to the worldview of our culture." In *The Upside-Down Kingdom*, Donald Kraybill argues that the kingdom of God is inverted when compared with the generally accepted values of American society. He writes, "Following Jesus means not only a turning around in some personal habits and attitudes, but most fundamentally it means a completely new way of thinking—a new logic. To follow Jesus means a complete upsetting of the assumptions, logic, values, and presuppositions of the dominant culture." Thus the Christian's mindset changes when informed by Scripture. Definitions of success are inverted as self-sacrifice replaces self-seeking, compassion supplants ambition, sharing overcomes consumption, enemies are loved not hated and status hierarchies are flattened.

What's a Christian to Do?

The conformity research has implications for Christian lifestyle. Most fundamentally this social psychological literature questions our individualism, our refusal to recognize that we are interdependent and that we do influence each other. The illusion of independence pervades the church. We not only underestimate the problem of conformity to this world, but when we do recognize it our attempt to deal with it is often misguided. We think the solution is found in developing greater independence; we teach our children, "Dare to be a Daniel; dare to stand alone."

Living as Christians is necessarily a community task. It requires social support. Without a sustaining environment it is hard to develop and even more difficult to maintain a Christian lifestyle. Being created social means that we need to be nourished; we must be encouraged by each other to live our commitments. It's tough to maintain one's Amish identity while living alone in San Francisco.

Social influence is not inherently evil. Without doubt our actions are shaped by the people around us. But this very fact that can work against a Christian lifestyle can also work to enhance it. Consider a variation of the Milgram obedience study: Three teachers, rather than one, were assigned the task of punishing the learner. Two of the three teachers were confederates who had been told to disobey the experimenter after the learner's first vehement protest. In this situation, the obedience of the remaining teacher usually dropped dramatically.

From the compliant two-thirds in the original study it fell to 10 per cent. Milgram concluded that "the mutual support provided by men for each other is the strongest bulwark we have against the excesses of authority." Ironically, the majority of defiant subjects denied that the confederate teachers' action was the critical factor in their own defiance. This again illustrates that we are often unaware of others' influence.

Other studies have produced similar findings when the unanimity of the group is broken by having one member give a dissenting view. People provided with a single ally, a partner, show much more allegiance to truth than those who stand alone against the group. Hence disciples sent out two by two are provided mutual support in challenging the existing social order.

Observations of small groups, together with recent laboratory experiments, also indicate that when like-minded people interact, their initial tendencies intensify. For example, as members of diet groups discuss their mutual problem, their shared desire to cut their food consumption may heighten the commitment of each. In one laboratory study separate groups composed of relatively prejudiced or un-prejudiced students were asked to respond—both before and after discussion—to issues involving racial attitudes, such as property rights versus open housing. Discussion among like-minded students increased the initial gap between the two groups. Each group became stronger in its own convictions.

Christian fellowship can heighten spiritual identity, especially when members concentrate their interaction among themselves. As Thomas à Kempis recognized long ago, "a devout communing on spiritual things sometimes greatly helps the health of the soul especially when men of one mind and spirit meet and speak and commune together." Peter and Paul, freed from jail, met with their fellow believers and then went out to preach with even greater boldness. The chief dynamic of John Wesley's Methodist movement was the weekly small group meeting. Those who heard the powerful preaching but did not experience the support of the group sooner or later reverted to their former ways.

The Importance of Christian Community

If people are to live distinctively Christian lives, the spirit of individualism must be overcome. Loyalty to Christ is next to impossible without a relationship to his body, to a fellowship of Christians who contribute to each other's upbuilding. Although time and again we are reminded that the New Testament church was a believing *community*, we have lost this perspective. As Andrew Kuyvenhoven has observed, "Many of us become positively uneasy when we are made to realize that God wants us to contribute to the 'upbuilding' of others—by word and deed. It is certainly a lot easier to 'attend church' than to 'be church.'" Arthur Gish puts it even more strongly: "The church should not accept confessions of faith and commitments without providing nurture and support to help people keep their promises. We fail people by not supporting and helping them keep their commitments."

The fellowship of believers is necessary, however, not only for the support it provides, but also for defining what Christian commitment means in terms of everyday living. Jim Wallis suggests that Christians have often made their stand against culture in the wrong places. "Twentieth century evangelicals," he writes, "have largely ignored the most basic conflicts between the gospel and the American culture while carefully clinging to carefully defined separations from the world over trivial matters of personal behavior." Richard Foster has argued that one of the great tasks confronting the Christian is not "Do I conform or not?" but "Which issues demand nonconformity and which issues do not?"

Defining a Christian pattern of living is difficult and is necessarily a community task. We need each other. And while the identification of general principles will be important, more than this is needed. Even after we have absorbed the general rules we stumble over their application.

For example, a group may identify resisting materialism as a general goal, but what does that mean in terms of lifestyle? Perhaps, as Hendrik Hart and Ron Sider have suggested, we learn to practice community by dealing with specific issues and by starting in small ways. Within the church a few families who know they are spending too much might meet together to make changes in the way they live. They can discuss family finances and evaluate family budgets. Expenditures for houses, cars and vacations can be discussed honestly in terms of individual needs and the needs of God's kingdom. Tips for simpler living can be shared. And when decisions are reached, the people in the small community can encourage, support and pray for one another.

Separate groups might form to address other issues or problems. Those who are horrified at racism or concerned about the threat of nuclear holocaust might consider practical ways they could implement their Christian confession. Such groups need not become cliques nor judgmental of those in the larger Christian community. To combat that possibility, Hart suggests that the small communities remain open and that from time to time families change projects.

So, in taking seriously Paul's call for nonconformity, let's realize that neither anticonformity nor independence is the goal. Rather, as a community we seek a new conformity and another influence, that of Jesus Christ. In his letter to the Philippians, Paul makes it clear: "Being in full accord and of one mind, . . . have this mind among yourselves, which is yours in Christ Jesus" (Phil 2:2, 5 RSV). This will happen only as we seek the Lord together.

Questions

1. Why do people conform to those around them?
2. In what circumstances is conformity good? When is it bad? How can you decide the difference? What does one risk by choosing not to conform?
3. The title of this selection suggests that conformity is "a way out." Explain what the author means.

Shooting an Elephant

George Orwell

George Orwell was a brilliant author, essayist, and reviewer, whose titles include Animal Farm *and* Nineteen Eighty-Four. *This selection, based on his experiences as a law officer for the British Empire in Burma, is one of his best essays. When an elephant goes on a rampage and Orwell is pressured into shooting it, he begins to understand the true nature of his role in that foreign culture.*

In Moulmein, in Lower Burma, I was hated by large numbers of people—the only time in my life that I have been important enough for this to happen to me. I was sub-divisional police officer of the town, and in an aimless, petty kind of way anti-European feeling was very bitter. No one had the guts to raise a riot, but if a European woman went through the bazaars alone somebody would probably spit betel juice over her dress. As a police officer I was an obvious target and was baited whenever it seemed safe to do so. When a nimble Burman tripped me up on the football field and the referee (another Burman) looked the other way, the crowd yelled with hideous laughter. This happened more than once. In the end the sneering yellow faces of young men that met me everywhere, the insults hooted after me when I was at a safe distance, got badly on my nerves. The young Buddhist priests were the worst of all. There were several thousands of them in the town and none of them seemed to have anything to do except stand on street corners and jeer at Europeans.

All this was perplexing and upsetting. For at that time I had already made up my mind that imperialism was an evil thing and the sooner I chucked up my job and got out of it the better. Theoretically—and secretly, of course—I was all for the

Burmese and all against their oppressors, the British. As for the job I was doing, I hated it more bitterly than I can perhaps make clear. In a job like that you see the dirty work of Empire at close quarters. The wretched prisoners huddling in the stinking cages of the lock-ups, the grey, cowed faces of the long-term convicts, the scarred buttocks of the men who had been flogged with bamboos—all these oppressed me with an intolerable sense of guilt. But I could get nothing into perspective. I was young and ill-educated and I had had to think out my problems in the utter silence that is imposed on every Englishman in the East. I did not even know that the British Empire is dying, still less did I know that it is a great deal better than the younger empires that are going to supplant it. All I knew was that I was stuck between my hatred of the empire I served and my rage against the evil-spirited little beasts who tried to make my job impossible. With one part of my mind I thought of the British Raj as an unbreakable tyranny, as something clamped down, in *saecula saeculorum*, upon the will of prostrate peoples; with another part I thought that the greatest joy in the world would be to drive a bayonet into a Buddhist priest's guts. Feelings like these are the normal by-products of imperialism; ask any Anglo-Indian official, if you can catch him off duty.

One day something happened which in a roundabout way was enlightening. It was a tiny incident in itself, but it gave me a better glimpse than I had had before of the real nature of imperialism—the real motives for which despotic governments act. Early one morning the sub-inspector at a police station the other end of town rang me up on the phone and said that an elephant was ravaging the bazaar. Would I please come and do something about it? I did not know what I could do, but I wanted to see what was happening and I got on to a pony and started out. I took my rifle, an old .44 Winchester and much too small to kill an elephant, but I thought the noise might be useful *in terrorem*. Various Burmans stopped me on the way and told me about the elephant's doings. It was not, of course, a wild elephant, but a tame one which had gone "must." It had been chained up, as tame elephants always are when their attack of "must" is due, but on the previous night it had broken its chain and escaped. Its mahout, the only person who could manage it when it was in that state, had set out in pursuit, but had taken the wrong direction and was now twelve hours' journey away, and in the morning the elephant had suddenly reappeared in the town. The Burmese population had no weapons and were quite helpless against it. It had already destroyed somebody's bamboo hut, killed a cow and raided some fruit-stalls and devoured the stock; also it had met the municipal rubbish van and, when the driver jumped out and took to his heels, had turned the van over and inflicted violences upon it.

The Burmese sub-inspector and some Indian constables were waiting for me in the quarter where the elephant had been seen. It was a very poor quarter, a labyrinth of squalid bamboo huts, thatched with palmleaf, winding all over a steep hillside. I remember that it was a cloudy, stuffy morning at the beginning of the rains. We began questioning the people as to where the elephant had gone and, as usual, failed to get any definite information. That is invariably the case in the East; a story always sounds clear enough at a distance, but the nearer you get to the scene of events the vaguer it becomes. Some of the people said that the elephant had gone in one direction, some said that he had gone in another, some professed not even to have heard of any elephant. I had almost made up my mind that the whole story was a pack of lies, when we heard yells a little distance away. There was a loud, scandalized cry of "Go away, child! Go away this instant!" and an old woman with a switch in her hand came round the corner of a hut, violently shooing away a crowd of naked children. Some more women followed, clicking their tongues and exclaiming; evidently there was something that the children ought not to have seen. I rounded the hut and saw a man's dead body sprawling in the mud. He was an Indian, a black Dravidian coolie, almost naked, and he could not have been dead many minutes. The people said that the elephant had come suddenly upon him round the corner of the hut, caught him with its trunk, put its foot on his back and ground him into the earth. This was the rainy season and the ground was soft, and his face had scored a trench a foot deep and a couple of yards long. He was lying on his belly with arms crucified and head sharply twisted to one side. His face was coated with mud, the eyes wide open, the teeth bared and grinning with an expression of unendurable agony. (Never tell me, by the way, that the dead look peaceful. Most of the corpses I have seen looked devilish.) The friction of the great beast's foot had stripped the skin from his back as neatly as one skins a rabbit. As soon as I saw the dead man I sent an orderly to a friend's house nearby to borrow an elephant rifle. I had already sent back the pony, not wanting it to go mad with fright and throw me if it smelt the elephant.

The orderly came back in a few minutes with a rifle and five cartridges, and meanwhile some Burmans had arrived and told us that the elephant was in the paddy fields below, only a few hundred yards away. As I started forward practically the whole population of the quarter flocked out of the houses and followed me. They had seen the rifle and were all shouting excitedly that I was going to shoot the elephant. They had not shown much interest in the elephant when he was merely ravaging their homes, but it was different now that he was going to be shot. It was a bit of fun to them, as it would be to an English crowd; besides they wanted the meat. It made me vaguely uneasy. I had no intention of shooting the elephant—I had merely sent for the rifle to defend myself if necessary—and it is always unnerving to have a crowd following you. I marched down the hill, looking and feeling a fool, with the rifle over my shoulder and an ever-growing army of people jostling at my heels. At the bottom, when you got away from the huts, there was a metalled road and beyond that a miry waste of paddy fields a thousand yards across, not yet ploughed but soggy from the first rains and dotted with coarse grass. The elephant was standing eight yards from the road, his left side towards us. He took not the slightest notice of the crowd's approach. He was tearing up bunches of grass, beating them against his knees to clean them and stuffing them into his mouth.

I had halted on the road. As soon as I saw the elephant I knew with perfect certainty that I ought not to shoot him. It is a serious matter to shoot a working elephant—it is comparable to destroying a huge and costly piece of machinery—and obviously one ought not to do it if it can possibly be avoided. And at that distance, peacefully eating, the elephant looked no more dangerous than a cow. I thought then and I think now that his attack of "must" was already passing off; in which case he would merely wander harmlessly about until the mahout came back and caught him. Moreover, I did not in the least want to shoot him. I decided that I would watch him for a little while to make sure that he did not turn savage again, and then go home.

But at that moment, I glanced round at the crowd that had followed me. It was an immense crowd, two thousand at the least and growing every minute. It blocked the road for a long distance on either side. I looked at the sea of yellow faces above the garish clothes—faces all happy and excited over this bit of fun, all certain that the elephant was going to be shot. They were watching me as they would watch a conjuror about to perform a trick. They did not like me, but with the magical rifle in my hands I was momentarily worth watching. And suddenly I realized that I should have to shoot the elephant after all. The people expected it of me and I had got to do it; I could feel their two thousand wills pressing me forward, irresistibly. And it was at this moment, as I stood there with the rifle in my hands, that I first grasped the hollowness, the futility of the white man's dominion in the East. Here was I, the white man with his gun, standing in front of the unarmed native crowd—seemingly the leading actor of the piece; but in reality I was only an absurd puppet pushed to and fro by the will of those yellow faces behind. I perceived in this moment that when the white man turns tyrant it is his own freedom that he destroys. He becomes a sort of hollow, posing dummy, the conventionalized figure of a sahib. For it is the condition of his rule that he shall spend his life in trying to impress the "natives," and so in every crisis he has got to do what the "natives" expect of him. He wears a mask, and his face grows to fit it. I had got to shoot the elephant. I had committed myself to doing it when I sent for the rifle. A sahib has got to act like a sahib; he has got to appear resolute, to know his own mind and do definite things. To come all that way, rifle in hand, with two thousand people marching at my heels, and then to trail feebly away, having done nothing—no, that was impossible. The crowd would laugh at me. And my whole life, every white man's life in the East, was one long struggle not to be laughed at.

But I did not want to shoot the elephant. I watched him beating his bunch of grass against his knees, with that preoccupied grandmotherly air that elephants have. It seemed to me that it would be murder to shoot him. At that age I was not squeamish about killing animals, but I had never shot an elephant and never wanted to. (Somehow it always seems worse to kill a *large* animal.) Besides, there was the beast's owner to be considered. Alive, the elephant was worth at least a hundred pounds; dead, he would only be worth the value of his tusks, five pounds, possibly. But I had got to act quickly. I turned to some experienced-looking Burmans who had been there when we arrived, and asked them how the elephant had been behaving. They all said the same thing: he took no notice of you if you left him alone, but he might charge if you went too close to him.

It was perfectly clear to me what I ought to do. I ought to walk up to within, say, twenty-five yards of the elephant and test his behavior. If he charged, I could shoot; if he took no notice of me, it would be safe to leave him until the mahout came back. But also I knew that I was going to do no such thing. I was a poor shot with a rifle and the ground was soft mud into which one would sink at every step. If the elephant charged and I missed him, I should have about as much chance as a toad under a steam-roller. But even then I was not thinking particularly of my own skin, only of the watchful yellow faces behind. For at that moment, with the crowd watching me, I was not afraid in the ordinary sense, as I would have been if I had been alone. A white man mustn't be frightened in front of "natives"; and so, in general, he isn't frightened. The sole thought in my mind was that if anything went wrong those two thousand Burmans would see me pursued, caught, trampled on and reduced to a grinning corpse like that Indian up the hill. And if that happened it was quite probable that some of them would laugh. That would never do. There was only one alternative. I shoved the cartridges into the magazine and lay down on the road to get a better aim.

The crowd grew very still, and a deep, low, happy sigh, as of people who see the theatre curtain go up at last, breathed from innumerable throats. They were going to have their bit of fun after all. The rifle was a beautiful German thing with cross-hair sights. I did not then know that in shooting an elephant one would shoot to cut an imaginary bar running from ear-hole to ear-hole. I ought, therefore, as the elephant was sideways on, to have aimed straight at his ear-hole; actually I aimed several inches in front of this, thinking the brain would be further forward.

When I pulled the trigger I did not hear the bang or feel the kick—one never does when a shot goes home—but I heard the devilish roar of glee that went up from the crowd. In that instant, in too short a time, one would have thought, even for the bullet to get there, a mysterious, terrible change had come over the elephant. He neither stirred nor fell, but every line of his body had altered. He looked suddenly stricken, shrunken, immensely old, as though the frightful impact of the bullet had paralysed him without knocking him down. At last, after what seemed a long time—it might have been five seconds, I dare say—he sagged flabbily to his knees. His mouth slobbered. An enormous senility seemed to have settled upon him. One could have imagined him thousands of years old. I fired again into the same spot. At the second shot he did not collapse but climbed with desperate slowness to his feet and stood weakly upright, with legs sagging and head drooping. I fired a third time. That was the shot that did for him. You could see the agony of it jolt his whole body and knock the last remnant of strength from his legs. But in falling he seemed for a moment to rise, for as his hind legs collapsed beneath him he seemed to tower upward like a huge rock toppling, his trunk reaching skywards like a tree. He trumpeted, for the first and only time. And then down he came, his belly towards me, with a crash that seemed to shake the ground even where I lay.

I got up. The Burmans were already racing past me across the mud. It was obvious that the elephant would never rise again, but he was not dead. He was breathing very rhythmically with long rattling gasps, his great mound of a side painfully rising and falling. His mouth was wide open. I could see far down into caverns of pale pink throat. I waited a long time for him to die, but his breathing did not weaken. Finally I fired my two remaining shots into the spot where I thought his heart must be. The thick blood welled out of him like red velvet, but still he did not die. His body did not even jerk when the shots hit him, the tortured breathing continued without a pause. He was dying, very slowly and in great agony, but in some world remote from me where not even a bullet could damage him further. I felt I had got to put an end to that dreadful noise. It seemed dreadful to see the great beast lying there, powerless to move and yet powerless to die, and not even to be able to finish him. I sent back for my small rifle and poured shot after shot into his head and down his throat. They seemed to make no impression. The tortured gasps continued as steadily as the ticking of a clock.

In the end I could not stand it any longer and went away. I heard later that it took him half an hour to die. Burmans were bringing dahs and baskets even before I left, and I was told they had stripped his body almost to the bones by the afternoon.

Afterwards, of course, there were endless discussions about the shooting of the elephant. The owner was furious, but he was only an Indian and could do nothing. Besides, legally I had done the right thing, for a mad elephant has to be killed, like a mad dog, if its owner fails to control it. Among the Europeans opinion was divided. The older men said I was right, the younger men said it was a damn shame to shoot an elephant for killing a coolie, because the elephant was worth more than any damn Coringhee coolie. And afterwards I was very glad that the coolie had been killed; it put me legally in the right and it gave me sufficient pretext for shooting the elephant. I often wondered whether any of the others grasped that I had done it solely to avoid looking a fool.

Questions

1. How would you describe Orwell's moral dilemma?
2. Why did he feel pressure to shoot the elephant?
3. Why did the natives want him to shoot the elephant?
4. In what ways had Orwell become a "hollow, posing dummy"?

The Reuben Option

Allan Boesak

Allan Boesak lives in Cape Town, South Africa, where he writes and speaks widely on issues of racial justice. This selection is taken from his book Walking on Thorns. *Here Boesak looks carefully at the biblical figure of Reuben, half brother of Joseph and defender of Joseph's life when his other brothers desired to put him to death. But Reuben's motives for defending Joseph are suspect at best. He seems to be more interested in his own welfare than that of his brother. This is the dilemma of the church today. Boesak calls it "the Reuben option."*

But when Reuben heard it, he delivered him out of their hands, saying: "Let us not take his life. "And Reuben said to them: "Shed no blood; cast him into this pit here in the wilderness, but lay no hand upon him"—that he might rescue him out of their hand, to restore him to his father.

Genesis 37:21,22

Joseph was the favourite son of his father. He was, of course, the son of Rachel, Jacob's first and real love. He was also the son of his father's old age—not simply the son Rachel bore to him when he was already well on in years, but also the son who was such a comfort to him in his old age.

Joseph is special. All God's promises to Abraham and all the hopes of Jacob are now centred in this favourite son. His name means "add"—he is added, by the love and grace of God, a special gift from God which reshapes everything.

Joseph's birth marks a decisive change in the life of Israel. This son is a sign to Jacob that the promise of God still works in his life and in his body. Joseph is the last, because little Benjamin does not feature here. Once again we see the wonderful inversion of life's order by Yahweh: the last becomes first. That is why Joseph receives from his father the multicoloured robe with the long sleeves, a sure sign that he is the chosen one, the "crown prince," the one who will lead the family.

Spoiled, too young to do hard work, Joseph easily becomes a tattletale. Able to get away with things the older brothers are not permitted, his actions elicit the chagrin of his brothers. But that clearly is not the main reason for their hatred and jealousy. The real reason is something else: Joseph dreams.

Joseph dreams, but in a real sense he is only the bearer of dreams. The dream is Yahweh's dream, for Israel, for the world. The dream is a vision of history being inverted, undermined, changed against all odds. Joseph's dream is a power which neither tradition nor force can resist. It is a dream in which the impossible happens, the weak becomes strong, the lowly is raised up, the powerless is crowned with glory.

The brothers hated him because the dream threatened them. "They hated him, and could not speak peaceably with him" (vs.4), a wonderfully loaded phrase. Not only were they "unkind" to him, they could never be *at peace* with him; he was no longer a brother, he became an enemy. The decision to kill him does not really surprise us, it is almost inevitable.

Jacob provides the opportunity by sending Joseph to his brothers as they were tending flock near Shechem. "Here comes the dreamer," they say. Literally, here comes the lord, the master of dreams. A "master of dreams" is one who uses dreams to manipulate and intimidate others. The dreams now are not really visions, they are an instrument with which to gain control over others. As a sorcerer would use his powers, preying on superstition and the deep-seated fears of his victim, so Joseph is accused of using his dreams to intimidate and to control both his father and his brothers. They do not see his gift as a gift of God; for them it is not God's way of revealing the divine purposes for the chosen family and for the whole created world. They can only see Joseph's dream as a threat to the present order in which they have the upper hand. It is no longer a petty family quarrel—it is a life and death struggle. They simply *had* to kill him.

Reuben is not with his brothers in their strident demand that Joseph be put to death. He sounds so reasonable, so responsible—especially responsible. He emerges as Joseph's protector, saving him from certain death so that he could bring him back to Jacob.

Or so it seems. In reality, Reuben's role is much more ambiguous. He is the eldest, and therefore has special responsibilities. He is the one who must protect the family when the father is not present. He must also protect the family name and honour.

But Reuben's record is not all that clean. He seems to have shown little of the older brother's sense of responsibility as the tension builds up between Joseph and his brothers, and, by implication, the tension between the brothers and the father. There is no reconciling word, no attempt to mend the relations. No sign that he was trying to restrain his brothers as the grumbling grew more and more ominous. Even worse, Reuben has long since lost the confidence of his father, and his rightful place as the eldest, by sleeping with Bilha, Jacob's concubine.

What made him commit this grievous sin, "shaming his father's bed"? Was it a calculated move to secure for himself the headship of the clan, a strategy that was not uncommon in the ancient East where the successor to the throne inherited also the harem? This act of Reuben's was probably more than passing passion; it was perhaps in the nature of the declaration of a take-over. For Reuben, Israel was no longer "father"; he was an old man, a rival who stood in his way to the top. With infinite sensitivity, in words pregnant with tragedy, the narrator simply notes: ". . . and Israel heard of it" (Gen. 35:22).

So now Reuben engages in deception to save his brother. More for his own sake than Joseph's. Is it meant to restore Joseph to his father, or to restore Israel's faith in his eldest son? "Let us not spill blood," Reuben says, "let us throw him into the pit." He appears to speculate on the effect of the superstitious fear over the spilling of blood, something we find expressed in Genesis 9:6—as if murder would go unpunished as long as no blood is spilled.

But Reuben dares not choose openly for Joseph, he does not want to give up his popularity with his brothers now, and their support later, for his headship of the clan. So he sacrifices on two altars, as it were. He desperately wants to regain his father's favour, but he cannot risk alienation from his brothers. He knows what is right, he knows what he must do, but his hidden interests weigh too heavily on the other side. So Reuben opts for the feeble role of the "responsible" brother; his aim is to keep both sides happy, to do enough to salve his own conscience, but not enough to save the life of his brother.

Joseph is sold into slavery, and slavery is only a different kind of death. The fact that Joseph, many years later, can say that "it was not you who sent me here, but God" (45:8) does not alter this situation. Neither Joseph nor Reuben could have known this. The grace of God which turns evil into good can never be an excuse for our continued sinfulness. Reuben is not presented here as an evil man. He is not a murderer. No, he is presented as concerned and responsible. As Walter Brueggemann says: "Reuben is presented as responsible, but cowardly, and the killers of the dream will not be restrained by a responsible coward."

This, I think, is the agony of the church: we know what we should be doing, but we lack the courage to do it. We feel we ought to do it and we cannot. We are afraid to make choices, so we are constantly on the look-out for compromises. We are paralyzed by the need to be all things to all people, to be a church where all feel welcome all the time, and so we sacrifice on both altars. We stand accused by a history of compromises always made for the sake of survival.

We have justified slavery, violence and war; we have sanctified racism and split our churches on the issue of the preservation of white supremacy. We have discriminated against women and kept them servile whilst we hid our fear of them behind claims of "masculinity" and sanctimonious talk about Adam and Eve. We have grown rich and fat and powerful through the exploitation of the poor, which we deplored but never really tried to stop. All in the name of Jesus Christ and his gospel. Now this same gospel speaks to us, and we can no longer escape its demands. It calls us to love and justice and obedience. We would like to fulfill that calling, but we do not want to risk too much. The Reuben option.

The Reuben option: Take a stand, but always cover yourself. The problem cannot be ignored, so let us do something about it, but always in such a way that it does not hurt us too much. Take a stand; use the right words in the resolutions taken by the synod and the general assembly, but also make sure that you build into those resolutions all the necessary safeguards—just in case. Don't antagonize people too much, especially those in the church who have money. Opt for peace, but don't confuse that with justice.

The Reuben option: How often do we face it in my own country and in my own church! We know we have to say that we are against injustice, racism and apartheid. We know that we must work for the kingdom of God, work in such a way that people's humanity will be restored, but we are afraid to join the struggle for liberation, to participate actively in that struggle. The risks are too many. Let us pass resolutions against apartheid, but let us frame them in such a way that we can defend ourselves when the white church threatens to withdraw its money.

The Reuben option: Opt for justice, work against racism, but in such a way that we will not cause too much tension in the church. Was that not how the world church functioned for many years? Think of all the controversy and the conflict over the World Council of Churches' Programme to Combat Racism. We came close to losing our unity on that issue, we almost jeopardized our whole Christian witness on it. So the churches went through agonizing times. How do we support the PCR and yet do it in such a way that no one (especially those conservatives who hold the purse strings) can accuse us of giving money to "terrorists"? To our shock we discover that we have to choose constantly between the interests of those who can afford to make television programmes "exposing" the PCR and the interests of the oppressed, the poor and the weak, the victims of exploitation and racism, who also happen to be our brothers and sisters in the Lord.

The Reuben option: Have a programme for hungry children, collect millions and spend them on the poor. "Give and feel good!" is the legend on a poster from one charitable organization, with a picture of a little black child, arms grotesquely thin, protruding stomach, tears rolling down the cheeks. Yes, indeed. But to use all our energy, our resources, our ingenuity, to work honestly and openly to change an economic system that by its very nature cannot and will not give the poor a chance to become fully human? That we cannot do, because then we become "involved," and we have to look with new eyes at the systems on which our budgets are based.

The Reuben option: We face that ourselves. I know that we are called to serve God's kingdom in terms of peace and justice and human dignity. But how difficult it is when this call stands in the way of our ambition! When we live under the threat of death every day, when we are always only one step away from being "picked up," when they tell us that our name is "on the list" because we are a danger to "Christian civilization"—how difficult it is then to make that choice! And I have discovered that the choice for commitment and obedience is not made once for all. It is a choice that has to be made every day.

The Reuben option. And so we invent little excuses and we dress them up as theological arguments about church and politics, violence and non-violence, personal and public morality and, above all, responsibility. We call ourselves evangelical and ecumenical and fight one another; in the meantime the poor continue to be exploited, the weak continue to be trampled upon and the innocent continue to die. And we *know* we are being unworthy of the gospel.

"It is so difficult!" someone will say. Indeed it is. We are not "merely" human, we are *human!* But we are not the church of Reuben, we are the church of Jesus Christ. Are we not therefore able to do more than we think we can? Are we not those who will move mountains if we have faith "like a mustard seed"? Are we not those called by Jesus Christ to do his work in the world? Are we not those saved by him, and has he not made known to us "the mystery of his will" (Eph. 1:9) ?

I know we sometimes say: the situation is more complex than we think; we have to be careful, because the most important thing is the survival of the church. I would, however, like to submit to you that the survival of the church is none of our business. It is God's business. We must simply learn to trust God to take care of it. Why should we be so worried about the survival of the church? Maybe because for us that often means: don't antagonize those who give the most money. Sometimes it means: don't antagonize the powers that be. But do we really believe that any earthly power can destroy the church of Jesus Christ? No, the survival of the church is *not* our main problem. Our main problem lies within ourselves, and with our difficulty to be faithful and to be obedient, to love justice and mercy and to walk humbly with our Lord.

Kaj Munk was a pastor of the church in Denmark. He became the spiritual force behind the Danish resistance to Hitler at the time of the Nazi occupation. In January 1944, they took him away one night and shot him like a dog in the field, but his life and death continued to inspire the Danes in their struggle for freedom. To me, Kaj Munk is one of the great men in the recent history of the Christian church. He reminded his fellow pastors of what they needed in a world where the choices were becoming more stark, more painful, more unavoidable day by day. "What is therefore the task of the preacher today? Shall I answer: faith, hope and love? That sounds beautiful. But I would rather say: courage. No, even that is not challenging enough to be the *whole* truth. . . . Our task today is recklessness. . . . For what we as (church) lack is most assuredly not psychology or literature. We lack a holy rage. . . ."

A holy rage. The recklessness which comes from the knowledge of God and humanity. The ability to rage when justice lies prostrate on the streets and when the lie rages across the face of the earth. A holy anger about things that are wrong in the world. To rage against the ravaging of God's earth and the destruction of God's world. To rage when little children must die of hunger while the tables of the rich are sagging with food. To rage at the senseless killing of so many and against the madness of militarism. To rage at the lie that calls the threat of death and the strategy of destruction "peace." To rage against the complacency of so many in the church who fail to see that we shall live only by the truth, and that our fear will be the death of us all. . . . To restlessly seek that recklessness that will challenge, and to seek to change human history until it conforms to the norms of the kingdom of God.

And remember, says Kaj Munk, "the signs of the Christian church have always been the lion, the lamb, the dove and the fish. But *never* the chameleon." And remember too: the church is the chosen people of God.

But the chosen shall be known by their choices.

Questions

1. What is the Reuben option? Describe it in your own words. How does Reuben, Joseph's brother, exemplify "the Reuben option"? What was Reuben trying to protect—the life of Joseph or his own reputation?
2. What personal factors contribute to the Reuben option? What role do other people play? What is at stake?
3. What personal qualities are necessary to reject the Reuben option in the choices one makes?

A Chicken Sexer's Tough Choices

George K. Brushaber

George K. Brushaber is president of Bethel College and Seminary. This selection appeared as a column in the evangelical magazine Christianity Today. *Brushaber says that a few choices in life are clear-cut, like those of the chicken sexer. Most, however, are very complex because many alternatives and variables have to be considered. Those choices are like the ones made by the hide grader. In all of our choices, we need godly discernment.*

It was a long time ago, but I remember one contestant on television's "What's My Line" whose occupation completely stumped the panel. With a triumphant grin on his face, the guest finally identified himself as a "chicken sexer" employed in a hatchery to sort newborn chicks by sex.

Years later I toured a hatchery and observed a chicken sexer at work. At the rate of a thousand or more per hour, he grasped each fuzzy yellow chick and identified its gender instantly. Female chicks went to the hen houses to produce eggs. The roosters-to-be, on the other hand, started out on their inexorable journey toward the congenial colonel's secret blend of 13 herbs and spices. Although I observed him for a long time, I never determined how the chicken sexer made his judgment so quickly and surely. Was it because he had only two choices open to him?

At about that same time, I toured a leather warehouse. Hides from all over the world were sorted and then distributed to artisans who would fashion thousands of different leather products. In the center of the frantic warehouse activity, amid piles and piles of hides, stood the "hide grader." Constantly moving among the hundreds of bundles, the hide grader made a judgment about each hide. To me, they all looked the same. Yet the hide grader sorted them into 20 or more different categories. Without pausing in his sorting, he spoke of differences in color, smell, weight, pliability, and strength.

The key to the hide grader's judgments was more than these characteristics, I learned. It was the grader's ability to assess accurately for each hide how it could best be treated and "worked." He envisioned what that hide could become. He discerned its potential for usefulness and beauty.

"Do you reject many hides?" I asked.

"Nope, not me," he said. "Anybody can sort out the junk. I only work with the good stuff and make sure it ends up the very best it can be."

The chicken sexer and the hide grader go about their work not too many miles apart. Both judge quickly and confidently. Yet their decision-making processes differ. The chicken sexer chooses between two clear alternatives. The hide grader's options are complex, measured in nuances and degrees, laden with value and vision.

Life's choices are like that. Some choices—actually only a few—have two straightforward options. I choose between true and false, right and wrong. It is a relatively easy matter, even though I sometimes choose wrongly.

Usually, however, choosing is difficult. Judgment, insight, and vision are necessary. I must practice discernment. And sometimes I can only hope to discern the least among several evils.

Choosing among a host of alternatives, each encrusted with emotions, habits, and entangling considerations, is painfully hard. Alternatives may be full of promise or full of threat. Seldom can I anticipate all the consequences. Sometimes I am not even aware of all the alternatives available. Time for reflection is always short. I must judge, decide, act. That is my predicament. Paul understood our great need for discernment. He prayed for the Philippian believers that they would have both the knowledge and the discernment necessary to minister in faithfulness to Christ. The thrust of Paul's prayer on behalf of the Philippians was not only that they might have the discerning capacity to make the best choices, but also that they might become the best people, growing always more into the likeness of Christ. That is what I want for myself.

The older I get the more I realize that discernment comes as a gift from God. As discernment comes to characterize me more, I will choose those courses of action that will really matter. With God's help I can decide with confidence the more excellent way. I even dare to hope that my family, colleagues, and casual acquaintances, including the chicken sexer and the hide grader, will recognize that God has increased my capacity for genuine discernment. Pray as Paul did that I may increasingly become a man who discerns the mind of Christ and acts upon it.

Questions

1. Give an example of a significant, but clear-cut choice that you have had to make recently. Was the choice easy to make? Did you make the right decision? What happens when other people influence you to make a decision that you know is wrong?
2. Give an example of an important and not-so-clear-cut choice that you have had to make recently. What made the decision difficult? What were your options? Did you make the right decision? Did other people influence your decision?
3. Are "chicken-sexer decisions" easier to make than "hide-grader decisions"? Why or why not?

Prayers of Steel

Carl Sandburg

Carl Sandburg is among the best known American poets of modern times. Sandburg enjoyed traveling around the U.S. giving lectures, playing his guitar, and reading his poetry. He also was very interested in the life and times of Abraham Lincoln. One of his books on Lincoln, The War Years, *won the Pulitzer Prize. This poem expresses a Christian prayer to be transformed into a tool suitable for restoration and renewal in the kingdom of God.*

Lay me on an anvil, O God.
Beat me and hammer me into a crowbar.
Let me pry loose old walls.
Let me lift and loosen old foundations.

Lay me on an anvil, O God.
Beat me and hammer me into a steel spike.
Drive me into the girders that hold a skyscraper together.
Take red-hot rivets and fasten me into the central girders.
Let me be the great nail holding a skyscraper through blue
nights into white stars.

Questions

1. What do you think is the anvil in this poem? What is the skyscraper?
2. What does the poet wish to accomplish as a crowbar? As a steel spike?
3. What can you tell about the poet's attitude behind this prayer/poem? Is there a sense of complete commitment to God?

3
Exploring Issues

Work

Working People's Voices

Studs Terkel

Studs Terkel is a celebrated American author who collects much of his material by tape recording interviews with common people all across the country. He used this technique to research a book on World War II for which he won the Pulitzer Prize. These selections are taken from his book Working, *in which people talk about their jobs and how they feel about them.*

Mike LeFevre

It is a two-flat dwelling, somewhere in Cicero, on the outskirts of Chicago. He is thirty-seven. He works in a steel mill. On occasion, his wife Carol works as a waitress in a neighborhood restaurant; otherwise, she is at home, caring for their two small children, a girl and a boy. . . .

I'm a dying breed. A laborer. Strictly muscle work . . . pick it up, put it down, pick it up, put it down. We handle between forty and fifty thousand pounds of steel a day. (Laughs) I know this is hard to believe—from four hundred pounds to three- and four-pound pieces. It's dying.

You can't take pride any more. You remember when a guy could point to a house he built, how many logs he stacked. He built it and he was proud of it. . . .

It's hard to take pride in a bridge you're never gonna cross, in a door you're never gonna open. You're mass-producing things and you never see the end result of it. (Muses) I worked for a trucker one time. And I got this tiny satisfaction when I loaded a truck. At least I could see the truck depart loaded. In a steel mill, forget it. You don't see where nothing goes.

I got chewed out by my foreman once. He said, "Mike, you're a good worker but you have a bad attitude." My attitude is that I don't get excited about my job. I do my work but I don't say whoopee-doo. The day I get excited about my job is the day I go to a head shrinker. How are you gonna get excited about pullin' steel? How are you gonna get excited when you're tired and want to sit down?

It's not just the work. Somebody built the pyramids. Somebody's going to build something. Pyramids, Empire State Building—these things just don't happen. There's hard work behind it. I would like to see a building, say, the Empire State, I would like to see on one side of it a foot-wide strip from top to bottom with the name of every bricklayer, the name of every electrician, with all the names. So when a guy walked by, he could take his son and say, "See, that's me over there on the forty-fifth floor. I put the steel beam in." Picasso can point to a painting. What can I point to? A writer can point to a book. Everybody should have something to point to.

Sharon Atkins

A receptionist at a large business establishment in the Midwest. She is twenty-four. Her husband is a student. "I was out of college, an English Lit. major. I looked around for copywriting jobs. The people they wanted had majored in journalism. Okay, the first myth that blew up in my face is that a college education will get you a job."

. . . You come in at nine, you open the door, you look at the piece of machinery, you plug in the headpiece. That's how my day begins. You tremble when you hear the first ring. After that, it's sort of downhill—unless there's somebody on the phone who is either kind or nasty. The rest of the people are just non, they don't exist. They're just voices. You answer calls, you connect them to others, and that's it.

I don't have much contact with people. You can't see them. You don't know if they're laughing, if they're being satirical or being kind. So your conversations become very abrupt. I notice that in talking to people. My conversations would be very short and clipped, in short sentences, the way I talk to people all day on the telephone.

I never answer the phone at home. It carries over. The way I talk to people on the phone has changed. Even when my mother calls, I don't talk to her very long. I want to *see* people to talk to them. But now, when I see them, I talk to them like I was talking on the telephone. It isn't a conscious process. I don't know what's happened. When I'm talking to someone at work, the telephone rings, and the conversation is interrupted. So I never bother finishing sentences or finishing thoughts. I always have this feeling of interruption. . . .

The machine dictates. This crummy little machine with buttons on it—you've got to be there to answer it. You can walk away from it and pretend you don't hear it, but it pulls you. . . . Your job doesn't mean anything. Because *you're* just a little machine. A monkey could do what I do. It's really unfair to ask someone to do that.

Nora Watson

Jobs are not big enough for people. It's not just the assembly line worker whose job is too small for his spirit, you know? A job like mine, if you really put your spirit into it, you would sabotage immediately. You don't dare. So you absent your spirit from it. My mind has been so divorced from my job, except as a source of income, it's really absurd.

As I work in the business world, I am more and more shocked. You throw yourself into things because you feel that important questions—self-discipline, goals, a meaning of your life—are carried out in your *work*. You invest a job with a lot of values that the society doesn't allow you to put into a job. You find yourself like a pacemaker that's gone crazy or something. You want it to be a million things that it's not and you want to give it a million parts of yourself that nobody else wants there. So you end up wrecking the curve or else settling down and conforming. I'm really in a funny place right now. I'm so calm about what I'm doing and what's coming. . . .

She is twenty-eight. She is a staff writer for an institution publishing health care literature. Previously she had worked as an editor for a corporation publishing national magazines.

She came from a small mountain town in western Pennsylvania. "My father was a preacher. I didn't like what he was doing, but it was his vocation. That was the good part of it. It wasn't just: go to work in the morning and punch a time clock. It was a profession of himself. I expected work to be like that. All my life, I planned to be a teacher. It wasn't until late in college, my senior year, that I realized what the public school system was like. A little town in the mountains is one thing. . . .

"My father, to my mind, is a weird person, but whatever he is, he is. Being a preacher was so important to him he would call it the Call of the Lord. He was willing to make his family live in very poor conditions. He was willing to strain his relationship with my mother, not to mention his children. He put us through an awful lot of things, including just bare survival, in order to stay being a preacher. His evenings, his weekends, and his days, he was out calling on people. Going out with healing oil and anointing the sick, listening to their troubles. The fact that he didn't do the same for his family is another thing. But he saw himself as the core resource in the community—at a great price to himself. He really believed that was what he was supposed to be doing. It was his life.

"Most of the night he wouldn't go to bed. He'd pull out sermons by Wesley or Spurgeon or somebody, and he'd sit down until he fell asleep, maybe at three o'clock in the morning. Reading sermons. He just never stopped." (Laughs.)

I paper the walls of my office with posters and bring in flowers, bring in an FM radio, bring down my favorite ceramic lamp. I'm the only person in the whole . . . building with a desk facing the window instead of the door. I turn myself around from all that I can. I ration my time so that I'll spend two hours working for the Institution and the rest of the time I'll browse. (Laughs.)

I function better if they leave me alone more. My boss will come in and say, "I know you're overloaded, but would you mind getting this done, it's urgent. I need it in three weeks." I can do it in two hours. So I put it on the back burner and produce it on time. When I first went there, I came in early and stayed late. I read everything I could on the subject at hand. I would work a project to the wall and get it really done right, and then ask for more. I found out I was wrecking the curve, I was out of line.

The people, just as capable as I and just as ready to produce, had realized it was pointless, and had cut back. Everyone, consciously or unconsciously, was rationing his time. Playing cards at lunch time for three hours, going sun bathing, or less obvious ways of blowing it. I realized: Okay, the road to ruin is doing a good job. The amazing, absurd thing was that once I decided to stop doing a good job, people recognized a kind of authority in me. Now I'm just moving ahead like blazes.

I have my own office. I have a secretary. If I want a book case, I get a book case. If I want a file, I get a file. If I want to stay home, I stay home. If I want to go shopping, I go shopping. This is the first comfortable job I've ever had in my life and it is absolutely despicable.

I've been a waitress and done secretarial work. I knew, in those cases, I wasn't going to work at near capacity. It's one thing to work to your limits as a waitress because you end up with a bad back. It's another thing to work to your limits doing writing and editing because you end up with a sharper mind. It's a joy. Here, of all places, where I had expected to put the energy and enthusiasm and the gifts that I may have to work—it isn't happening. They expect less than you can offer. Token labor. What writing you do is writing to order. When I go for a job interview—I must leave this place!—I say, "Sure, I can bring you samples, but the ones I'm proud of are the ones the Institution never published."

It's so demeaning to be there and not be challenged. It's humiliation, because I feel I'm being forced into doing something I would never do of my own free will—which is simply waste itself. It's really not a Puritan hang-up. It's not that I want to be persecuted. It's simply that I know I'm vegetating and being paid to do exactly that. It's possible for me to sit here and read my books. But then you walk out with no sense of satisfaction, with no sense of legitimacy! I'm being had. Somebody has bought the right to you for eight hours a day. The manner in which they use you is completely at their discretion. You know what I mean? . . .

For all that was bad about my father's vocation, he showed me it was possible to fuse your life to your work. His home was also his work. A parish is no different from an office, because it's the whole countryside. There's nothing I would enjoy more than a job that was so meaningful to me that I brought it home.

Questions

1. Mike LeFevre, Sharon Atkins, and Nora Watson are obviously unhappy in their jobs. What are they looking for? Can they get it from their work?
2. If you find yourself in such a job, what are some specific things that you might try to do to make the job more meaningful?

In Fulltime Fishmonger Service

Calvin G. Seerveld

Calvin Seerveld is an author and teacher at the Institute of Christian Studies in Toronto. This selection was published in The Banner. *Seerveld describes the working environment in his father's fish market in the 1930s. He says that his father was "in fulltime service for the Lord—prophet, priest, and king in the fish business." He suggests that Christian workers should also see their labors in that same biblical sense.*

My father is a seller of fish. We sons know the business, too, having worked from childhood in the Great South Bay Fish Market, Patchogue, Long Island, New York, helping our father like a quiver full of arrows. It is a small store, and it smells like fish.

I remember a Thursday noon long ago when my dad was selling a large carp to a prosperous Jewish woman, and it was a battle to convince her. "Is it fresh?" It fairly bristled with freshness, had just come in, but the game was part of the sale.

They had gone over it anatomically: the eyes were bright, the gills were a good color, the flesh was firm, the belly was even spare and solid, the tail showed not much waste, the price was right—finally my dad held up the fish behind the counter, "Beautiful, beautiful! Shall I clean it up?" And as the Jewish lady grudgingly assented, ruefully admiring the way the bargain had been struck, she said, "My, you certainly didn't miss your calling."

Unwittingly she spoke the truth. My father is in fulltime service for the Lord—prophet, priest, and king in the fish business. And customers who come in the store sense it. Not that we always have the cheapest fish in town! Not that there are no mistakes on a busy Friday morning! Not that there is no sin! But this: that little Great South Bay Fish Market—my father and two employees—is not only a clean, honest place where you can buy quality fish at a reasonable price and with a smile, but it is also a store with a spirit, a spirit of laughter, of fun, joy *inside* the buying and selling that strikes an observer pleasantly. And the strenuous week-long preparations in the back room for Friday fish-day are not a routine drudgery interrupted by "rest periods," but again, a spirit seems to hallow the lowly work into a rich service, *Godsdienst* (God-service, Dutch word for *worship service)*, in which it is good to officiate.

When I watch my dad's hands, big beefy hands with broad stubby fingers each twice the thickness of mine (they could never play a piano), when I watch those hands delicately split the back of a mackerel or with a swift, true stroke fillet a flounder close to the bone, leaving all the meat together; when I know that those hands dressed and peddled fish from the handlebars of a bicycle in the grim 1930s, cut and sold fish year after year with never a vacation through fire and sickness, thieves and disaster, weariness, winter cold and hot muggy summers, twinkling at work without complaint, past temptations, struggling day in, day out to fix a just price, in weakness often but always in faith consecratedly cutting up fish before the face of the Lord; when I see that, I know God's grace can come down to a man's hand and the flash of a scabby fish knife.

Let me go one step further. The dirtiest job in the fish store is Friday's late load-up of the truck with a dozen large, metal barrels full of fish scraps, bones, guts and leftovers, rotting boxes, other refuse and seaweed, and the six-mile drive to the city dump outside of town. It looks like a movie set for Dante's Inferno as you approach the dump past uninhabited scrublands, with wildcat fires scattered about its perimeter, grotesque mountains of sliding cans and rubbish, and animated bulldozers poking and pushing and cursing through the smoke. You back the truck up in rather soft sand to the edge of the cavernous hole, not too close lest it give way, but right to the brink, throw open the doors, and then one by one try to tip the heavy cans of slops over your leg down into the abyss without slopping all over your shoes and pants and without losing the can in the pit or falling in yourself. I've sometimes thought as I stood there stinking in the summer heat, catching my breath in a maze of flies, eyes smarting from the stench and smoke, what a perfect place for Chaucer's line on the yeoman, "But it was joye for to seen hym swete!"

That's biblical! I am not romanticizing but am putting work in a biblical perspective so strange to modern thought: the meanest work can be done to the Lord and is a holy service. My brothers and I at work in the dumps, laughing and struggling, happy to be bodily alive there too—it is like a little hallelujah chorus sung by the South Bay Fish Market, the kind of earthly hallelujah, priestly service, angels fain would sing, but which God has reserved for the believing man, the Christian worker.

That man or woman has missed his or her calling whose daily work is not a thanksgiving to the living God. The person whose work is thanksgiving, praise of the God of heaven and earth, has a daily joy, a solace, unmeasurable in human coin. I am not saying that the Bible automatically sanctions any old job. Rather, the Bible calls workers to hallelu the Lord in whatever job they have and promises that the Spirit of God will sanctify the work itself of those who respond in faith to the divine calling. I know, the increasingly mechanized and specialized factory work is making it more and more difficult for workers to understand their jobs as sacred callings. That is why the fellowship of the working saints is all the more imperative! The hairs of our heads are numbered to God Almighty. The intents of our hearts are privy to God alone, and the Lord probes intently, jealously, the work of our hands. All of it. Because we were bought with his own Son's blood, we belong completely to our God. If we lose this biblical vision, we perish from his sight.

I remember it this way, from my name: *Seerveld* is a medieval nondescript place name like *van den Berg* (from the mountain). Some serfs scattered about on lands outside the feudal lord's castle were probably called *des heren veld* (of the lord's field). In time the initial *d* dropped off, the *h* was left out, and the rest smoothed out to *seerveld* (a field of the lord). God has thoughtfully provided me, it seems, with a kind of gentle reminder of my creaturely working status. All I am is a nondescript field of the Lord for God to plow and cultivate and bring forth fruit in; God asks me only to be responsive, hallelujahing ground, a place for the Holy Spirit to have free play in. Everyone—van den Berg, van der Vennen, van der Ploeg—should also be *des Heren veld*. That is our *logical* service, says the Scriptures.

Questions

1. Describe the atmosphere in the fish market. How did Seerveld feel about working there? Why do you think the customers could sense it, too?
2. What was it about the fish market that gave it a spirit of joy, laughter, and fun? Did it have to do with the type of work—or the type of worker?
3. What does it mean to "hallelu the Lord in whatever job we have"?

Why Work?

Bruce Shelley

Bruce Shelley is a church history professor at Denver Seminary. This selection appeared in the magazine Christianity Today. *He writes that most North Americans these days think work is just a necessary evil, a "mere means to personal pleasure." People don't expect to get much satisfaction out of their jobs anymore. In contrast, the Bible has a lot to say about work. Shelley points out several biblical principles and concludes that quality, honesty, and care in our daily work are vitally important for the Christian worker.*

In April 1988, national news wires reported the death of a self-educated janitor named Lawrence Hummel, who wore his lawyer's hand-me-downs but left over $600,000 to Bethany College in northern West Virginia, where he mopped floors for 30 years.

Hummel had amassed a million-dollar fortune from the stock market with knowledge gleaned from discussions with professors and from economics classes at the college. Even so, to the end of his life Hummel continued to live frugally .

"If you saw him and talked with him," said Joseph Gompers, his lawyer, "you might confuse him with a bum. But he wasn't. He was a warm, compassionate person who cared about people" (*The Denver Post*, April 20, 1988).

The story made news because Lawrence Hummel was different; according to the standards of contemporary American culture, he was even something of a misfit. He saw no need to turn his wealth into any of the normally accepted symbols of the American dream: clothes, travel, homes, or cars. Work, for Hummel, had a higher purpose. Thoughtful Christians have always claimed the same thing—that work has a purpose beyond paychecks and perks.

Restless in the workplace

Contemporary American culture would give several reasons for work. Perhaps the prevailing one is traceable to Adam Smith's classic treatise, *The Wealth of Nations*. In 1776 the Scottish professor of moral philosophy argued that people work because it is in their enlightened self-interest. "Every individual," Smith wrote, "is continually exerting himself to find out the most advantageous employment for whatever capital he can command." Capitalism, based on Adam Smith's views, then, harnesses our innate selfishness for the "common good."

While capitalism in America has changed dramatically in the last two generations, evidence of the creativity and productivity that it has fostered abounds. We are surrounded by the promises and rewards of the American dream: appliances, cars, conveniences, and toys of all shapes and sizes.

At the same time, thoughtful observers of the American scene have become acutely aware of the dark side of all this: widespread addiction to self-interest, the passion for consumer products, and the empty spirit of today's worker. Many Americans pursuing the economic dream of hot tubs, condos, and money market accounts are apparently growing restless in the workplace.

One recent poll, conducted for Robert Half International, a New York based accounting, data-processing, and recruitment firm, indicated that one out of four Americans is unhappy in his or her job. The reasons? Workers most often mentioned their need for greater recognition, more money, less stress, and a better boss.

This frustration in the workplace comes in large part because people feel the squeeze of two conflicting attitudes toward work.

On the one hand, Americans are influenced by the images from our economic culture that portray the workplace as a source of happiness and personal fulfillment. Even when we are not sure how to define work, we know that it is linked somehow with a sense of self. What we *do* is supposed to describe what we *are*.

When an American meets someone for the first time, within minutes the question is asked, "What do you do?" The frequency of the question points to our idolization of jobs in America. We even assess a person's worth according to his or her employment.

In the 1970s, Studs Terkel wrote a hefty volume titled *Working* in which he let scores of workers describe their feelings about their jobs. It was obvious that most of them nurtured the dream that they would somehow "find themselves" in their work; and when they suddenly found themselves on the list of the unemployed, they were devastated.

Terkel quoted John R. Coleman, president of Haverford College, who probably expressed the trauma of unemployment best. He had taken an unusual sabbatical in 1973, during which he worked at menial jobs. While working as a porter-dishwasher, he was fired.

"I'd never been fired," he recalled, "and I'd never been unemployed. For three days I walked the streets. Though I had a bank account, though my children's tuition was paid, though I had a salary and a job waiting for me back in Haverford, I was demoralized."

On the other hand, recent years have convinced many Americans that work can never be satisfying in itself. Many of us endure work only so long as it promises a satisfactory private life. Work, more recent American culture would have us believe, is simply a necessary evil of physical existence, a mere means to personal pleasure.

Americans subscribing to this line of thinking live from one coffee break to another. When it comes to weekends, "TGIF," they say: "Thank God, it's Friday!" Work is the place to accumulate the cash for another escape to Maui or the Bahamas. So a job for these Americans is always a barrier to happiness, never a way of happiness.

Can't we catch the same attitude in our television commercials? Not long ago one of them showed four friends in their fishing clothes, surrounded by a breathtaking mountain scene. They were sitting around a warm, glowing fire. The fish were in the skillet and the beer was on ice. With everyone smiling, one of the men held up a chilled can and said, "It just doesn't get any better than this."

The point is obvious: Life isn't found on the job accomplishing something significant. It is found instead with the boys, outdoors, on a weekend, with food and a special beer.

The frustration behind this understanding of work has led hosts of Americans today to abandon the traditional Puritan work ethic. . . . They work with no overarching purpose. . . .

Work in the Bible

What is the Christian alternative to the raw self-interest of the American dream? The Bible teaches that work is ordained of God, for our benefit.

That is the significance of the Christian view of work. In their book *Why Work?* (Baker), John Bernbaum and Simon Steer summarize the biblical teaching with five basic principles:

First, *work is God-ordained.* According to the Genesis story of Creation, the command to work comes from One who is himself a worker. Work was not a result of sinful rebellion; it was a part of God's original intention for human beings. According to Genesis, God commands humanity to "fill the earth and subdue it. Rule over the fish of the sea and the birds of the air and over every living creature" (Gen. 1:28, NIV). We work, then, because God intended us to work.

Second, *as a result of fundamental human rebellion against God, work no longer brings the fulfillment and joy God intended.* Human rebellion is reflected in human work. Work can now become a means of exploitation and oppression, or it can become an idol.

The teacher of Ecclesiastes is a striking example of our human frustration. "I built houses for myself," he writes, "and planted vineyards. . . . I bought male and female slaves. . . . I amassed silver and gold for myself. . . . Yet when I surveyed all that my hands had done . . . everything was meaningless, a chasing after the wind" (Eccles. 2:4-11, NIV).

Third, *Jesus Christ has redeemed our work from the curse.* That the incarnate God worked at a carpenter's bench is a striking testimony to the sanctity of the workplace.

Fourth, *for the Christian, work is to be done as a service to Christ.* "Slaves," wrote the apostle Paul, "whatever you do, work at it with all your heart, as working for the Lord, not for men, since you know that you will receive an inheritance from the Lord as a reward. It is the Lord Christ you are serving" (Col. 3 : 22-24, NIV) .

Finally, *the Bible tells us that work not only brings glory to God if done for him, but has moral benefits as well.* In 2 Thessalonians 3:10-12, Paul tells us that we should work in order to provide for ourselves and our families. And in Ephesians 4:28 he urges believers to undertake work that is useful, that we may have "something to share with those in need."

A Christian's view

In our time it is almost impossible for Americans to see how their work can be useful and serve the community at large. The growth of cities and the organization of labor have "privatized" work. In the last two generations, Americans have come to look upon their work almost exclusively in terms of personal advantages. Any benefit for the community— beyond economic growth— has largely dropped from view.

Christians, however, are governed by a higher conception of work. In the collect for Labor Day, the Episcopal Book of Common Prayer entreats God, " So guide us in the work we do, that we may do it not for self alone, but for the common good." This concern for the "common good" can make work more than a private enterprise.

"The entrepreneur who creates hundreds of new jobs," writes Denver's Catholic Archbishop J. Francis Stafford in *This Home of Freedom*, "is performing a morally good act: he or she is giving fellow human beings an opportunity to exercise their capacity for honest work. Workers who perform their duties conscientiously and well, and trade unions which bargain in good faith for the rights of workers, are also moral agents, contributing to the integrity of the workplace."

We should remember that the colonial Puritans who shaped so much of our thinking about work spoke of work as *vocation*. The word carries the thought that our work is a calling from God. The Lord himself, it implies, has a purpose for every person's work, whether as a nurse, a pilot, a social worker, a lawyer, a mechanic, or, as Jesus, a carpenter.

Certain vocations, it is true, more directly influence the thinking and viewpoints of people in society. Teachers, scriptwriters, politicians, editors, judges, artists, and ministers all fall into this category; they address questions of life and its meaning. Because Christians hold a special view about the kind of creatures we are and what is in store for us in the future, Christians in these "meaning-of-life" vocations carry a special responsibility to communicate the Christian view of the world. And when they do, they will make a difference in American life.

In many other vocations the questions of ultimate purpose and human destiny never affect the quality of the work itself. A plumber's work itself, for example, never addresses the question of life's meaning. But in these sorts of vocations, the Christian reflects his or her faith in another way, through the care given to the work itself. A Christian plumber therefore works honestly and does the best work he can.

Quality is job one

Whether we directly influence others in our jobs or reflect our faith more indirectly through our handiwork, Jesus' workbench suggests to us something about the importance of the quality of our daily work. Who, after all, can imagine Jesus turning out shoddy work?

The biblical term for carpenter suggests a craftsman. In the earlier days, and still today in many places, in small towns like Nazareth, there were village craftsmen, handymen who could repair a gate, build useful cabinets, or make a set of table and chairs.

That is the kind of work Jesus did. The drawers of the cabinets ran smoothly, the yokes were well balanced, the boxes were square, and the toys were sturdy and safe.

Why does that sound like "the good old days"? Has quality slipped from the American workplace?

Addison H. Leitch, the late Presbyterian professor at Gordon-Conwell Seminary, wrote not long before he died about how he once made himself unpopular at a college convocation at the end of a semester when everyone was getting ready to go home for the holidays.

"Suppose," Leitch said, "that the last man to check out the jet plane on which you will fly home did his job just as faithfully as you have done yours here during the last semester."

A groan went up. The students all knew that the man on the jet can be depended on to do the *right* thing.

But *did* they know that? In a day of dirty restaurants, trains that crash, television repairmen who don't "fix it," police who take bribes, and students who lift books from libraries, how did they know that the maintenance man would do his job?

Quality is a Christian concern because for the Christian the daily job is a daily offering to God. It is never a mere matter of personal choice.

That perspective is vital today. Americans are trying to conduct business, run companies, and get ahead with little concern for standards of right and wrong. Morality, we like to think, is a personal matter. "The business of America is business," some say.

But Christians know better. Like Lawrence Hummel, they have an unusual view of work. They hold that the gospel brings responsibility, dignity, and purpose to what happens in the shop or office. Jesus Christ, their Savior and Model, was, after all, a carpenter. And God has purposes for our work that go far beyond our day-to-day tasks.

Questions

1. Contrast the Christian and the secular reasons for working. Why are they so different?
2. What five biblical principles concerning work are suggested by Bernbaum and Steer?
3. How did Lawrence Hummel's view of work differ from that of most North Americans? Does his view differ from yours? In what ways?

Justice and the Opportunity to Work

Richard C. Chewning, John W. Eby, Shirley J. Roels

This selection appears as a chapter in the book Business Through the Eyes of Faith. *The authors believe that everyone should have an equal opportunity to work, but discrimination (because of race, sex, physical ability, and age) in our society severely limits job access for many people. Christians should lead the way in developing antidiscrimination policies in the workplace.*

Work Is a Healing Process

One of our company customs is to have an appreciation dinner for people who retire. Some time ago, a man with a congenital hip problem retired. He has walked with a severe limp all his life. At the dinner we were sitting next to each other. I asked him, "Arthur, do you have pain all the time?"

"Yes, I do."

"How many years have you had this pain?"

"All my life—for sixty-five years."

"How could you work with all that pain?" I asked him.

He put his hand on my shoulder. "The trouble with you healthy people is that you don't realize that work is a healing process."

Everyone Deserves to Work

Isn't it going a bit too far to suggest, that work is a healing process? Most of us would do anything we can to avoid work. Or would we? One of the really difficult things about being sick is that we cannot work. Even children get bored after several days' vacation from school because they do not have work to do.

When Adam and Eve were created God gave them the responsibility to take care of the garden (Genesis 2:15). They were given authority over all the animals. Work is a natural and important part of life. It is through work that we are creative and that we produce products or provide services that benefit ourselves and others. The ability to work is a gift from God. God worked in creating the world. Because we are created in God's image, we find meaning and fulfillment in work too.

There are many kinds of work. Some are organized and provide salary; other work is volunteer, such as with the United Way or the church. Some kinds of work, like cooking and yard work, come because we are part of families. Some work is honored and publicly acclaimed; other work, such as caring for an invalid grandparent, often goes unnoticed.

Access to meaningful work is a fundamental consideration of economic justice because work is so central to our purpose in the world. Salaried work is also the primary means in our society for getting the money we need to live.

In ancient Israel there were three ways in which people were given access to productive capacity. In that agrarian society land was the most important resource. First, the land was divided between the tribes by lot (Numbers 26:55-56; 33:54; Joshua 13-19). Not everyone got exactly the same amount or quality. The tribe of Dan, for example, got one of the smallest inheritances, but was the second largest group. And Manasseh, who was to get a double share, ended up with approximately six times as much land as his brother Ephraim's tribe. The tribes were not equal in their starting points.

Within each tribe those with greater need were given greater resources. The families within the individual tribes were to divide the land so that the larger families in each tribe would get more land than the smaller families (Numbers 26:53-54; 33:54). Within the families of each tribe there was a principle of equality at work.

The Jubilee principle was established to rearrange access to resources and the work associated with them. Every fifty years all land was to revert to the original holder's family so that no family would be permanently disinherited or refused access to the means of production (Leviticus 25:15-41). This principle meant that poor judgment, material inequalities, or misconduct of one generation would not have perpetually negative effects on subsequent family generations. Despite initial inequalities, God wanted everyone in Israel to work and have access to productive resources.

There is probably no greater dehumanizing force in the world than structures that deny employment, for whatever reason, to those who want to work and are able to do so; or structures that prohibit certain groups of people from gaining promotions or from moving into upper levels of responsibility.

We will specifically address four kinds of discrimination that affect our society: race, sex, physical disability, and age.

Racial Discrimination

All societies have some kinds of racial discrimination. Until very recently South Africa had a system of job reservation that reserved jobs beyond specified levels for white people. A black person could get a job in an automobile repair shop doing menial work and handing tools to the mechanic as long as he worked under the direction of a white person. But no matter how much experience he had or how much he knew, he could not get a job that required supervising others or total responsibility for the job.

Our society has no laws that foster discrimination in this blatant way, but many subtle forces lead to similar results. De facto discrimination places artificial impediments to job access or promotion. It gives one group advantages God never intended. It is a contrived system that makes some groups superior to others.

Racial discrimination has been a major barrier to employment opportunities over the centuries. Majority and powerful groups have found some way to exploit minority groups whenever there were ways to distinguish between the groups.

Sometimes discrimination is based on color, such as when whites discriminate against blacks. Sometimes discrimination is based on physical differences, such as between Europeans and Asians. Heritage, religion, and ethnicity were factors in the Nazi discrimination against Jews.

The problems created by discrimination continue long after the direct practice is changed. Slavery has been illegal in this country for more than a century. There have been laws for several decades against job discrimination based on race. Yet the effects of earlier discrimination remain.

Families who years ago were not able to enter college cannot pass on to their children the attitudes and advantages they missed. People forced to live in poverty because of housing and job discrimination experience structural forces that prevent them from developing skills, habits, and attitudes that help them get good education and jobs.

The Bible is clear on two points regarding reparation for past wrongs. Those individuals who are responsible for injury are to be held personally accountable for making restitution, and those who suffer a definable loss are due payment (Exodus 22:1-15). Also, nations and groups of people who discriminate incur long-term costs of such discrimination. South Africa is experiencing severe economic difficulties because of its failure to use the resources of the black population. There is continual political instability and fear among the whites because of the unjust policies.

As a part of their contribution to society businesses must find ways both to eliminate current discriminatory practices and to catch up for past wrongs. God wants everyone to have meaningful and productive work and to have access to productive resources. We should be leading the charge to hire a diverse multicultural work force.

Sex Discrimination

Sex discrimination also limits opportunities for women and, to a lesser extent, men. Some policies discriminate against single people. Some years ago a Christian organization provided benefits such as medical insurance to men on its staff, but not to married women—because they assumed the women would receive those benefits through their husbands! That kind of blatant discrimination is no longer legal, and it was certainly never right.

Both men and women are created to enjoy the gift of meaningful and productive work (Genesis 1:26-27). Proverbs 31:10-31 describes a very successful and industrious married woman. She was something of a superwoman, who probably had a number of servants to help get everything done. In the agrarian society of biblical times women worked beside their husbands. In the Bible God gave many commands to correct role stereotypes that had developed. The stereotype would have suggested that women had primary responsibility for children. Yet God gave fathers special responsibilities for educating children. The need for fathers to love their children was given special attention by John the Baptist when he called the fathers of his day back to a loving care for their children (Luke 1:17). It was not assumed that fathers should place their career ahead of their love for their children. Both mothers and fathers must wrestle with the tensions that can build up as they seek to balance God's creation mandates regarding family, work, and worship, and as they break out of the role stereotypes of the past.

The Bible really takes a very revolutionary stance for the culture in which it was written. It portrays godly women in a variety of work situations that defy tradition. The church at Corinth included Lydia, a seller of purple-dyed cloth (Acts 16:13-15), who was a significant commercial merchant. Deborah was a judge (Judges 4-5). Jesus affirmed Mary when she chose to do traditional male activities, worship and study, rather than the traditional female work of preparing the meal (Luke 10:38-42). Paul writes that in Christ there is neither male nor female (Galatians 3:28).

Traditional assumptions about women's work patterns are changing in our culture. Unfortunately, though, some of the traditional assumptions are still used by some employers to justify limited job placement for women, lower pay scales, slow promotions, and other policies that restrict equity in employment. Christians should take the lead in finding ways to balance the tensions between family and work by striving to eliminate sex discrimination in the workplace, and at the same time finding creative ways for both men and women to share family responsibilities.

Discrimination Against the Disabled

People with disabilities are created in the image of God just as much as star athletes or homecoming queens. Yet psychological as well as physical barriers have been placed in their access to the workplace. They experience discrimination because of thoughtless assumptions that disabled people will be less productive or that they really don't want to work.

Such stereotypes are further reinforced by the fact that many people feel uncomfortable around people who are disabled. Because they have not taken the time to work through their own emotions, they don't know what to say to disabled people. Ignorance fosters feelings of insecurity, and the able-bodied end up revealing their own emotional handicaps.

Because there are certain costs associated with employing disabled persons, such as health insurance premiums or special equipment and facilities, some firms have not hired them. This has meant a loss both to business and to society. Disabled people have lost dignity and the sense of worth that comes from making a contribution to society. Society has lost the economic and social contribution disabled workers could have made.

Affirming the authenticity of the disabled does not mean that business must become a charity. It simply means that business should be equitable. People with disabilities should be allowed to work and earn what their productivity will justify. If business would take the minimal step of hiring the disabled and paying them their worth, the overwhelming majority of the disabled would not only prove their worth economically but find their self-respect greatly enhanced. What is not equitable is to deny them access to the marketplace and force them to remain nonproductive.

Age Discrimination

For many years Dick was employed as a book salesman for a Christian book publisher. He was very good at his job. He met and exceeded his quotas and got positive performance reviews. He was particularly good at selling Bibles.

Shortly after he turned fifty-five, however, his supervisor told Dick that he was sorry, but Dick was to be let go. Shortly afterward Dick learned that a younger person had been given his territory.

Dick tried to find out what had happened, but he couldn't get any information from the company. All he could conclude was that he was released because he cost too much. Because of his age and experience it cost the company more for his salary, health insurance, and other benefits than it would cost for a younger person. It looked to Dick as if he had been discriminated against because of his age.

Age discrimination is an increasing problem that hits older men and women at both ends of the job market: when they look for jobs (older workers generally have more experience and hence can ask a higher salary), and in situations like Dick's when they become eligible for benefits that are related to age. Both types of age discrimination are forbidden by law. But the problem persists because of the difficulty in proving that the real reason behind the failure to hire or the early release was age discrimination.

The Employee Retirement Income Security Act of 1974 (ERISA) was enacted largely because of mounting evidence that some employers were releasing older employees before a defined retirement date. ERISA mandated funding and provided vested interests in pension programs. Too many employers had been using economic downturns in their business as convenient opportunities to justify the release of senior employees before they became eligible for pensions.

Certainly an employer does have special obligations to a loyal employee who has given the most productive years of his or her life to the business. Age does bring with it a number of changes. Older employees are likely to file a disproportionate number of claims against their insurance coverage, because they tend to have more illnesses. They sometimes become less productive and less adaptable to change. On the other hand, they have valuable experience accumulated over many years. They are conscientious and loyal. Perhaps they could be assigned less physically demanding jobs. Or additional time could be taken to explain new procedures. Business should repay the faithfulness of long-term employees by being faithful to them.

The Right Employment Strategy

There are both moral and economic reasons for eliminating discrimination. The moral reasons are based on the fact that since all people are created in the image of God, they are responsible to do productive work. It is wrong to use discriminatory practices to deny individuals and groups of people the opportunity to work. The economic reasons are illustrated in the following story.

When you are handling $36,000 worth of hotel reservations every hour, it's important to have reliable staff on hand. You can't afford no-show employees. So when a winter storm paralyzed Atlanta last year, the Days Inns national reservation center followed its policy of transporting employees to and from the job. Interestingly it was only the "young and able-bodied" who needed help. The senior and wheelchair-bound workers all came in on their own steam.

That typifies the lodging chain's experience with "special sector employees" (mostly seniors and handicapped, with some homeless). The company began seriously recruiting this untapped sector of the work force four years ago and has found them to be more dependable and motivated than employees between eighteen and thirty-five. On weekends, for example, the no-show rate among the younger set can be as high as 40 percent; among seniors and disabled workers it's zero. "Their enthusiasm serves as a role model for the balance of the employees," says the company's vice-president of human relations.

Christians should take the lead in developing policies and

procedures that eliminate current discriminatory practices and that attempt to make up for past discrimination. Many Christians are doing just that. The U.S. Bishops' "Pastoral Letter on Catholic Social Teaching and the U. S. Economy," and the Lay Commission on Catholic Social Teaching's book, *Toward the Future: Catholic Social Thought and the U. S. Economy,* both address many of these issues with a deep concern for social justice for the less advantaged.

If we are to make progress in eliminating discrimination we must go beyond generalized good intentions to specific commitments, policies, and practices for affirmative action. The following list suggests some specific ideas that should be included in a plan.

1. A written commitment and goals for affirmative action and equal employment approved by the board of directors and top management.
2. The designation of a specific person with responsibility to implement the plan.
3. Constant monitoring of the plan for evaluating and measuring effectiveness and the designation of a specific person to carry this responsibility.
4. A profile of the numbers of women, racial minorities, and disabled in various employment categories and departments.
5. A description of procedures that are to be used in recruitment, employment, and promotion to assure fairness to all groups.

If we follow these steps, we will open doors to all who want to work. Skills will be available that otherwise would have been excluded. The greater diversity in the work force will enrich the workplace. Many strategies are available to accomplish this. One business owner might design a shift schedule to accommodate mothers who desire to see their children off to school. Another might hire minority employees via contacts in a local black church. Still others might redesign work stations for the elderly and wheelchair bound. The creative possibilities are endless.

Questions

1. What was the Year of Jubilee in the Old Testament? Why were the Israelites to observe it? What was its purpose?
2. What kinds of discrimination work against equal employment opportunities today?
3. Which type of discrimination commonly practiced today—race, sex, physical ability, age—do you think will be the last to go? Why?

Human Sexuality

How Do You Feel About It?
Lewis B. Smedes

Lewis Smedes is a theologian and writer who teaches at Fuller Theological Seminary in California. This selection is a chapter from his book Sex for Christians. *Smedes notes that sexuality has long been considered a threat to the Christian life. However, he points to the Bible as the place to gain a proper perspective on sexuality and the human life as a whole. It gives us an "understanding of who we are, what we tend to make of ourselves, and what we can be through grace."*

The toughest problem Christians have with sex is how to feel about their own sexuality. On this subject many of us are confused, confounded, and inconsistent. We may be sure that we know what is right or wrong about things people do with sex, especially things other people do. But few of us really are sure within ourselves about how we actually feel and how we ought to feel about the sexuality that is woven into the texture of our very beings. The most sex-frightened prude may secretly enjoy the sexual urges that pulsate within him/her. The most liberated person of our supposedly taboo-free age has residual tinges of shame about his/her sexuality. The one is ashamed of the urges he cannot help nourishing inside himself; the other is embarrassed by the shame he cannot get rid of. Few of us totally deny our sexuality. But we cannot find the way into a happy celebration of it either. We carry a complex mixture of feelings.

The average Christian has an especially hard time integrating his sexuality with his faith. He is dedicated to a Lord whose earthly life was celibate and whose messengers were not interested in reporting his attitudes toward sex. He is summoned to follow the Lord into purity and holiness, neither of which is usually allowed to include an enthusiastic summons to sexual fulfillment. He is informed and guided by Scripture, whose word on sexuality is not always specific and clear. He senses that he ought not feel right about anything that his Lord feels less than enthusiastic about. Does God like sex? Would Jesus be pleased with our restless urges, our fantasies, our irrational itching for sexual experience? Can we integrate sexuality with Christian sanctification? Can a Christian person think about the mystery of his own sexuality and rejoice and be glad in it?

Those who are sensitive to the tensions within life have always been saddled with the job of reconciling two competing currents within human experience. One current is vital, dynamic, moving, and restless: it is the spontaneous, palpable vitality of nature. Here we experience the irrational, sometimes upheaving, movement of nature toward birth and growth. On this side of life humanness throbs with needs for explosive release of energy, impulsiveness, and ecstasy. The other current is thoughtful, orderly, controlled, and rational. In it we experience the need for discipline, the desire to keep things in order and to mold raw life into shapes and forms designed by our minds. Here we want to keep vitality under control; here we discipline our impulses; here we fence in the restless drives that rise from the energy cells of life.

The reason Christians have a special problem is that the

tensions we feel in our sexuality often seem to fit Paul's label "the lusts of the flesh." If our lives are guided by the Spirit, we will not fulfill "the cravings of our lower nature" (Gal. 5:16). How, then can we bring our sexuality into Christian discipleship except as that murky side of us that ought to be put down by the Spirit? Christian commitment, it seems to many, places us on the side of God against our sexual drives. We may say that sexuality is good in itself, but only needs control. But the fact that it needs so much control easily creates the feeling that our sexuality is a threat to our Christian lives, a threat percolating up from the dark abyss of our old nature.

Some Christians feel that their sexuality is nature's strongest competitor for their loyalty to Christ: "You cannot love both God and sex." While they may not make it part of their creed, their feelings tell them that sexuality is not a sweet gift of creation but a bitter fruit of the fall. They are supported in this by a long antisexual tradition within Christianity. Augustine, to whom we otherwise owe more than most of us even imagine, interpreted the Christians' calling to struggle against evil as a calling to struggle against their sexuality. Intense desires for sexual fulfillment and intense pleasure from sexual action were for him marks of fallen man. Augustine could not imagine an innocent person in Paradise turned on sexually: a sinless Adam could never have been sexually aroused by a pure Eve; Adam and Eve could not have walked with God in the day and made spontaneous love at night. If we do this now it is only because we have not brought our bodies under the rule of Christ. The less one is driven toward sex and the less pleasure he receives from sexual expression, the more sure he can be of his own sanctification. The Lord, in his grace, tolerates our inconsistency; but we must know that he calls us to better, sexless things. This was how Augustine felt about sexuality. Some Christians still carry Augustine's feelings in their hearts; they can only hope that God tolerates their sexuality until their liberation from it in heaven.

Other Christians, who have perhaps grown up during the sexual revolution, have thrown off their guilt feelings about sexuality. But they have still not found a way to mesh their good feelings about sexuality into their commitment to Christ. They are persuaded that Christ is somehow a friend of sexuality, but they suspect that the church is not. They live in a kind of duality: on one hand they feel right about affirming their sexuality, and on the other they accept a view of Christian faith in which sex, while not condemned, has no positive place. They accept restrictions on their sexual behavior but do not know how to thank God for their sexuality even within the rules of morality. They feel they have a right to enjoy their sexuality, but they don't know how it fits into their Christian life. And they resent the church's inability to help them celebrate their sexuality while respecting its limits and liberties.

. . . How does our sexuality fit into the same picture with God? This is really a way of asking how we are invited by God to feel about our sexuality within and not alongside our Christian faith. . . .

Sexual morality, first of all, has to do with how we ought to feel about ourselves as sexual beings. It has to do with our attitudes toward all the desires and pleasures, the needs and their satisfactions, that are bound up with our sexuality. A good sexual life has to do with more than how people act and by what rules they regulate their behavior. Many people who obey the traditional rules of Christian morality live a miserable sexual existence. Equally true is the fact that many liberated people who fly free and easy over all the traditional sexual moral codes are left barren and lonely as sexual persons. Coming to terms with how Christians are invited by their faith to feel about their sexuality ought to open the door to a kind of peace of conscience and personal enjoyment that is not alien to but an essential part of their Christian discipleship. However, plowing through to a Christian celebration of sexuality is not all that easy; nor is the way through the Bible and tradition all that clear.

At this point, I ought to say something more about what I mean by sexuality. Sexuality refers to what we are, not only what we do. What we are cuts across what we do, to be sure; some of us never really come to terms with what we are until we begin doing. Few of us are ever sure of how we feel about what we are until after we do something that reveals something new about ourselves. An adolescent may not really come to terms with his sexual feelings in any deep sense until he masturbates or engages in petting. Some people do not really confront their feelings about sexuality until they discover the freedom to talk about it late in life. Some people never face up to their feelings. But even though we often are plugged into our feelings only after we act, our feelings about what we *are* can be distinguished from our sense of right and wrong concerning what we *do*.

Our sexuality penetrates several dimensions of our lives. The first level of sexuality is physical—partly neurological, partly a matter of hormones, and partly a matter of touch, taste, sight, and smell. What do we experience when we experience sexuality on this level? We feel caught up in the pulsating vitality of body-life: we are part of the rising and falling of sheer physical dynamics and tension. We feel a tension that is not easily relaxed, an urge that is not easily quenched, a desire that is not easily satisfied, a chafing within that is not easily soothed. And all this is focused—sometimes only vaguely—on our genitals or breasts. In the process we may fantasize about a particular person, but the aiming of our desire at that person is secondary to the vague and undirected desire. We do not *choose* to be involved in this tension; it comes with us as part of our sexuality, part of our selves. In this level of our being, we seem far removed from the spiritual life. Here we deal with spontaneous, unchosen urges that can easily seem like a threat to everything we value as Christian—prayer, devotion, purity, beauty, and the love of God. The question is whether it *must* be felt as a threat to the life of the soul.

Our sexuality always leads us beyond the physical stage to a far more personal need: we are driven inexorably into a desire for personal, intimate involvement with another person. The glandular urge, it turns out, is the undercurrent of a need for sharing ourselves with another person. Sexuality throbs within us as movement toward relationship, intimacy, companionship. The desire is more than a wish for somebody's fingers to play with our bodies, though it is that also; it is an exciting desire, sometimes a melancholy longing, to give ourselves in trust to another. We want to expose our whole selves to another and to be trusted with another person's self-exposure to us; we want to stretch out and reach into another person so that the other can add himself to what we are; we want to probe into the mystery of another person's being. It is also a feeling that we cannot be complete until we give ourselves to another person. This is to say that our biological sexuality is lifted into personal *eros*.

This brings us to still another level of our sexuality: the need for self-knowledge. We need to explore the mystery of another person in order to get inside the mystery of ourselves. The two—the biological and the inter-personal—must come together as our passage into self-knowledge. Our sexuality whispers a promise that if we could really get close to it, really express it, really satisfy it, we would come into our own as persons. This is why, in some fuzzy sense, everyone associates sexual maturity with growing up. The intuition is that knowing oneself as a person is tied up with knowing another person sexually. Our sexuality, then, is a biologically rooted urge to answer the ancient counsel: "Know thyself."

Is there more? There probably is. There is probably more to our sexuality than meets the eye or is open to our conscious experience. Why have people often associated sex with religion, as though somehow sex were the gateway to God? What distorted vision of reality led those ancient Canaanites to their shrines of prostitution? What was it, on the other hand, that led Paul to see marriage as an illustration of how Christ relates to the church and to see sexual intercourse as a mysterious life-uniting act that so radically altered the partners' individual existence that they became one flesh? Christianity knows that we do not get to God through ecstasy of the flesh. But the ecstasy of sexual fulfillment is not absolutely unlike the ecstasy of religious experience, otherwise it would not have been so often identified with it. Is there more to our sexuality than the share we have in animal nature, more than the urge for personal union, more even than the discovery of our selves? Is there more than meets the eye of the sexologist?

Our sexuality is hard to categorize because it spills over into so many levels of our life. But hard as it is to catch it in a neat verbal net, we know that it is woven into all that we are as personal creatures of this world. The question is how we should value it, how we should feel about it, how we should relate it to our conviction that to love and serve God and our neighbor is the one thing necessary.

We must turn to the Bible. But where shall we turn, and how shall we read? Must we look for texts that will tell us how to feel? We will be hard put to find many; the Bible does not spell out divine theories of sexuality. Nor is it a book with only one response to sexuality: its several writers always write in response to the needs and conditions of their situation. Many Old Testament writers have one eye slanted toward the pagan religions, and their warnings against certain sexual practices are often a warning against a religion that turns worship into a sex orgy. Jesus talks amid legalistic Jews, reminding them that sexual chastity is not bought simply by avoiding illegal acts. Further, he sees marriage as rooted in creation and thus evidently thinks very highly of it. Paul, on the other hand, expecting Christ to return soon, at first sees no great value in marriage, except as a way to cabin and control sexual drives.

If there is one clear endorsement of sexual passion—besides the Song of Solomon—it is Proverbs 5:18-19:

> "Rejoice with the wife of thy youth. Let her be as the loving hind and pleasant roe; let her breasts satisfy thee at all times; and be thou ravished always with her love." (KJV)

True, the point of this verse is that a young man should enjoy the embrace of his own wife, rather than be "ravished with a strange woman." But the proverb hardly hints that a man should be ashamed of a sexuality that nudges him toward sensual pleasure. On the other end of the spectrum is the vision of Revelation 14, whose spiritual heroes at the throne of the Lord are chaste elders who were not "defiled with women," but who followed the Lamb faithfully (Rev. 14:4). The impulses that push us toward sexual union are not given a celebrative boost here. The rest of the Bible deals with sexuality somewhere between the boundaries of Proverbs 5:18 and Revelation 14:4.

Sexuality is not something that biblical writers are concerned about in any explicit way, nor does one sense that they were hung up with shame about it. One gets the impression from the Old Testament that the glandular urge was simply assumed as part of male life that had to be put under some limits; female sexuality is hardly recognized. In the New Testament, sexual promptings seem to be more of a threat; it seems far more important to avoid fornication than to fulfill sexual need. The erotic desire for sharing the intimate presence of another person is not a large part of the New Testament scene.

Marriage, for instance, is not lauded as a partnership entered for the enrichment of the lives of the partners. It is, for Paul at least, a way of domesticating sexuality so that it will not spill over into the sin of fornication. Marriage is much more than this, of course. Those splendid passages in Ephesians and Colossians about marriage lift it to a plateau where it can be compared to Christ's union with his church. The marriage *status* has enormous meaning for Paul. But a reader would not get the word from him that sexual union is a gateway to personal enrichment and voluptuous delight. One would not easily guess that Paul might advise a frustrated couple to seek therapy in order to get more pleasure from their sexual union.

In contrast, we live in a time when all levels of sexuality are given top billing in life. Romantic love, the personal side of erotic desire, is accepted as the most beautiful promise in life. Erotic relationships are valued for their potential of happiness. If there is one message we have all heard in our time, it is the tantalizing news that sexuality is a good thing. But for many of us the message has not gone below our mind. We may admit it with our minds, but our feelings carry a suspicion that sexuality is an embarrassment to genuinely Christian people. We still feel uneasy, restless, embarrassed by the vital urges within us. But either way—as a promise or a problem—sexuality has become a major concern. It is at, or near the top of our priorities. We have been talking about it, viewing it with alarm, disturbed by what we see around us, and stimulated by what we feel within us. But we have not yet—many of us—come to terms with it.

The writers of the Bible did not make sexuality a major theme. They had more urgent matters on their minds; they were responding to the great acts of God for human salvation. They were not divinely inspired to theorize about sex. But it was just because they were bringing the good news for the whole person that they could not help saying something about human sexuality.

How then can we read the Bible as an informing light for our sexual lives? This is a pivotal question. I think, in the first place, that we can let the gospel open up a *perspective* for us on human life as a whole. The message of Christ gives us a point of view, a vista from which to understand and evaluate our total experience as human beings. It informs our attitudes, shapes our values, and points to our goals. It also speaks to us about our origins as body-persons, and about our inevitable tendency to distort life. And it offers the possibility of liberation from the powers of distortion and inhumanity. In short, what we look for first is not a theory of sexuality nor a set of rules for sexual behavior; we look for an understanding of what we are, what we tend to make of ourselves, and what we can be through grace. And then we can fit our sexuality and our sexual behavior into the biblical pattern and the biblical perspective. What we want, then, is not sexual information first of all, but a view and an attitude toward our sexual lives that is informed by the gospel as a whole.

The wrong way would be to look only for biblical texts that tell us what to do and what not to do in sex. There are rules, to be sure. And any Christian will take them seriously. But what we need to find out is whether there is an insight, a vision, that tells us what the deeper significance of sexuality and sexual behavior is. For instance, we want to know more than the New Testament rules about extramarital sex; we want to know the New Testament insight into the significance of sexual intercourse. Only then can we make sense of the rules. It is a mistake to think of the New Testament as a new revelation of rules for sexual behavior. The New Testament is a message of grace; it is the gospel of freedom in Christ. Through it we come face to face with God's movement toward us so that we can move toward him and toward each other.

Questions

1. How does Smedes define sexual morality?
2. Why does Smedes insist that our sexuality be understood in terms of what we *are* as well as what we *do?*
3. How can the expression of one's sexuality become a source of true joy for the Christian?
4. How would you answer someone who argues that the sexual drive conflicts with true devotion to Christ?

Love, Sex, and the Whole Person

Tim Stafford

Tim Stafford is a popular Christian author. These selections are taken from Stafford's widely-read column published in Campus Life *magazine. Stafford answers letters from real people who have questions about their sexuality. Here Stafford addresses questions about premarital sex, necking, homosexuality, date rape, abortion, AIDS, and masturbation.*

Why . . . should *this* kind of juncture of two bodies be so much more serious than *this* kind—say, shaking hands?

Thomas Howard, *An Antique Drum*

Nobody can really do what the prostitute and her customer try; nobody can go to bed with someone and leave his soul parked outside.

Lewis Smedes, *Sex for Christians*

My girl friend and I are juniors in college. We have gone together since we were freshmen, and have restrained ourselves as far as having sex is concerned. Last spring we got engaged. We plan to be married as soon as we graduate.

But it has been harder and harder to keep from going all the way. Sometimes Julie and I talk about it and we feel really frustrated. Lately she's been saying things like "I wish I could understand what's wrong with it." It's not like she comes out and says she'd like to have sex, but I think if I wanted to she'd be willing. And really, I want to, but I'm also afraid. I've always expected to wait for marriage. Now I'd feel better if we just went ahead. Then at least we wouldn't be frustrated.

I'm starting with this question because it includes all the "What-if?" factors. I spent four years in coed dorms, and I've sat in hours-long discussions trying to hold up the Christian outlook on sex. I know how the arguments go. I've had mine battered with that insistent "What-if?"

"*What if* they're using birth control, and there's no fear of pregnancy? Then would it be right?"

"*What if* they really love each other, and don't feel any guilt?"

"*What if* they're going to get married?"

"What's wrong with sex before marriage, if sex is supposed to be beautiful?"

Good questions, all of them. So consider this guy who wrote to me. You have to feel compassion for him. He and his fiancée are planning to be married. Presumably they really love each other, and aren't just infatuated. Presumably they are thoughtful enough to use birth control effectively, and don't have to worry about VD. Besides which, it appears to them that waiting for marriage is tearing up their relationship. The frustration is too much to take.

I could have started with a more typical case: a pair of high school juniors who've been together three months, feel madly in love, and think they might go all the way soon. The typical couple is a lot younger, less thoughtful and less committed than the couple who wrote to me. Often one is more crazy about sex than about his partner, or they are both more in love with love than with each other. If so, you can expect their relationship to split within a few months.

But I want to take on the ideal situation. If premarital sex is a bad idea for this engaged couple, it's bad for everyone.

I'm going to assume all the "What-ifs?" by considering this couple first. And I'm also going to assume one thing about you: you're not interested in a second-rate relationship. I assume you're searching for the most loving, sexually fulfilling relationship two humans are capable of—marriage as marriage is meant to be, and not as it is commonly lived.

I say "marriage" because I can't see any way around it. If

you are in love with someone that deeply, you're going to want to live together. You're going to want to share everything. And you're certainly not going to be content to let the relationship drop after a few years. You're going to want to stay together forever, if it's that good. If your goal is the best, you'll ultimately choose the state of committed living together we call marriage.

Unless that is your goal, what I say won't help much. I can't prove to you that sex before marriage will make you miserable. I can't prove you will end up tearing out your hair from the guilt. You know better. Some people do end up miserable, but you know others who have sex and don't regret it.

But I believe they are missing something. They are missing their best chance at the deep, soul-satisfying love we all want. Even this couple, in love and engaged to be married, is in danger of missing out on the best. I'm going to list six reasons why couples ought to wait.

When you're in love, the frustration of waiting is hard to take. But have you thought of the ways it could help your relationship?

For one thing, sex is a way of expressing love. But it's not the only way, or even the most helpful. To build a relationship takes time—time talking and doing things together. When you're sleeping together but not living together, sex tends to take over to the exclusion of other ways of expressing love. But when you put off sex, you can channel that love energy into getting to know each other better.

The best relationships aren't formed in pressure-free environments anyway. Yes, waiting for sex can be frustrating, but many things in life are frustrating. The question is, what as a couple do you do with those pressures? Do you handle them creatively? Do they tear you apart or push you closer together? If you can't learn to help each other grow through this pressure, are you really suited to help each other through the other pressures of life? Marriage ultimately is going to force you to "wait" on many things you want.

Waiting doesn't have to be grim. If you see it as a challenge, it can almost be fun. And it certainly is good experience.

An engagement period is, by its nature, a period of testing—of partial commitment. You still can back out, and whether you like to believe it or not, you might. Something like 50% of the people who get married have been engaged at least once before. That means many engagements don't work out. If you do break up, it will be much more painful if you've already had sex together. Breaking any engagement is traumatic; with sex involved, it can be worse. Do you want to risk that pain? Or risk it for your fiancée?

This is true for any relationship, engaged or not: breaking up when you've had sex together is much more emotionally tearing. Sex brings you together in ways you can't predict. It does change you. We all know, somewhere inside, that those who have made love weren't meant to be torn apart. But there is no guarantee anywhere—not in feelings of love, not in the words "I love you," not even in an engagement—that your relationship is going to go all the way to marriage.

Intercourse is not necessarily that wonderful the first few times, even in marriage. It takes time (often years), patience, and ideal conditions for many people to have a genuinely fulfilling experience.

The Sorenson Report, the most complete sociological study of teenage sexuality available, asked girls who had had their first intercourse before marriage to choose words to describe their reaction. They chose words like "afraid," "guilty," "worried," and "embarrassed" before any others. Words like "happy," "joyful," and "satisfied" came substantially further down the list. No one is saying your fiancée will feel like that, but the odds are for it. Have you considered the complications it will bring to your relationship if your first sex experience is bad for one or both of you?

It's hard enough to handle failure like that inside marriage. Outside, there is little time to deal with it. Unless you're living together, you've got to get dressed and separate. And you lack the security about the future that newlyweds feel, having just said their vows. You also usually lack the privacy and security that are likely to help sexual success along. Failures are more likely outside marriage than in. And they're complicated by the problem of guilt, which sneaks in and surprises people when they least expect it. The result of having sexual failures now could be a lot harder on both of you than the present frustrations. It could even break up your relationship .

If you're planning marriage, you must be looking forward to a whole new life of sharing together. It's not just sex, of course: it's *life*. That includes work, cooking, choosing where to live, vacations, and probably even the creation of new human beings. It's a whole: sex can't be separated from the rest of it, and you don't want to separate it.

When you're thinking in terms of a lifetime, the year or so of your engagement is a relatively short period. How do you want that lifetime to begin? With a great celebrative party, or furtively, secretly? Do you want to sneak into sex, or would you rather start with a honeymoon to enjoy it, with all the time and privacy in the world? Do you want it to begin when you're only partly sure you're doing the right thing, when there are still some doubts in the back of your mind? Or when you stand together in front of all your friends and say, in effect, "It's right for us to be together for all time, and we're completely dedicated to that. You help us and hold us to it." The contrast between the two ways of beginning is so great, it seems to me to be worth quite a bit of waiting.

By having sex you're relieving the frustration of putting it off, but you're also relaxing the attractive tension that keeps you together.

The sexes are called opposite because in many ways they are. Usually they have different ways of looking at things. They have different interests. Yet there is an attraction that brings them together.

Think of the most boring subject you can. Algebra? Copper production? Then put yourself in a small room with an attractive member of the opposite sex to talk about that subject. I'll guarantee that subject will acquire a sudden fascination.

Sure, it's biological. Most people don't feel it until they're older than twelve. But it's nothing to be ashamed of. It's something to be excited about and thankful for, because God made it to be that way. I'm not really talking about the need for release from sexual tension. Sexual attraction goes far beyond that. It's the desire to probe and understand the mystery of another person. It's the kind of tingling conversation in which you want to talk and listen at the same time, in which you want to swallow sentences whole. It's an intense unsatisfiable curiosity, a sense that you're being drawn up and out of yourself into a whole new world you have to explore; it's an itch that is pure joy to scratch but that can't ever be scratched enough. And sexual intercourse is the culmination of this urge. It's a delightful, healthy urge, and a practical one too: it brings male and female together. And it keeps them together, urging them to put more time and effort into exploring the other's personality.

But what happens if you go all the way with the urge? What happens if you have sex?

Several things can happen. First, powerful emotions can appear. They're different for different people. Some feel naked and ashamed. Others feel confused and bewildered. Often people suddenly feel as though their partner is a stranger to them. There is the distinct feeling, for many, that something has changed; they have "lost" something. Intercourse turns out to be more than something physical. They thought it would be simply one step beyond making out, but it turns out to be a spiritual act. What it comes down to, I think, is a feeling of having stumbled into a place you never imagined existed, and for which you weren't ready.

It's a strange experience, even in marriage, when your partner and you "know" each other as well as you possibly can, and have committed yourselves unbreakably to each other. Outside of marriage, it sometimes makes you feel as though you've made yourself naked for a stranger.

And that can be followed in time by boredom. You have gone "all the way." There's no more mystery about your partner: you've satisfied your curiosity. Or so you think. Actually, sex in that sense is lying to you. It doesn't reveal anything: it only expresses what love and understanding is already there. Nevertheless, you feel as though the relationship is fulfilled, and sooner or later you begin to realize it isn't all that fulfilling. You've done the ultimate, and the ultimate wasn't enough. No curiosity or desire to probe the mystery of the other person pulls you back together. Boredom sets in.

This doesn't happen right away. Sex is meant, after all, to be the ultimate expression of love, and it certainly can feel like it. The first time it may be tremendous. Even if it isn't tremendous, at least it's the first time. That in itself is exciting.

But that can change with time. Your relationship tends to plateau at the level it has already reached. You don't lose interest in sex, but if your relationship isn't very deep, you do lose interest in your partner. Your curiosity is gone. Much of your time together is dominated by sex. No longer is intense energy put into exploring each other's personality. Eventually a breakup comes, often painfully. Or (what may be worse) you go on to marriage simply from a sense of duty. The joy is gone.

Of course, some of this attractive tension dies with married couples too. But there are a million other things to hold you together then—legal things, social things, the fact that you live together and share everything. And the fact that you share all of life forces you to continue to explore each other, to grow. That growth revives the attraction, giving it new dimension. . . .

One other thing:

Premarital sex will erode your relationship with God. Maybe you don't care. If not, skip this. But if God means much to you, then this fact may affect you more than anything else.

You can't listen to what God says and go out and do the opposite too often. The joy of relating to Him will fade. Prayer and Christian fellowship will mean less. They usually will die a quiet death. You may not even realize it until you wake up in the middle of the night and wonder where God has gone.

I have been dating Karen for seven months, and we have had a beautiful, fantastic relationship. I told her when I first started to take her out that I didn't want to get involved in premarital sex. She agreed. You have to understand what kind of girl she is—sweet and very innocent. I love her very much and I know she loves me.

On New Year's Eve she came over to my house. She was up in my room looking it over and we just started to neck on my bed. She had on a low-neck dress and before I knew it I was in it. After we realized what we had done, we both told each other we were sorry, but then she told me that she wasn't. We both agreed that we enjoyed it and that it made us love each other all the more. We both said that we wouldn't do it again. Can you explain this situation to us? Do you think that it happened for a certain purpose? Do you think that God made it happen? I have never done this kind of thing before and it really has us both down.

Some people would find it humorous that a sweet, innocent girl who just happened to be in a low-cut dress happened to be in her boyfriend's bedroom where they "just started to neck," and where "before he knew it" he was inside her dress. But if I laugh, I'm also laughing at myself. Often enough I've found myself doing things I hadn't planned on. Yet looking back, I also see that subconsciously I had been making preparations all along. It leaves me feeling a little like a hunter, caught in a noose which swoops him off his feet upside-down. As blood rushes to his head and he dangles helplessly, he remembers that he set the trap himself last week.

Couples play these games too much: they just happen to be in an empty house, and then without warning they find themselves making out, and then, to their surprise, they find themselves going further than they'd planned. Considering the physical exertion and teamwork required, it's astonishing how many couples go too far "by accident."

So did God make it happen? You could make a far better case that you two made it happen—with a dose of help from an active, normal sex drive.

The interesting part is your surprise that you enjoyed it, and that it "made us love each other all the more." (By that last phrase I presume you mean you felt closer to each other—that the emotions were warm.) But what could you expect? God made sex for, among other things, pleasure and the expression of love. There is no "on/off" switch activating this the day you get married. Sex feels good anytime. It should always give you warm, intimate feelings. If that weren't true, I don't think it would be any problem for people to stick with the biblical idea of waiting for marriage. As a matter of fact, many people experience sex and have the same reaction you did: "Hey, that's not so bad! In fact, it's wonderful! All those puritans must have been keeping this thing off limits because they didn't want me to enjoy myself."

The reason some kinds of sexual expression ought to be kept in marriage isn't because they don't feel good outside of marriage. It's that they are too big for anything less than the quality of relationship you find in a committed, loving, Christian marriage.

My problem is different from most, and I don't know what to do. I am constantly being driven by homosexual desires. I don't even like to print that, but I guess I must say it. I know God loves me, but somehow I just can't seem to get things together. Why am I this way in the first place? People don't know how I hurt on the inside.

I've tried to help myself but I can't. I'm terribly lonely. I've thought about talking to my minister, but I can't. He thinks I'm a terrific guy. If he only knew what I am going through.

Due to receiving many letters like this one, I feel queasy when I hear people joke about homosexuals. I wonder if someone is listening who is driven deeper into hating himself. You might be surprised—I know most people would be—at the number of people, Christian and non-Christian, male and female, who feel driven by homosexual desires and are confused and sick over it. Though it is not "normal," it is common.

If you are troubled by this kind of desire, I want to begin by repeating what you already know: that the Bible considers homosexual actions wrong. There isn't a great deal of material dealing with it; in the Old Testament it simply is declared off-limits, and that is carried over in the New Testament. The only passage that gives a hint of *why* it is wrong is Romans 1:26,27. There Paul discusses homosexuality in the context of a civilization that has turned its back on God, and has succeeded in twisting so far away from what it ought to be that it has exchanged what is "natural" for what is "unnatural." Paul probably is thinking of the story of creation in Genesis, where God made man in His own image "male and female." We're sexual people—that's what's "natural"—and sex was made to be between male and female. The trouble with homosexuality is that it doesn't let males be male and females be female, because male and female only mean something in relationship to each other. I don't mean that homosexuals are sick because some act effeminate—though the fact that some do might tell us something. I mean that they are closed off to their full human identity by not discovering themselves in relationship to the opposite sex. We learn something about ourselves and about God through the wonderful erotic attraction and interaction of male and female. We learn even if we never marry, for we take part in those interactions at other levels.

That is the basic threat—that you would lose out on part of your identity. Your true identity in Christ isn't homosexual. Some experts say nearly everyone has homosexual desires to some extent. But the sexual focus of our lives ought to be the opposite sex, for that is how we discover more about ourselves.

There isn't any condemnation of homosexual tendencies in the Bible. Being attracted to your own sex is a temptation, a unique and difficult one. But temptation isn't sin; so long as you resist acting out your desires, or inflaming your mind by dwelling on them, you're not sinning. In fact, you may be growing closer to God by trusting Him for strength.

Nor does the Bible give any hint that homosexual sins are any worse than other kinds. If you look at the verses following Romans 1:26,27, you see that envy and gossip are in the same class.

So if you're sorry for past actions and have confessed them to God, and if you're ready to continue resisting temptation, with God's help, you're as good in God's eyes as anyone else.

But I know that assurance, while it helps, doesn't solve the problem. I imagine the central problem is expressed in the words, "I'm terribly lonely." That's a very common reaction. You can't talk to anyone because of the fear and the shame. You envy those who have normal dating relationships, but getting romantic with a girl just doesn't do much for you. You're afraid to get close to a guy, because you're not sure you could handle the temptations. Besides, if the guy found out, he might be totally repulsed. You end up closed off from the rest of the world, feeling miserable and lonely, full of self-pity. You wonder, "Why was I made this way?"

To that last question I don't think there's any final answer. One thing is clear: *It's not your fault.* Some researchers think it's an innate condition; others think it's psychological, the result of an overbearing mother or something like that. No one knows what causes it, and no one knows why God has let it come to you. My own suspicion is that its cause has a lot to do with the kind of sexually confused society we live in. Walter Trobisch, a writer who lived in Africa for many years says homosexuality is almost unknown there, except perhaps in port cities where there has been a Western influence. But if homosexuality is part of a willful condition in our society that doesn't mean you're personally accountable. The condition has been given to you. You're accountable for how you respond.

Some homosexuals say that the right way to respond is "naturally." That is, "You have the condition; therefore, act it out. Be true to yourself." I think they're wrong, but why?

There are some obviously unhealthy aspects of homosexuality: the pick-up bars, the affected behavior, the short-lived relationships based on physical appearance. But there are also homosexuals who have tried to make the best of their condition by forming permanent "marriages" with someone of the same sex, giving love and affection just as they see married couples doing. Isn't that "natural" for them?

We may yet see compelling reasons why it is not "natural." But right now all I can say is that the Bible doesn't see it that way. The "natural" thing—the thing to do if you want to affirm who you really are, as God made you—is to resist homosexual temptations and try to affirm heterosex as much as it's possible for you. I don't expect non-Christians to accept this. But if we follow the Bible—and personally, I have found it to be far more reliable than my own logic—we have to follow it in saying that homosexual acts are unnatural.

Why are you tempted by them, while others aren't? Only God knows.

But it may help to realize that other people ask the same identical "Why? Why was I made this way?" Crippled people ask it; ugly people ask it; mute people ask it. In fact, nearly everyone asks it at one time or another. But it isn't a question that helps you. Self-pity only makes the situation worse.

I know a guy who has cerebral palsy. He can't talk at all, his hands are twisted so that he can't use them, and even his feet are unsteady so that he can barely walk. Yet his mind is completely intact, and he's completed college now, typing papers with his toes. He's got a good sense of humor (he scribbles out his conversations on the floor with his feet) and most people who try talking to him can't resist liking him.

I asked him once what was the most important way a person could help someone like him. He didn't have to stop and think: he immediately wrote out with his foot, "Don't pity us." He knew pity would cripple him sooner than his disease. And the guy doesn't pity *himself* at all. He could. He has every reason to. But he won't. He's accepted himself the way he is, and gone ahead with his life.

From what I can see, those with homosexual desires have the same basic problem. Self-pity destroys them as much as anything. You must resist this, and consistently ask God to help you resist it.

Then you can pray for God to change you. There are many homosexuals who've been "healed," some overnight, some over a long period of time. It doesn't happen to everyone, but it does happen to some. One guy wrote, "He has not only changed my sexual-physical desires, but also my ways of thinking, my actions and mannerisms, my interests and my self-image. His power is fantastic. It is also available to anyone. He has proven this in my life by giving me increasing heterosexual desires that have never before been present. God still changes lives today. I praise Him and thank Him. He has miraculously changed me!"

And there are others who tell the same story. I have to say that God doesn't change everyone. But do not give up on God. Be honest with Him day after day. Ask Him for help.

I'd recommend being honest with another person, too. This is very difficult because of the tragic attitudes many Christians have toward homosexuals. Pray this over carefully. The risks are great, but I think you should take them. Experiencing someone else's growing acceptance of you is part and parcel of growing to accept yourself. When you find someone you believe you can talk to, make sure you explain fully to him how afraid you are he'll reject you. Chances are he will initially be taken aback. But if he understands the need, and is really a mature Christian, he'll be willing to help you.

Finally, it's important to develop a life style you can survive with. True, normal romance and marriage look pretty appealing. But it's made very clear in the Bible that some people are called by God to remain single, and that isn't considered a second-class life style. It hardly could be, since Jesus and Paul chose it.

The single life can be completely fulfilling. But like a good marriage, it takes work. You can't sit around waiting for a fulfilled life to be delivered in the mail. You have to deliberately cultivate the friendships (and often a group of friends is the best option) and interests that make life seem worth living. Every unmarried person faces this—you are no different from the rest of us.

Perhaps 1 Corinthians 10:13 will help you: "But remember this—the wrong desires that come into your life aren't anything new and different. Many others have faced exactly the same problems before you. And no temptation is irresistible. You can trust God to keep the temptation from becoming so strong that you can't stand up against it, for he has promised this and will do what he says. He will show you how to escape temptation's power so that you can bear up patiently against it" (LB).

I'm a 17-year-old girl, and I have a problem. Today I had sex with this guy. Before then I was a virgin, and I was proud of it. It made me feel that I had respect for myself, and guys respected me because I was different from other girls.

I know that what I have done is a sin in God's eyes. But I never thought I would ever do this. I was always the one who said, "I can control myself; I have a lot of self-control." I always said that the man I have sex with will be the man I marry.

I have asked God to forgive me and I know he will.

But my question is, How can I feel that I have been washed clean of this sin and become close to God again, and not yield to this temptation anymore? I want to know for a fact, without a shadow of a doubt, that God has forgiven me, and I want to feel better about myself again.

The Bible tells us that "If we claim to be without sin, we deceive ourselves and the truth is not in us. If we confess our sins, he is faithful and just and will forgive us our sins and purify us from all unrighteousness" (1 John 1:7-9).

I cannot guarantee that you will never yield to this temptation, or any other, again. I can guarantee that temptation will never be totally beyond your ability to resist. But I know that temptations will come—real temptations. A real temptation is one you're quite capable of giving in to. There are no people who have so much self-control (as you thought you had) that they don't have to worry about temptation. We are all vulnerable, 24 hours a day.

So I can't guarantee you a sinless tomorrow. I can guarantee you a forgiven tomorrow, simply because that is what God promises in black and white. If you want forgiveness, he gives it without limit.

How you feel about it is another story. Experience has taken you down a peg in your own estimation. That's probably going to make you feel rotten. You're probably not going to feel the same self-confidence and pride you felt before. But maybe that's just as well, if your confidence was built more on your opinion of yourself than on God's loving grace. That's an unrealistic self-confidence, and you can do better without it.

After all, as the Bible says, "If we claim to be without sin, we deceive ourselves." That means that each and every one of us has weaknesses—not merely potential weaknesses, but weaknesses we've given in to. If we don't know it, we're self-deceived.

My prayer is that you can rebuild your self-confidence and pride on a different basis. I hope it will depend less on your self-control and more on the way God gives you self-control each day. I'd urge you particularly to seek out someone—a mature, caring individual—whom you can talk to honestly and pray with regularly. If you're to experience forgiveness and build a new self-image, and not give in to temptation again, you need some other people to help you. Don't try to walk alone.

I would like to share with you the biblical insight the Lord has given me on the subject of masturbation. From the beginning of seventh grade until the middle of my sophomore year in college, I was addicted to masturbation. I was very confused and full of guilt. I (like so many of your readers) questioned whether or not it was a sin. For most of those years I tried to quit, but to no avail. I have since been able to stop masturbating. The following are the insights that God has shown me:

First, masturbation is a sin. The last part of Romans 14:23 says, ". . . for whatsoever is not of faith is sin." If we have any question in our minds as to an activity's wholesomeness we should refrain from it. If we aren't 100 percent convinced that something is not sinful, then to us it should be viewed as sin. Guilt also is an indicator. If our heart condemns us, then we have no confidence toward God, and we will not receive from him the answers to our prayers (1 John 3:19-22).

The next insight: You can quit. For years I struggled to claim victory, but my efforts were unfruitful. Take notice of the words "I," "me" and "my" in their following contexts. I have found the Bible to be true when it says, ". . . not by might, nor by power, but by my Spirit says the Lord of Hosts" (Zechariah 4:6). Or, ". . . apart from me you can do nothing" (John 15:5). I've found that if I "set the Lord continually before me . . . I will not be shaken" (Psalm 16:8). If I concentrate on godliness rather than on overcoming the temptation to masturbate, it is much easier to claim the victory. Sure the temptations will come now and then; but if I "submit . . . therefore to God . . ." I can ". . . resist the devil, and he will flee . . . ." (James 4:7). We must not forget the first part of that verse: "Submit yourselves therefore to God. . . ."

I couldn't agree more with your last paragraph. Of course, what you say applies to more than masturbation. It applies to everything a Christian does. In all that we do, in word or deed, we should concentrate on the glory of God, not on ourselves. That's what following Jesus is all about.

I know your experience will be intensely interesting to many readers who find themselves unable to stop masturbating, no matter how they try. Whenever I've written about masturbation in the last few years, I've asked those who have been able to quit to write and share how they did it. (I usually ask them to wait until they've quit for a year before writing, since some people will tell you about the tremendous once-and-for-all victory they had over temptation starting yesterday.) I usually hear from a handful of people; that's not many, considering that hundreds of thousands read this column each month. Yet some do write to me, demonstrating that while masturbation may be very difficult to control, it is not impossible. Those who write almost always say something similar to what you have reported—that they were able to stop masturbating by taking their thoughts off of it and concentrating instead on the power and love of God. I'm glad that focusing on him is transforming your life.

But I would caution you against viewing your experience as

a technique that can be used by anyone to solve any problem. In my experience, it doesn't work that neatly. Even if it did, I'd be very leery of any tendency toward a push-button God. I wouldn't want to encourage people—I'm sure you don't either—to manipulate God-thoughts in their minds in order to control their masturbation. Keeping your thoughts focused on God has to be genuine, not just a technique for control.

When I read your understanding of masturbation as sin, I have to disagree. I'm afraid that you've misapplied Romans 14:23. Notice that Paul doesn't say (as you suggest he might), ". . . whatever you aren't absolutely confident is right is sin." Paul says, "Whatsoever is not of *faith* is sin." Faith isn't confidence in your ability to know right from wrong. It's confidence in God. Paul is saying that whenever you engage in an activity that erodes your trusting faith in God, that's off the mark. Whether it's "right" or "wrong" is irrelevant. If it's destroying your faith, it's wrong for you.

Applying that to a specific situation isn't always straightforward. For instance, it's a fact that some people who've been sexually abused as children feel tremendously guilty whenever they get close to someone of the opposite sex. Should they then consider relating to the opposite sex a sin? Of course not. Guilt feelings are worth checking out, but they're not an infallible guide. In the passage from 1 John that you quoted, the point John is making is really quite the opposite of what you draw from it. He is saying that "in whatever our heart condemns us"—basically, however guilty we may feel—"God is greater than our hearts" and wants to reassure us of his reality in our lives. If we're living loving lives, John says, we'll be reassured of where we stand with God, regardless of our self-condemning thoughts.

That's how it is with masturbation. It deeply disturbs many people. They feel guilty, and wonder whether they're even Christians since they can't quit. But God is greater than our guilt feelings. I believe he wants to reassure those who condemn themselves because of this. In fact, they belong— body and soul—to him.

I can understand your misinterpretation. Superficially, Paul's words in Romans 14 would seem to say that anyone who has doubts about masturbation should consider it a sin. However, a more careful reading of Paul's words will reveal that his deep concern is that people not be shaken in their faith. In the situation he was writing about, peer pressure led people to do things they considered sinful, and the result was confusion and uncertainty about their status before God. Paul was quite sure that what they were doing wasn't really sinful, but he was very anxious that their faith not be disturbed. So he told those applying peer pressure to cut it out, since they were leading their brothers and sisters into sin. "Sin" was whatever destroyed or disturbed faith.

That's different from the situation most people face with regard to masturbation. They aren't considering whether they should take it up or not. They're already masturbating, and can't stop. Drumming into their heads that masturbation is a sin won't help them stop. It will only increase the amount of "not-faith" in their lives, making them doubt whether they belong to God. That's exactly the result Paul is aiming *against* in Romans 14:23. I'm not talking theoretically here. I've heard from too many people who absolutely loathe themselves, and doubt the reality of God in their lives, because they can't quit a "sin" that the Bible never bothers to mention. I don't want to encourage that self-loathing. I want them to put it behind them.

I prefer to take your solution to masturbation without your understanding of it as a sin. I say to all: Concentrate on God, on his strength. his love and his glory, and stop worrying about masturbation. If you want to quit and you can, do so. If you want to quit and you can't, then know that this is not the most important issue in life. I'm quite sure that most of the finest Christians you know masturbated when they were young. It didn't hurt them. If God cared about masturbation so much, he would have said so. He's much more concerned that you grow deeper in your love for him.

Two weeks ago I went with my Campus Crusade group to hear Josh McDowell. He spoke to over 600 students, counselors and parents on the topic, "Why Wait?" Everyone listened in complete silence as he rattled off terrifying statistics about sexually transmitted diseases. And I wondered how many people, like me, listened for purely personal reasons. How many of them were fearful for things they'd already done, for damage they can't undo to their young bodies?

I am only 18 years old, and I don't live in a big city where AIDS runs rampant. (In fact, my town may not even be on the map.) But I have had eight sexual partners in the past year, all from different backgrounds. I thought nothing of it at the time; I was just "sowing wild oats," looking for something I wasn't supposed to have. I had never been involved with sex and alcohol before, and I'm not now. There was just that one year in my life when I took leave of my senses and went literally wild.

Now I'll be wondering about that year for perhaps 15 more (Josh said that AIDS can stay dormant for that long). It wasn't Josh's "nightmare" lecture that got me to stop indulging in sex. (Actually, it was your "Why Wait?" article of last summer.) But it was Josh who scared me to death. I'd never thought about the consequences. Young people, especially Christians, think they're immune to serious diseases and anything fatal. And if you don't go to a Christian college, it's easy to give in to the "college mentality"—"eat, drink, and sleep with Mary." At least for a while, you want to try what you've never had before. After all, everyone else does it; so you figure, "I'm young—young people are supposed to do this, aren't they?"

It's not a matter of feeling guilty. I've worked that out with God, and I know I'm forgiven. But I don't want to know if I am infected, for fear I might find out I'm going to die. Even though we must reap what we sow, I don't think I could handle knowing. Thinking back on the past year, I was really out of control. I could have used Josh's sermon then! Yet, it's like it had to happen—like the only way you'll know poison will kill you is if you take it. I know that sounds suicidal, but for some people that's true. Some make it to the hospital in time to have their stomachs pumped; some don't. I thought I was one who made it in time, but I suppose I still have to find out.

Analogies aside, I think you get the picture. I don't believe I'm overreacting. Nowadays, you can't overreact. Anytime you sleep with someone (outside of a faithful marriage)—even if you know that person—you're at risk. Knowing I was forgiven, I looked forward to a future doing what God wanted me to do. To having a husband, a best friend, with whom I could make passionate love whenever we wanted for the rest of our lives. Now, when I think about the future, I get scared. I get depressed. I don't see anything.

If I'm in this situation, others must be too. This is never discussed: What does a Christian with AIDS do? Can you imagine how scared I am? Now that you know most of the story, you can make something positive of this for your column. I need, I suppose, something positive. I feel like my future may not be.

First, let's talk medicine. It's true, as Josh McDowell said, that AIDS can lie dormant in your body for a long time. (Fifteen years is an estimate. AIDS hasn't been under study that long.) However, that doesn't mean you have to wait 15 years to find out whether or not you have been infected with the AIDS virus. You can be tested accurately within a few months of your last possible exposure. I strongly recommend having the test taken. You'd be far better off facing one excruciating moment of truth than a hundred such crises for years to come.

If you have been infected, you need time to face the possibility of death. If you haven't, then you can truly put your past behind you. So long as you're unsure, every cold will be a crisis with you wondering, *Is this the beginning of AIDS?* Your uncertainty will block any serious relationships with the opposite sex. How can you think about marriage if you don't know whether marriage might bring the death of your husband? After all, you might infect him. I'm convinced that uncertainty is much worse than certainty, no matter how bad the certainty turns out to be.

I'd agree with you that overreacting to AIDS is impossible for someone who is considering whether to be sexually promiscuous. As Katie Leishman put it in *The Atlantic*: If there were a thousand guns on a table and only one of them was loaded, how many people would pick up one, point it at their head, and pull the trigger if the prize were a toaster? No matter how small the risk of infection may be the life-and-death consequences of AIDS make cheap thrills extremely expensive.

However, for people like you who are looking at their past, it is possible to overreact to AIDS. There is a real possibility you've been infected with a disease that will kill you. But there's a much better chance that you haven't been infected. I think you've let the situation get out of perspective; so much so that your fears have overcome common sense, which says, "Get tested. Then decide what to do next."

Now, let's talk spiritually. The apostle Paul wrote in Romans 8:38-39, "I am convinced that neither death nor life, neither angels nor demons, neither the present nor the future, nor any powers, neither height nor depth, nor anything else in all creation, will be able to separate us from the love of God that is in Christ Jesus our Lord." *Neither death nor life* can keep you from experiencing God's love. If you have contracted AIDS, you will experience God's love in death quite soon. If you don't get AIDS, you will experience God's love in death sooner or later, since we all die.

Either way, Paul's words put AIDS in perspective. Paul is saying that the great variable in life isn't a deadly disease. The great variable is whether you have accepted God's forgiveness and salvation. He is saying that there is something far more powerful than AIDS: God's love.

That means you do have a future, one that doesn't depend on what your test results show. You have a future with God, in his love. You ask what a Christian with AIDS should do? First he needs to confess and repent for any wrong actions he's done. He needs to ask for, and receive, God's forgiveness. If that's happened, he can do just what a Christian with cancer or leukemia or any deadly disease would do. He can draw closer to God through prayer and worship and Bible reading, in order to experience more deeply God's love in both life and death.

I worry that Christians will overreact to AIDS by basing their whole argument against premarital sex on it. AIDS isn't the reason I believe sex should be kept for marriage. Premarital sex is wrong because it isn't right—it isn't the way God designed for us to live. AIDS is just one more indication that sex outside of marriage goes against the original design.

If and when an AIDS vaccine is discovered, sex outside of marriage will still be wrong. It will be wrong for the same reason it was wrong before AIDS appeared: because sex is an intimate, soul-exposing experience meant to be shared with one beloved person in a relationship throughout life. Sex outside of marriage puts that one relationship at risk.

I'm 18 years old and have been dating my boyfriend very seriously for about six months. We plan to get married in four or five years, and we love each other very much. We also plan to wait until we get married to have sex with each other.

I am a virgin, he is not. He had been dating his old girlfriend for five years when they "went too far." Soon after that, they broke up because they realized they did not really love each other. About three weeks after they broke up, she called to tell him she was pregnant with his child. Because they were so young (they were both 16), their parents would not let them see or talk to each other. Her parents forced her to have an abortion, despite my boyfriend's pleas to keep the baby.

He feels very guilty about this, and is very scared that, although he has asked for forgiveness, God will not allow him to have any more children. He also feels that he broke the commandment stating, "Thou shalt not kill" and wonders if he will be able to get to heaven. This bothers him constantly, and he often cries about it when I am with him. What can I do to help ease his pain? Will God allow him to have children now? Will he be able to get to heaven?

The Bible is very clear: "If we confess our sins, [God] is faithful and just and will forgive us our sins and purify us from all unrighteousness" (1 John 1:9). The only condition on that promise is confession, and your boyfriend has done that. "If anyone is in Christ, he is a new creation; the old has gone, the new has come!" (2 Corinthians 5:17).

As far as God is concerned, what your boyfriend did is finished. It's understandable that he still feels regret and guilt, but you should encourage him not to tarnish God with his bad feelings. If God has pronounced him not guilty, why would he turn around and punish him? God's purpose in sending his Son was not to condemn us for our sins, but to save us from them (John 3:16). He's done that with your boyfriend.

Your boyfriend may need to talk to a pastor or trained Christian counselor in order to work through his feelings and let the good news of God's forgiveness sink in. God offers us a new beginning precisely so we don't have to continually punish ourselves—or fear his punishment.

I have been feeling a great deal of guilt recently from a situation that happened about two years ago. I really need help; it's tearing me up inside. It all started when I was going out with Greg. We got into an argument over something really stupid, and that night I ended up going over to my friend Sarah's house. Her parents weren't going to be home and she wanted some company.

Sarah and I were eating pizza and watching movies when her boyfriend stopped by with his friend Norm. I had never met Norm before in my life. The boys came in and joined us for the pizza and movie. We were all having a great time. Then Sarah told me that she and Clint would be right back and they left the room. I had no idea where she was going, and having never met Norm before, I felt uncomfortable being by myself with him. We sat and watched the movie for a while, and then all of a sudden he jumped on top of me and started kissing me. I was real scared because he was so forceful, and I didn't know what to do because he wouldn't stop, even when I resisted.

Norm didn't take me all the way that night, but he took advantage of me. I cried for so long after the incident because I felt so violated physically. I never told anyone about this, and I'm hurting badly right now. I think it is from the guilt of going farther than I had ever in my dreams imagined, and knowing I didn't want to. Please offer me help on how to deal with this now.

In most if not all states, what you describe is a felony.

Norm could be arrested, tried and imprisoned. What he did can be called date rape, sexual abuse or other names, but by any name it is a horrible deed that should never be tolerated.

One reason girls keep quiet about it is that they feel guilty. They sometimes ask themselves whether they did something to encourage the Norms of the world. They blame themselves. But in reality, nothing could justify his behavior. I want to emphasize that you are not guilty, no matter how you feel. Norm is.

It's normal to feel the wounds, even two, three, four years later. Some people can be affected by a night like that for the rest of their lives. That's why it's important that you get counseling, immediately. If you don't know of a professional family counselor, you can ask your pastor, your doctor or your school counselor to refer you to someone. They will keep your request absolutely confidential, and you don't even need to tell them what you want a counselor for. Just say. "It's a personal matter, and it's very important that I see a trained professional." You need very much to talk to someone who can help you work through the consequences.

Just one last comment: It sounds to me as though you were set up. While you aren't to blame for what happened to you, in the future remember this: You have the right to act on your feelings any time you feel uncomfortable with a guy. You don't owe anybody an explanation. Just get out of the situation. Get up and leave. If someone asks where you're going, say, "I have to do something," or "It's personal." And keep walking .

Questions

1. Why does Stafford say couples should wait for marriage before having sex?
2. Does necking usually "just happen"? Or does it take a certain amount of preplanning? Why?
3. Why is it wrong to joke about homosexuality?
4. What assurance does the Bible give that once we have

repented of sin, we will never commit that sin again? If there is no assurance that we won't sin again, how does the Bible deal with our sinfulness? How does one know that God has forgiven a confessed sin?

5. What does Stafford advise a girl to do who is in an uncomfortable situation with a guy? Is his advice good advice?
6. The focus of abortion is often on the mother of the child. In what ways can abortion affect the father of the child?
7. Stafford says that even if a cure for AIDS is discovered, sex before marriage is still wrong. Why?
8. On what grounds does Stafford say masturbation is not a sin? How does he counsel Christians who despise themselves because they cannot stop masturbating?
9. What help does the Bible give to persons who struggle with guilt or frustration over their sexual lives?

Earthkeeping

Why Smaller Refrigerators Can Preserve the Human Race

Appletree Rodden

Appletree Rodden has done research in biochemistry and worked as a member of a German ballet company. This essay was first published in the magazine Harper's. *Rodden makes the case that large refrigerators are more harmful than helpful in a number of ways.*

Once, long ago, people had special little boxes called refrigerators in which milk, meat, and eggs could be kept cool. The grandchildren of these simple devices are large enough to store whole cows, and they reach temperatures comparable to those at the South Pole. Their operating costs increase each year, and they are so complicated that few home handymen attempt to repair them on their own.

Why has this change in size and complexity occurred in

America? It has not taken place in many areas of the technologically advanced world (the average West German refrigerator is about a yard high and less than a yard wide, yet refrigeration technology in Germany is quite advanced). Do we really need (or even want) all that space and cold?

The benefits of a large refrigerator are apparent: a saving of time (one grocery-shopping trip a week instead of several), a saving of money (the ability to buy expensive, perishable items in larger, cheaper quantities), a feeling of security (if the car breaks down or if famine strikes, the refrigerator is well stocked). The costs are there, too, but they are not so obvious.

Cost number one is psychological. Ever since the refrigerator began to grow, food has increasingly become something we buy to store rather than to eat. Few families go to market daily for their daily bread. The manna in the wilderness could be gathered for only one day at a time. The ancient distaste for making food a storage item is echoed by many modern psychiatrists who suggest that such psychosomatic disorders as obesity are often due to the patient's inability to come to terms with the basic transitoriness of life. Research into a relationship between expensive corpulence and the size of one's refrigerator has not been extensive, but we might suspect one to be there.

Another cost is aesthetic. In most of Europe, where grocery marketing is still a part of the daily rhythm, one can buy tomatoes, lettuce, and the like picked on the day of purchase. Many European families have modest refrigerators for storing small items (eggs, milk, butter) for a couple of days, but the concept of buying large quantities of food to store in the refrigerator is not widely accepted. Since fresh produce is easily available in Europe, most people buy it daily.

Which brings to mind another price the large refrigerator has cost us: the friendly neighborhood market. In America, time is money. A large refrigerator means fewer time-consuming trips to the grocery store. One member of a deep-freeze-owning family can do the grocery shopping once or twice a month rather than daily. Since shopping trips are infrequent, most people have been willing to forgo the amenities of the little store around the corner in favor of the lower prices found in the supermarket.

If refrigerators weren't so large—that is, if grocery marketing were a daily affair—the "entertainment surcharge" of buying farm fresh food in a smaller, more intimate setting might carry some weight. But as it is, there is not really that much difference between eggs bought from Farmer Brown's wife and eggs bought from the supermarket which in turn bought them from Eggs Incorporated, a firm operated out of Los Angeles that produces 200,000 eggs a day from chickens that are kept in gigantic warehouses lighted artificially on an eighteen-hour light-and-dark cycle and produce one-and-a-half times as many eggs—a special breed of chickens who die young and insane. Not much difference if you don't mind eating eggs from crazy chickens.

Chalk up Farmer and Mrs. Brown as cost number four of the big refrigerator. The small farmer can't make it in a society dominated by supermarkets and big refrigerators; make way for superfarmers, super yields, and pesticides (cost number five).

Cost number six of the big refrigerator has been the diminution of regional food differences. Of course the homogenization of American fare cannot be blamed solely on the availability of frozen food. Nonetheless, were it not for the trend toward turning regional specialties into frozen dinners, it might still be possible to experience novelty closer to home.

So much for the disadvantages of the big refrigerator. What about the advantages of the small one? First of all, it would help us to "think small." . . . The advent of smaller refrigerators would set the stage for reversing the "big-thinking" trends brought on with the big refrigerator, and would eventually change our lives.

Ivan Illich makes the point in *Tools for Conviviality* that any tool we use (the automobile, standardized public education, public-health care, the refrigerator) influences the individual, his society, and the relationship between the two. A person's automobile is a part of his identity. The average Volkswagen owner has a variety of characteristics (income, age, occupation) significantly different from those of the average Cadillac owner. American society, with more parking lots than parks, and with gridded streets rather than winding lanes, would be vastly different without the private automobile. Similar conclusions can be drawn about any of the tools we use. They change us. They change our society. Therefore, it behooves us to think well before we decide which tool to use to accomplish a given task. Do we want tools that usurp power unto themselves, the ones called "non-convivial" by Illich?

The telephone, a "convivial tool," has remained under control; it has not impinged itself on society or on the individual. Each year it has become more efficient, and it has not prevented other forms of communication (letter writing, visits). The world might be poorer without the telephone, but it would not be grossly different. Telephones do not pollute, are not status symbols, and interact only slightly (if at all) with one's self-image.

So what about the refrigerator? Or back to the more basic problem to which the refrigerator was a partial answer: what about our supply of food? When did we decide to convert the emotion-laden threat of starvation from a shared community problem (of societal structure: farm-market-home) to a personal one (of storage)? How did we decide to accept a thawed block taken from a supermarket's freezer as a substitute for the voluptuous shapes, smells, and textures of fresh fruits and vegetables obtained from complex individual sources?

The decision for larger refrigerators has been consistent with a change in food-supply routes from highly diversified "trails" (from small farms to neighborhood markets) to uniform, standardized highways (from large farms to centrally located supermarkets). Desirable meals are quick and easy rather than rich and leisurely. Cullinary artistry has given way to efficiency, the efficiency of the big refrigerator.

People have a natural propensity for running good things into the ground. Mass production has been a boon to mankind, but its reliance on homogeneity precludes its being a paradigm for all areas of human life. Our forebears and contemporaries have made it possible to mass-produce almost anything. An equally challenging task now lies with us: to choose which things of this world should be mass-produced, and how the standards of mass production should influence other standards we hold dear.

Should houses be mass-produced? Should education? Should food? Which brings us back to refrigerators. How does one decide how large a refrigerator to buy, considering one's life, one's society, and the world, and not simply the question of food storage ?

As similar questions are asked about more and more of the things we mass-produce, mass production will become less of a problem and more of a blessing. As cost begins to be measured not only in dollars spent and minutes saved, but in total richness acquired, perhaps smaller refrigerators will again make good sense. A small step backward along some of the roads of "technological progress" might be a large step forward for mankind, and one our age is uniquely qualified to make.

Questions

1. What are the costs of owning a large refrigerator? Rank these in order of importance to you.
2. In what ways is a refrigerator a convivial tool? Name other convivial tools.
3. What are the characteristics of nonconvivial tools? Name three nonconvivial tools.
4. Do you think mass production is more a problem or a blessing in our Western culture? Why?

A Letter on Strip Mining
Harvey and Nancy Kincaid

Harvey and Nancy Kincaid live near Buffalo Creek in West Virginia. Mrs. Kincaid has spoken publicly in opposition to strip mining. Her letter was read before the West Virginia State Legislature, and it helped persuade lawmakers to pass the Anti-Strip Mining Bill in that state.

Gentlemen:

I don't believe there could be anyone that would like to see the strip mines stopped any more than my husband and myself. It just seems impossible that something like this could happen to us twice in the past three and one half years of time. We have been married for thirteen years and worked real hard at having a nice home that was ours and paid for, with a nice size lot of one acre. Over the thirteen years, we remodeled this house a little at a time and paid for it as we worked and did the work mostly ourselves. The house was located about a quarter of a mile off the road up Glenco Hollow at Kincaid, Fayette County, West Virginia, where it used to be a nice, clean neighborhood.

Then the strippers came four years ago with their big machinery and TNT. I know that these men need jobs and need to make a living like everyone else, but I believe there could be a better way of getting the coal out of these mountains. Have you ever been on a mountaintop and looked down and seen about five different strips on one mountain in one hollow?

My husband owns a Scout Jeep and he can get to the top of the strip mines with the Scout. I would like to invite you to come and visit us sometime and go for a ride with us. It would make you sick to see the way the mountains are destroyed.

First they send in the loggers to strip all the good timber

out and then they come with their bulldozers. If their engineers make a mistake in locating the coal they just keep cutting away until they locate the seam of coal. When the rains come and there isn't anything to stop the drainage, the mountains slide, and the spoil banks fall down to the next spoil bank and so on until the whole mountain slides. There is a small creek in the hollow and when the spring rains come, its banks won't hold the water.

So where does it go?—into people's yards, into their wells, under and into their houses. You have rocks, coal, and a little bit of everything in your yards. When the strippers came they started behind our house in the fall sometime before November. There was a hollow behind our house and we asked them not to bank the spoil the way they did, because we knew what would happen when the spring rains came. My father-in-law lived beside us and the property all ran together in a nice green lawn—four acres.

But the rains came in the spring and the spoil bank broke and the water and debris came into our property every time it rained. It would only take a few minutes of rain and this is what we had for three years.

Then the damage comes to your house because of so much dampness. The doors won't close, the foundation sinks and cracks the walls in the house, your tile comes up off your floors, your walls mold, even your clothes in your closets. Then your children stay sick with bronchial trouble, then our daughter takes pneumonia—X-rays are taken, primary T.B. shows up on the X-ray. This is in July of two years ago. About for a year this child laid sick at home. In the meantime we have already filed suit with a lawyer in Oak Hill when the water started coming in on us, but nothing happens. For three years we fight them for our property—$10,000. The lawyer settles out of court for $4,500. By the time his fee comes out and everything else we have to pay, we have under $3,000 to start over with.

So what do we have to do? Doctor's orders, move out for child's sake and health. We sell for a little of nothing—not for cash, but for rent payments, take the $3,000 and buy a lot on the main highway four miles up the road toward Oak Hill.

The $3,000 goes for the lot, digging of a well and a down payment on a new house. Here we are in debt for thirty years on a new home built and complete by the first of September. We moved the first part of September and was in this house *one month* and what happens? The same strip company comes up the road and puts a blast off and damages the new house— $1,400 worth. When they put one blast off that will crack the walls in your house, the foundation cracked the carport floor straight across in two places, pull a cement stoop away from the house and pull the grout out of the ceramic tile in the bathroom. This is what they can get by with.

How do they live in their $100,000 homes and have a clear mind, I'll never know. To think of the poor people who have worked hard all their lives and can't start over like we did. They have to stay in these hollows and be scared to death every time it rains. I know by experience the many nights I have stayed up and listened to the water pouring off the mountains and the rocks tumbling off the hills.

I remember one time when the strippers put a blast off up the hollow a couple years ago and broke into one of the old mines that had been sealed off for 30 years. They put their blast off and left for the evening. Around seven o'clock that evening it started. We happened to look up the hollow, and thick mud—as thick as pudding—was coming down the main road in the hollow and made itself to the creek and stopped the creek up until the creek couldn't even flow.

The water was turned up into the fields where my husband keeps horses and cattle. I called the boss and told him what was happening and the danger we were in and what did he say? "There isn't anything I can do tonight. I'll be down tomorrow." I called the agriculture and they told us, whatever we did, not to go to bed that night because of the water backed up in those mines for miles.

This is just some of the things that happen around a strip mine neighborhood. But they can get by with it, unless they are stopped. Even if they are stopped it will take years for the trees and grass—what little bit they put on them—to grow enough to keep the water back and stop the slides.

Mr. and Mrs. Harvey Kincaid

Questions

1. Describe the various problems the Kincaids encountered after the strip miners came in. What were they finally forced to do? What did they then encounter?
2. How did the strip mining operations affect the mountains, valleys, and streams of that area?
3. How did the Kincaids try to stop the miners? Why do you think they were unsuccessful in stopping the mining operations?
4. Do you think the Kincaids believe that all strip mining is bad? Why or why not?

"A Handful of Mud": A Personal History of My Love for the Soil

Paul W. Brand

Paul W. Brand worked in a Christian leprosy clinic in Vellore, India, for 18 years. More recently he has been head of rehabilitation at the U.S. Public Health Service leprosy hospital in Carville, Louisiana. He has also co-authored two books, Fearfully and Wonderfully Made *and* In His Image.

I grew up in the mountains of South India. My parents were missionaries to the tribal people of the hills. Our own life was about as simple as it could be, and as happy. There were no roads. We never saw a wheeled vehicle except on our annual visit to the plains. There were no stores, and we had no electricity and no plumbing. My sister and I ran barefoot, and we made up our own games with the trees and sticks and stones around us. Our playmates were the Indian boys and girls, and our life was much the same as theirs. We absorbed a great deal of their outlook and philosophy, even while our parents were teaching them to read and write and to use some of the tools from the West.

The villagers grew everything they ate, and rice was an important food for all of us. The problem was that rice needs flooded fields in the early stages of growth, and there was no level ground for wet cultivation. So rice was grown all along the course of streams that ran down gentle slopes. These slopes had been patiently terraced hundreds of years before, and now every terrace was perfectly level and bordered at its lower margin by an earthen dam covered by grass. Each narrow dam served as a footpath across the line of terraces, with a level field of mud and water six inches below its upper edge and another level terrace two feet below. There were no steep or high drop-offs, so there was little danger of collapse. If the land sloped steeply in one area, then the terraces would be very narrow, perhaps only three or four feet wide. In other areas where the land sloped very little, the terraces would be very broad. Every one of the narrow earth dams followed exactly the line of the contours of the slope.

Every few feet along every grassy path were little channels cut across the top of the dam for water to trickle over to the field below. These channels were lined with grass and were blocked by a grassy sod that the farmer could easily adjust with his foot to regulate the flow of water. Since each terrace was usually owned by a different family, it was important to have some senior village elder who would decide whether one farmer was getting too much or too little of the precious water supply.

Those rice paddies were a rich soup of life. When there was plenty of water, there would be a lot of frogs and little fish. Herons and egrets would stalk through the paddy fields on their long legs and enjoy the feast of little wrigglers that they caught with unerring plunges of their long beaks. Kingfishers would swoop down with a flash of color and carry off a fish from under the beak of a heron. And not only the birds enjoyed the life of the rice paddies—we boys did too. It was there that I learned my first lesson on conservation.

One day I was playing in the mud of a rice field with a half-dozen other little boys. We were catching frogs, racing to see who would be the first to get three. It was a wonderful way to get dirty from head to foot in the shortest possible time. But suddenly we were all scrambling to get out of the paddy. One of the boys had spotted an old man walking across the path toward us. We all knew him and called him "Tata," meaning "Grandpa." He was the keeper of the dams. He walked slowly, stooped over a bit, as though he were always looking at the ground. Old age is very much respected in India, and we boys shuffled our feet and waited in silence for what we knew was going to be a rebuke.

He came over to us and asked us what we were doing. "Catching frogs," we answered.

He stared down at the churned-up mud and flattened young rice plants in the corner where we had been playing, and I was expecting him to talk about the rice seedlings that we had spoiled. Instead he stooped and scooped up a handful of mud. "What is this?" he asked.

The biggest boy among us took the responsibility of answering for us all. "It's mud, Tata."

"Whose mud is it?" the old man asked.

"It's your mud, Tata. This is your field."

Then the old man turned and looked at the nearest of the little channels across the dam. "What do you see there, in that channel?" he asked.

"That is water, running over into the lower field," the biggest boy answered.

For the first time Tata looked angry. "Come with me and I will show you water."

We followed him a few steps along the dam, and he pointed to the next channel, where clear water was running. "That is what water looks like," he said. Then he led us back to our nearest channel, and said, "Is that water?"

We hung our heads. "No, Tata, that is mud, muddy water," the oldest boy answered. He had heard all this before and did not want to prolong the question-and-answer session, so he hurried on, "And the mud from your field is being carried away to the field below, and it will never come back, because mud always runs downhill, never up again. We are sorry, Tata, and we will never do this again."

But Tata was not ready to stop his lesson as quickly as that, so he went on to tell us that just one handful of mud would grow enough rice for one meal for one person, and it would do it twice every year for years and years into the future. "That mud flowing over the dam has given my family food every year from long before I was born, and before my grandfather was born. It would have given my grandchildren food, and then given their grandchildren food forever. Now it will never feed us again. When you see mud in the channels of water, you know that life is flowing away from the mountains."

The old man walked slowly back across the path, pausing a moment to adjust with his foot the grass clod in our muddy channel so that no more water flowed through it. We were silent and uncomfortable as we went off to find some other place to play. I had gotten a dose of traditional Indian folk education that would remain with me as long as I lived. Soil was life, and every generation was responsible for preserving it for future generations.

Over the years I have gone back to my childhood home several times. There have been changes. A road now links the hill people with the plains folk, for example. But traditional ways still continue. The terraced paddy fields still hold back the mud. Rice still grows in the same mud, and there is still an overseer called Tata—although he is one of the boys I used to play with sixty-five years ago. I am sure he lays down the law when he catches the boys churning up the mud, and I hope the system lasts for years to come. I have seen what happens when the old order breaks down, as it did in the Nilgiri Hills. I remember going there for a summer holiday with my family in 1921, when I was a boy.

The Nilgiri Hills, or Blue Mountains, were a favorite resort of the missionaries from the plains during the hot season. We hill folk did not need any change of climate, but we went because of the fellowship. The Nilgiris were steep and thickly forested, with few areas level enough for cultivation, even with terraces. The forestry service was strict and allowed no clearing of the trees except where tea plants or fruit or coffee trees were to be planted. These bushes and trees were good at holding soil, and all was well. I can remember, as a child, the clear streams and rivers that ran down the valleys, and the joy of taking a picnic to the waterfalls and wading in the pools.

Thirty years later—in the 1950s—I was back in India, now a doctor and a missionary myself, with a wife and a growing family. Now I was living on the hot plains at Vellore Christian

Medical College. Everything about India brought back memories, but what I longed for most were the mountains, to remind me of my childhood. My wife and I started a tradition of taking our children to the Nilgiris every summer holiday, and they reveled in the cool air and enjoyed the forests and mountain peaks. But something was different, or soon became so.

A new breed of landowners began to take possession of the mountain forests. During the great struggle for independence in India, a number of people had suffered imprisonment, and they now claimed rewards from a grateful country. Free India had much goodwill but little money, so it gave land to these political sufferers, and some of that land was the forests of the Nilgiri Hills. These new landowners had not been farmers before. They had never known any Tata to teach them the value of mud. They wanted to make money, and make it fast. They knew that the climate was ideal for growing potatoes, and that there was a market for them. So they cleared forests from sloping land and planted potatoes. Two, even three crops could be harvested every year, and they made good money. But the land suffered. Harvesting potatoes involves turning over the soil, and monsoon rains often came before the new crop could hold the soil. . . .

One summer holiday our bus struggled up the winding road, and the heat of the plains gave way to cool breezes. We looked for the streams and waterfalls that I had loved. But now the water looked like chocolate syrup; it oozed rather than flowed. What we were seeing was rivers of mud. I felt sick.

There was a dear old Swiss couple, Mr. and Mrs. Fritschi, who lived in Coonoor, on the Nilgiri Hills. They had been missionaries of the Basel Mission in Switzerland but were long retired and now owned a nursery of young plants and trees. They loved to help and advise farmers and gardeners about ways to improve their crops. It seemed to me that these devoted people would know if there was some way to advise the landowners about ways to save their soil. I went to ask Mr. Fritschi about the havoc that was being wrecked by potato farming and to find out if there was anything that we could do. Mr. Fritschi despaired about the new landowners. His eyes were moist as he told me, "I have tried, but it is no use. They have no love of the land, only of money. They are making a lot of money, and they do not worry about the loss of soil because they think it is away in the future, and they will have money to buy more. Besides, they can deduct the loss of land from their income tax as a business depreciation." In the United States today this would be called agribusiness rather than farming, and indeed, the attitudes of agribusiness are much the same.

Thirty more years have passed, and my children have grown up and scattered, and we have left India. But we love it still, and every year I go back to visit my old medical college in Vellore and take part in the leprosy work there. I don't really enjoy going back to the Nilgiri Hills anymore, although many parts of them are still beautiful. I look up to the slopes that used to be covered with forests and then were planted with potatoes year after year. There are large areas of bare rock now, of no use to anybody. The deforested areas that still have some soil look like stretches of gravel. The streams and springs that ran off from these areas ran clear sixty years ago, flowed mud thirty years ago, and today are dry. When the rains come, they rush over this land in torrents; the land floods, then goes dry. . . . Oh, Tata! Where have you gone? You have been replaced by businessmen and accountants who have degrees in commerce and who know how to manipulate tax laws, by farmers who know about pesticides and chemical fertilizers but who care nothing about leaving soil for their great-grandchildren.

Questions

1. Why did Tata rebuke the boys who were playing in the rice terrace?
2. How important was a handful of mud to the Indian villagers? Was it as important to the Nilgiri potato farmers? Why or why not?

3. Why didn't the potato farmers care about conserving the soil? How did they "explain away" their abuse of the land? Do you hear these same excuses offered today?

Redeemers of the Earth

Loren Wilkinson

*Loren Wilkinson has written a helpful biblical analysis of a
common disagreement. The question is: Are human beings
part of nature or apart from nature? Your answer to that
question most likely will govern your answer to the question
of how people are to relate to nature. Wilkinson covers the
issue well and provides a biblical analysis which may surprise you. Finally, some important Christians in history
have studied the issue; their views are helpful, too.*

I. The Disagreement: Apart from, or a Part of?

We humans are in the middle of a great disagreement over
our relationship to the rest of creation. It is not merely a
philosopher's quarrel, though it grows out of, or impacts
upon, a number of philosophical positions. Rather the disagreement runs through the center of some of our knottiest
personal and national decisions: nuclear energy, land-use planning, agricultural technique, personal consumption—in these
and countless other areas we find basic disagreements over the
place of humanity in nature. The underlying disagreement is
about both human nature and the human task: what we *are*
with regard to the rest of creation, and what we are *to do* with
it. My three-fold purpose in this paper is to clarify the nature
of the disagreement, to show how the Christian picture of man
points to a kind of resolution, and to survey some trends in
our society which are in harmony with that Christian resolution. But first, let us consider some examples of the problem:
Let us begin by looking at the disagreement over what man *is*.

On one side in this great debate are those who stress that
the most important factor in understanding the human condition is that we humans are fundamentally a part of nature.

This insight, coming particularly from various branches of biology, is confirming our unity with nature in a variety of astonishing, and sometimes disturbing, ways. When we eat, we are nourished by the protein-building chemistry of fish, birds, plants, and animals. When we drink, we are partaking of water which at some stage has been passed through or stored in living things. When we breathe, we take in oxygen which was not only purified by green plants, but which was, in the inception of our atmosphere, released by the action of life. The planet is like a vast organism—in some ways, like a vast cell—in which we are only one small part.

We are immersed, then, in nature: We are embedded in it, and it in us. Not only are we part of a vast, inter-reacting, and stable organism, but each of us is an organism made up of parts whose life is no more (or less) independent of their environment (which is our bodies), than we are independent of the earth. We are a part of that earth: This unity is the basic message, not only of the science of ecology, but of a host of movements, fads, and new consciousnesses. After generations of pretending our uniqueness we have discovered that the limits of our body are not our skin, but the whole living organism of the planet.

But there is another school of thought which stresses just the opposite. According to it, the most important thing to remember in understanding we humans is our difference from nature. Man is fundamentally apart from nature, as is demonstrated by his reason, his language, and above all, his ingenious abilities to manipulate and modify. And his difference is demonstrated also by the rapid alternation of the planet by human activity. Says theologian Harvey Cox, approvingly,

> Cities are the artifacts of man. But whereas they once formed mere islands in a vast sea of uncharted nature, today the balance is reversing itself. The world is becoming one huge interdependent city, in which jungles and deserts remain only with the explicit consent of a global metropolis.

But this is no tragedy, says Cox; it is the density of nature—

now is a thinking reie

to become what another theologian, Pierre Teilhard de Chardin, calls, "a solid sphere of homonized substance." Though the human biological heritage is a fact to be reckoned with, say these thinkers, the most obvious fact about man is his ability to rise *above* his biology: Biology is not destiny. We have taken our evolution into our own hands, and, for better or worse, are able to shape our future in a way unlike anything else in nature.

So much for the two basic positions about what man is. One groups says, "Man is a part of nature"; the other group says,"That may be true, but the most important fact about man is that he is apart from nature."

These two views of what man *is* are closely linked to two views of what man ought to *do*. It is here, in the realm of action that the deepest controversies emerge.

Those who say that man is a part of nature argue that he ought to live in harmony with it. Instead of creating new sources of energy we ought to learn to do what the rest of creation has always done: live within the limitations of the sun's energy. Instead of imposing a regime of chemical fertilizers and pesticides on our fields, we ought to farm them organically, minimizing the difference between the agricultural and the wild. In short, we need to recognize that we are a part of nature, and learn to live within that harmony.

But those who see man's essence as lying in his separateness from nature feel otherwise. Thinkers like Buckminster Fuller argue that drawing on the processes and energies of nature is a kind of starting motor, useful to crank up the engine of human ingenuity, which is our ability to do more and more with less and less. Man is the sort of creature who is always able to go beyond limitations and barriers. And Fuller's argument is convincing: There seems to be no real limit to our potential powers or accomplishments. Such ability to transcend natural limitations seems to lend both power and right to those who say that man ought to exercise his mastery over nature.

This then, is the debate. Some of us say that humanity is fundamentally a part of nature, and that we ought to learn to live more in harmony with it. And some of us declare that humanity is basically different from nature, arguing that we ought to exercise our power over nature so that it becomes raw material for human action. Perhaps the disagreement is most bitter over the question of technology. Though each of us unavoidably—and rather cheerfully—accepts a variety of technological accomplishments which make our life more comfortable, many people argue that technology has taken on a life of its own, which both destroys nature and alienates us from it.

On the whole, the dilemma appears to be inescapable, and is deeply rooted in the human condition. We are both a part of nature and apart from it; thus we destroy it and seek to preserve it. Is there any way that we can reconcile these apparent conflicts and live in less tension with ourselves and our planet? To seek an answer, let us consider the Biblical view of man.

II. The Biblical Picture of Man in Creation

When considered in the light of the problems I have just outlined, a striking fact about the creation account in Genesis 1 and 2 is that it gives support both for those who say that man is a part of nature, and those who say he is apart from it; likewise, it supports those who stress both man's need to live in harmony with the earth, and his right to manipulate it.

First of all, Genesis clearly teaches that humans are different from anything else in creation. This uniqueness is powerfully conveyed by the fact that only of humans is it said that they are made "in God's image": "And God created man in his own image, in the image of God He created them." Many have called this teaching a supreme example of human arrogance. But, like it or not, there is no teaching in Scripture more clear than this, and it stands at the very beginning of the Biblical record of God's dealings with man: Of all things in creation, man is uniquely like God; thus he stands apart from the world, is fundamentally different from it.

A further example of this unique status of the man in creation is in Genesis 2. There Eden is described as being created for man: "And the Lord God planted a garden toward the east, in Eden; and there He placed the man whom He had formed."

All things in the garden—which tradition has often considered to be the whole earth—are described as being placed there for man. In the first two chapters of Genesis then, man not only has a different status with regard to God; he has a different status with regard to the rest of creation. Creation is "for" him. It is this unique status of man in nature which many recent critics have said produced humanity's great destructive ability, and the kind of arrogance which is particularly evident in Western man. It is the burden, for example, of Lynn White in his famous article "The Historic Roots of Our Ecologic Crisis." Christianity, White argues, had taught that since man is the only thing in the universe which is like God, everything else is dis-godded, appropriate raw material for disposal by the one god-like thing in creation.

But there is another side to this picture of man's place in creation. Though he clearly is made as something different, and thus is apart from creation, he is also very clearly a part of it. First of all, man is made in the same order as everything else: He was made on the sixth day, after five days of creation: the process and pattern for his making were established in the making of stars, seas, fish, grass and birds—and he is like them. It is significant, too, that man is not the only thing made "on the sixth day": He shares a day of creation with the higher animals. Thus the ordered creation account parallels (as many biologists have noted) not only evidences of evolutionary progression, but also the fact of man's embeddedness in nature. For better or worse, and despite his god-likeness humans are *part of the process* of creation.

This fundamentally earthy nature of the human is suggested again in Genesis 2:

Then the Lord God formed man of dust from the ground, and breathed into his nostrils the breath of life; and man became a living being.

No English translation can catch the richness and depth of the Hebrew wordplay here: God made man, ADAM, from

ADAMAH, the dust of the ground. The same idea would be conveyed if we said in English, "God made *humans* from *humus*."

Thus however much we are to stress man's difference from the rest of creation, it is essential that we not lose sight of his essential likeness not only to God but to the earth and its creatures. Scripture teaches then, both that humans are apart from nature, and a part of it. Or, to use theological terms that are familiar in a different context, Scripture teaches both man's *transcendence* over nature, and his *immanence* in it.

So much then for the Genesis teaching on what man is; let us look at that teaching on what man *does*. What basis in Scripture is there for the current conflict about how man ought to treat nature?

First of all, we may note, along with many critics of Christianity, that the view of man as transcendent over nature is accompanied by a mandate which expresses, in the strongest possible terms, man's legitimate *dominion* over nature. Here the key statement is Genesis 1:28: "And God blessed them; and God said to them, 'Be fruitful, and multiply, and fill the earth, and subdue it; and rule over the fish of the sea and over the birds of the sky, and over every living thing that moves on the earth.'" Apart from the commands to be fruitful and multiply (which were given also to other creatures) two verbs here denote the action which man is especially supposed to exercise over nature. One is the Hebrew KABASH, here translated "subdue." It comes from a root meaning "to press down," or "bring into bondage," and it conveys the image of a conqueror placing his foot on the neck of the conquered. The other word, RADAH, here translated "rule," comes from a root meaning "to tread," or "to trample" (as in a wine press). Cognate words have meanings like "to chastise" or "prevail against." Both words clearly place man above the world, and portray him as in some way placing pressure on it. It is significant that both words convey things done with the feet, visually reinforcing the idea of man *over* nature. The idea of human uniqueness, conveyed in the teaching that man alone is made in God's image, is here supported by a picture of man as having a power and superiority over nature like that of the creating God, in whose likeness man is made. There is no way of softening the import of these words: They convey total power, a tyrant's power. It is like the power which God potentially has over His creation.

But once again, these forceful lording acts are not the only thing man is told to do. For in Genesis 2, other tasks are set for humanity: "Then the Lord God took the man and put him into the Garden of Eden to cultivate it and keep it" (Genesis 2:15).

Here, again two verbs (translated "cultivate" and "keep") set forth man's actions. "Cultivate" is the Hebrew word ABAD; it is variously translated "till," or "work," but it has the primary meaning of working *for* another. (It is the most common root for "servant" or slave.") The most literal reading would be "serve." Though the garden is planted to provide the needs of man, clearly man is placed in Eden to care for, even to *serve*, the garden. And the other word conveys the same sort of meaning. "Keep" translates the Hebrew SHAMAR—it is used to describe an action undertaken for the well-being of the thing kept. Thus the cherubim are told to "keep," "watch," or "guard" the garden after man's failure; and Cain, using this same verb, asks, "Am I my brother's keeper?"

Unmistakably, the meaning conveyed by both these words is that man is to care for the garden: His actions are to be undertaken at least as much out of concern for the welfare of creation as they are to be undertaken for the welfare of man.

Thus Genesis seems to contain support both for those who hold man's transcendence over nature, and for those who hold to his immanence in nature; likewise, it seems to confirm both those who say that man should alter nature for his own ends, and those who say that he should live in harmony with it. We have a very difficult time in understanding how the idea of total power over nature does not contradict the idea of service for nature. Likewise, we find it difficult to understand how we humans can be both transcendent over nature, and immanent in it.

But the whole of Biblical history, culminating in the life

and death of Christ, may be seen as a kind of answer to this dilemma: So also may be the fact that theologians have long said of God that He is both "transcendent" and "immanent." The key to understanding how man is to exercise legitimately both his transcendence and his immanence is thus to be found by looking at the transcendence and immanence of God. But before considering briefly God's dealings with creation as a basis for man's, let me point out one feature of the Genesis account which, I believe, holds a kind of key to the question both of man's nature and his task. It is in Genesis 2:19:

> And out of the ground the Lord God formed every beast of the field and every bird of the sky, and brought them to the man to see what he would call them; and whatever the man called a living creature, that was its name.

The most remarkable thing about this passage is the way in which God, who has spoken all things into being, here seems to *wait* "to see what man would call them." God the creator waits for man's word, man's LOGOS. Given the great significance which primitive peoples, generally, along with the Biblical writers, give to names, the impression is unmistakable that here God is in some ways *giving up* His creative role to man. Through the instrument of language, man is like the creator who, through His word, brought all things into being.

But let us look a bit more closely at this passage, from the perspective of man as transcendent and immanent, lord and servant. To name a thing is to exercise one's power over it. This linking of power with naming is an ancient belief, which we still sense in our reluctance to share our name with people we don't know. Thus naming is, on the one hand, an exercise of dominion: of human transcendence and manipulative power. On the other hand—especially given the great importance of naming among primitive people—to name a thing is to release it: Naming gives a kind of being. It creates a space in which the thing can appear. And of course, not just any name will do: It must be the right name—a name which reflects a knowledge of what that creature is. Such knowledge does not come from a lordly aloofness: It comes from an intimate knowledge—from being a part of, being *immanent* in the world of the thing one names. In naming, then, we catch a glimpse of the legitimate use of human power: It is appropriate for humans to stand apart from creatures, and to exercise this power over them; but it is also appropriate to exercise this power, in such a way as to clarify, to bring into the light, the unique selfhood of those things God made.

But this lesson, from naming, about the redemptive uses of power—is only implicit. We turn now to its more explicit appearance in Scripture—for indeed, the whole Biblical story may be understood as God's long lesson to man about the legitimate uses of transcendent power.

The culmination of that divine lesson is in the Incarnation of Christ. But before turning to that central Biblical event, let us consider two of many statements of the theme, both in the prophets.

The first is a familiar passage: Isaiah 53. The prophet begins, "Who has believed our report, and to whom has the arm of the Lord been revealed?" Frequent repetition has perhaps drained some of the significance from this astonished question. The prophet is saying, in effect, "You're not going to believe this." For his message is precisely the reversal of all human expectations about the use of power. It is astonishing that God, the Lord of the universe, should reveal His "arm" (that is, His power) not as a manipulating monarch, but as a servant: a servant who is involved with the pains and suffering of others to the extent that He endures them in His own flesh.

A second example of this long lesson that dominion does not mean exploitation is a less familiar passage in Ezekiel 34:

Then the word of the Lord came to me saying, "Son of man, prophesy and say to those shepherds, 'Thus says the Lord God, "Woe shepherds of Israel who have been feeding themselves! Should not the shepherds feed the flock? You eat the fat and clothe yourselves with the wool, you slaughter the fat sheep without feeding the flock. Those who are sickly you have not strengthened, the diseased you have not healed, the broken you have not bound up, the scattered you have not brought back, nor have you sought for the lost; but with force and severity you have dominated them."'"

Ezekiel 34:1-4

This last phrase, "with force and severity you have *dominated* them," uses the same verb that occurs in Genesis 1:28, describing the *dominion* man is to have over the earth. But in this passage it is clear that humans with power are *not* to exercise a dominion which fails to consider the welfare of the thing dominated. The passage is not a text on animal husbandry; yet the principles of a leader's legitimate power over his people are drawn from a shepherd's legitimate husbandry over his flock. The principle is the same in either case: A person with power who uses that power simply to increase his own benefit, and not also for the welfare of others, is using the power unjustly, *illegitimately*. Whatever "dominion" means, whatever human transcendence means, it cannot mean this sort of forcible imposition of one's will apart from the will and welfare of what is dominated.

The great example of a restored, corrected dominion is hinted at later in the chapter when God declares through Ezekiel,

Behold, I Myself will search for My sheep and seek them out. As a shepherd cares for his herd in the day when he is among his scattered sheep, so I will care for My sheep and will deliver them from all places to which they were scattered . . . I will seek the lost, bring back the scattered, bind up the broken, and strengthen the sick; but the fat and the strong I will destroy. I will feed them with judgment. . .

Ezekiel 34:11-16

The key phrase here is "in the day when he is *among* his scattered sheep." The passage inevitably recalls, for Christians, "the word which became flesh and dwelt among us"—or the frequent description of Christ as the good shepherd: "I am the good shepherd, and I know my own . . ." (John 10:14).

Thus, in Christ, the Christian is pointed unmistakably to another kind of dominion, another kind of transcendence. The God of the universe is redemptively among his sheep: immanent among them. And the full depth of this immanence is evident in one of the most powerful metaphors for Christ: not only is He the shepherd, but He is the *lamb* of God, who gave Himself for the life of the world.

These are all familiar passages, close to the heart of the Christian Gospel. They are perhaps too familiar for us to see clearly their implication for our stewardship of the earth. But the principle is clear: God demonstrates His transcendence— His dominion over man—by becoming, in Christ, redemptively immanent in human affairs: indeed, by becoming incarnate in the very flesh of the world He made. And this kind of dominion, rather than the dominion by force which uses everything for our own benefit, is to be the model for our own human use of power and transcendence—or, for our use of science and technology. We are to develop the power—which is legitimate in us, as it is in God—but are to use it redemptively; to enter, to understand, and to give names and freedom to the world we so transcend.

The great example of this radical idea of *transcendence* as *immanence* is at the heart of the Christian Gospel, for it is the life and death of Jesus. Let us consider, therefore, some of the things that the Incarnation can show us about the use of the earth.

First of all, the Biblical teaching on the Incarnation is that Christ was involved with *all* of creation, not just humanity. The totality of this involvement is suggested in John 3:16: "For God so loved the world that He gave His only begotten son. . . ." In this familiar passage, usually understood by Christians to refer only to human redemption, "world" is the translation of the Greek *kosmos*, whose broadest reference is not merely to the world of human affairs, but to the whole universe, as a harmoniously-related totality.

It is understandable that we be concerned primarily with human salvation: That is certainly the focus of the Gospel. But there are many passages in the New Testament which speak explicitly of Christ's involvement with the non-human world: "In the beginning was the word . . . All things were made through Him" (John 1:1 and 3); "In Him all things were created" (Col. 1:16); "In Him all things hold together" (Col. 1:17); ". . . the summing up of all things in Christ" (Eph. 1:10); "God has spoken to us through His Son . . . through whom he made the world" (Heb. 1:2).

However, the most striking picture of Christ's involvement in creation does not occur in the New Testament at all, but in the book of Proverbs. In a passage which has often been understood as referring to Christ, the personification of Wisdom declares:

> The Lord possessed me at the beginning of His way,
> Before His works of old.
> From everlasting I was established,
> From the beginning, from the earliest times of the earth . . .
> While He had not yet made the earth and the fields,
> Nor the first dust of the world . . .
> When He marked out the foundations of the earth;
> Then I was beside Him as a master workman;
> And I was daily His delight,
> Rejoicing always before Him,
> Rejoicing in the world, His earth,
> And having my delight in the sons of men.
>
> (Prov. 8:22-31 *passim.*)

This radical immanence of God in creation appears not only in these statements about Christ, but in the metaphors and the miracles associated with His ministry. Implicit in Christ's words and actions, is an awareness that here indeed is the creator of the universe: he who knows from the inside the secret chemistry that turns sunlight into grapes, and grapes into wine; who sustains the power that sends a vine's tendrils across a stone and knows the energies that hold stones together; his knowledge of life is so total that he lifts dead matter into living flesh. Christ has all this knowledge—and uses it as power. For, as creator and sustainer, He is both radically transcendent over and radically immanent in the stuff of creation. He is the power at work in each day of creation. Indeed, when we look at the most powerful metaphors applied to Christ, we see that the days of creation are recapitulated: Christ is the light of the world; He is stone; He is vine; He is grain of wheat; He is lamb; He is, above all, man.

That these are not merely random metaphors is confirmed by the miracles which Christ performs. In them He shows His power over the elements (as when He calms the sea), over basic biological processes (as when He turns water into wine), and over animal life (as the multiplication of fishes). In the words of C.S. Lewis:

> Look down into every bay and almost every river. This swarming undulating fecundity shows He is still at work. . . . It was He who at the beginning commanded all species "to be fruitful and multiply and replenish the earth." And now that day, at the feeding of the thousands, incarnate God does the same, does close and small, under His human hands, a workman's hands, what He has always been doing in the seas, the lakes, and the little brooks.

And of course, in the miracles of healing and resurrection, Christ demonstrates both His transcendence over, and His immanence in, human life.

Both as Creator, and as Redeemer, then, Christ is immanent in creation. The full pattern for this immanence is unfolded by Paul in Philippians 2, which speaks of God grasping not at Godhead, but taking the form of a servant. And in this crucial passage it is clear that this divine condescension is important not only for its role in the accomplishment of our Salvation, but also because it is through Christ's redemptive immanence among us that we have the power to be redemptively immanent in what we care for.

Do nothing from selfishness or empty conceit, but with humility of mind let each of you regard one another as more important than himself; do not merely look out for your own personal interests, but also for the interests of others. Have this attitude in yourselves which was also in Christ Jesus, who, although He existed in the form of God, did not regard equality with God a thing to be grasped, but emptied Himself, taking the form of a bondservant, and being made in the likeness of men. And being found in appearance as a man, He humbled Himself by becoming obedient to the point of death, even death on a cross.

(Phil. 2:3-8)

We Christians often apply this passage to our treatment of other humans. But the pattern—that superiority, dominion, transcendence are to be given up, for the purpose of service, suggests that we ought to reconsider our comfortable dominion over nature.

That it is God's intention for His people to have a redemptive role in nature is another neglected dimension of the Gospel: perhaps because its implications are so staggering, and the possibilities of misunderstanding and hence misusing our power are so great. But consider briefly a familiar passage in Romans 8. Following an assertion that we are not only children, but heirs of God, and fellow-heirs with Christ, Paul spells out one implication of what this inheritance might mean:

For the anxious longing of the creation waits eagerly for the revealing of the sons of God. For the creation was subjected to futility, not of its own will, but because of Him who subjected it, in hope that the creation itself also will be set free from its slavery to corruption into the freedom of the glory of the children of God.

(Rom. 8:19-21)

As creation was cursed through man, so also it will be blessed through man. Whatever else this difficult passage means, it clearly teaches that man has an actively redemptive role in creation, and one which has hardly yet begun to be played out. What we perceive now of creation is a groaning in the pains of childbirth: But creation itself, so this passage indicates, will one day share in *our* redemption—"in the freedom of the glory of the children of God."

The same idea is expressed in Hebrews 2. The writer begins by quoting most of Psalm 8, a familiar passage which sets forth in forceful terms man's superiority over nature:

> What is man, that Thou remembrest him?
> Or the son of man, that Thou art concerned about him?
> Thou has made him for a little while lower than the angels;
> Thou hast crowned him with glory and honor,
> And has appointed Him over the works of Thy hands;
> Thou has put all things in subjection under his feet.
>
> (Heb. 2:6-8)

When they occur in Psalm 8, these statements are clearly speaking of man. Here too, in Hebrews, they refer to man—but they describe only a partial, incomplete human dominion. As the writer explains: "For in subjecting all things to him [that is, mankind] He [God] left nothing that is not subject to him. But now we do not yet see all things subjected to him" (Heb. 2:8). The "not yet" is crucial, for it implies a progressive, steadily increasing, divinely-approved mastery of man over creation. But, though man has "not yet" had all things placed under his feet (and it is presumably for just such a dominion that creation is longing in Romans 8), "we *do* see Him who has been made for a little while lower than the angels, Jesus" (Heb. 2:9).

It is only a glimpse. But what these passages indicate is that creation waits for a legitimate liberating dominion by man. Such a dominion was what man was made for: Yet man failed, and only Christ has fulfilled that purpose. What is most startling and challenging for Christians, however, is the indication that such a legitimate, fulfilling mastery of creation is still the redeemed human's destiny. It is to be a mastery both as total as Christ's Lordship over us, and as redeeming, as self-giving, as Christ's death for us.

So we see, in Scripture, a resolution of that dilemma with which we opened this study: Man seems to be both a part of nature, and apart from it; it seems right for him both to manipulate it, and to live in harmony with it. And in the Christian Gospel we find, in Christ, the transcendent God who becomes immanent in the world for the world's sake: And that incarnation is presented as the power and the pattern for our own relationships with the world.

That was 2,000 years ago: And the dilemma is with us more intensely than ever before. Nevertheless, though our fall-enness continually tries to twist it into another problem, the Christian answer to this puzzle of our relationship to nature has been seen, and applied. Let us consider therefore some of those individuals and traditions in the history of Christian thought which have grasped the meaning of the Incarnation for our relationship to nature.

III. The Idea of Man as Redeemer of Nature in the History of Christianity

Of many possible examples, let us consider three: widely separated in space and time, but all part of the legacy of ortho-dox Christianity—Eastern Orthodoxy; the thought of St. Fran-cis and the Franciscans; and the Reformed theology of Abra-ham Kuyper. The earliest, and most continuous of these recog-nitions of the human redemptive role in creation is in Eastern Orthodox tradition.

Despite its generally other-worldly reputation among Western theologians, Eastern Orthodoxy has had, from near the beginning of its long divergence from the Western tradi-tion, a higher view of the created world. The reasons for this are complex, but an important factor is the refutation, in the ninth century, of the iconoclastic heresy: that movement which had as its main tenet the idea that no image should be made of Christ. In the process of suppressing the iconoclasts, the church formulated many explicit theological affirmations of the value of the created world. John of Damascus puts the Orthodox conclusion eloquently:

> In former times God, without body or form, could in no way be represented. But today, since God has appeared in the flesh and lived among men, I can represent what is visible in God. I do not venerate matter, but I venerate the creator of matter who became matter for my sake, who assumed life in the flesh, and who, through matter, accomplished my Salvation.

In Western theology there is nothing like this affirmation of the created world.

In Eastern thought, this affirmation is consistent with a higher view of the Incarnation—that it was in the divine purpose from the beginning, and not just a consequence of man's sin. And out of the higher view of matter implied by the Orthodox doctrine of the Incarnation came a clear doctrine of man's involvement in the progressive "deification" of nature. According to Maximus the Confessor:

> It was the divinely appointed function of the first man . . . to unite in himself the whole of created being; and at the same time, to reach his perfect union with God, and thus grant the state of deification to the whole creation.

The Orthodox thinkers are not explicit on what the "deification" of nature might mean. Generally, it seems to mean that both man and nature are to be a part of the eternal Kingdom of God and that nature's presence in that kingdom will depend on what man does with and in nature. But man has failed to be the agent for this "deification" of nature. In the words of the author of Hebrews, all things are "not yet" placed under his redeeming dominion. But (again, in keeping with the teaching of Hebrews) where Adam failed, Christ, the second Adam, succeeds—and becomes the model for all humanity. According to John Myendorff, a contemporary Orthodox thinker,

The restoration of creation is a "new creation," but it does not establish a new pattern, so far as man is concerned; it reinstates *man* in his original glory among creatures, and in his original responsibility for the world.

Vladimir Lossky, another contemporary Orthodox thinker puts it,

In his way to union with God, man in no way leaves creatures aside, but gathers together in His love the whole cosmos, disordered by sin, that it may at last be transfigured by Grace.

Thus, the theologians of the Eastern church grasped early the concepts both of man's transcendence over nature, and of the proper use to which that transcendence should be put: that is, as a means for the "deification" of the whole creation. And, equally important, the "deification" doctrine has remained, to this day, an important part of Eastern Orthodox thought.

But the driving energies of Christendom—indeed, of humanity in general—did not have their source in any such view of transcendence. It was rather in the West, impelled by an understanding of man as apart from creation, saved out of it, that the great eruption of human transcendence took place.

Nevertheless, there have been other movements, in Western Christendom, toward a similar affirmation of the human place in creation. A prominent one is in the thought of St. Francis, and the Franciscan tradition which originated in him.

In at least three ways, the life of St. Francis reveals a recognition, in Western Christianity, of the significance of the Incarnation for clarifying the human place in the world. The first is St. Francis' individuality. There was a quixotic individualism about St. Francis which makes him by far the best-known medieval figure. In an age which left little room for the assertion of selfhood, St. Francis stands out, across the centuries, as a person with a remarkably clear sense of self-identity. It is legitimate to say that Francis "transcends" his contemporaries in this way. Rather than fitting into the flow of the times, he stands out from them—and from nature. His own transcendent selfhood becomes a basis for the other, more commonly recognized distinctives of St. Francis' position.

The second of these distinctives, of course, is St. Francis' poverty. Francis and the Franciscans rediscovered the Christian example of servanthood, as is clear in the rule of St. Francis, which declares that

> Brothers . . . should seek the most humble jobs so that they are on the lowest rung of the economic ladder. They should be servants rather than masters . . . Under no conditions is a brother to hold money in any form.

In part, the rigor of this rule can be explained as a reaction against the perennial Christian forgetfulness of the poverty of Christ and His teaching about it. (Indeed, the rule was soon compromised even within Francis' own order.) But Francis' teaching is more than a reaction; it is a recovery of the basis of Christian ethics: that God Himself "took upon Himself the form of a servant" and made perfect his strength in weakness. A servant is immersed in, immanent in, the affairs of those he serves. Thus this emphasis on poverty and humility appears to be in tension with Francis' individuality; with his strong personality: but only superficially. For, in the Christian teaching on selfhood we are given transcendent selves in order to give them up, to be immanent redemptively in what we transcend. And nowhere is that redemptive immanence clearer than in the third aspect of St. Francis' teaching: his attitude towards nature.

There are abundant examples of Francis' attitude to non-human creation. Whether apocryphal or not, such stories as those of Francis preaching to the birds, or converting the wolf of Gubbo or calling a cicada to come rest on his hand, reflect Francis' basic insight: that humans share—and should share humbly—in created nature. In his everyday behavior, Francis attempted to be consistent in this attitude towards the earth. Thomas of Celano, in an early biography of Francis, writes:

When the brothers were cutting wood, he would forbid them to cut down the whole tree so that it might grow up again. He also ordered the gardeners not to dig up the edges of the gardens so that wild flowers and green grasses could grow and glorify the Father of all things . . . He picked up worms so they would not be trampled on, and had honey and wine set out for the bees in the winter season. He called by the name of *brother* all animals . . .

These attitudes are consistent with the great "Canticle of the Sun," which Francis wrote near the end of his life. That prayer is not, of course, a hymn *to* nature; it is unequivocally addressed to God: "Be praised my Lord, for all your creatures." But the creatures are spoken of with an affection which reveals Francis' sense of immanence among them. Because his life is so thoroughly directed to God, he can also direct it caringly into the things of the created world, and speak of Brother Sun, Sister Moon, Brother Wind, Mother Earth, Brother Fire, Sister Water, and (in a remarkably acute ecological insight) Sister Death. It has always been easy for Christians to recall that they are related to God in His image. Francis made it easier for them to remember that they are related to the earth as well.

Perhaps the most remarkable thing about St. Francis' ideas, however, is not their uniqueness in the Middle Ages, but the way in which they influenced subsequent thought. It is fashionable to say that St. Francis was an aberration in the Middle Ages—almost a heretic whose ideas about man's brotherhood with nature were quickly suppressed. But, in ways which are not frequently recognized, they had enormous influence on subsequent European thought. First of all, the Franciscans, through their emphasis on the ordinary, the humble and the immediate, influenced the direction of poetry in Western Europe—particularly in Italy and England. The vernacular lyric, which uses the detail of everyday life to express deep emotional and spiritual insights, thus owes its development in large part to Francis' rediscovery of man's kinship with nature. Thus it was, in part, Franciscan seeds which were to blossom,

500 years later, in Romanticism, and its flawed but renewed vision of the meaning of the creation for humans.

The other major impact of Franciscan thought was on philosophy—and through philosophy, on science. The great Franciscan philosopher was Bonaventure, who, unlike his better-known contemporary Aquinas, was remarkably open to the vision of God available in all created things. Said Bonaventure: "He therefore, who is not illumined by such great splendor of created things is blind . . . Open your eyes, therefore, that you may see our God in all creatures." The importance of such an attitude towards creation for the subsequent development of science is made clear in the words of Etienne Gilson:

> The Thomistic "form" begets a form in matter; it imposes that form upon a matter which submits to it; the Bonaventuran form rouses to life in the bosom of matter a potential form which that matter already contains.

That potential for matter to contain form intrinsically, inherently, is owing to the Franciscan-Bonaventuran reaffirmation of the importance of the Incarnation. And it was an idea which was especially fertile for those interested in investigating the natural world. Thus many of the roots of modern science lie in the Franciscans. Roger Bacon, Robert Grosseteste, and William of Occam were all Franciscans. The Franciscan sense of brotherhood with nature made a congenial environment for those who wanted to study nature. So it was, ironically, that Franciscan discovery of human kinship with nature which helped produce a way of knowing nature which, since the scientific revolution and subsequently, has produced that explosion of human transcendence which many people feel will destroy nature.

So much for the Franciscans. Let us consider now, very briefly, one more expression of the idea of man as redemptively immanent in nature—this time, in our own century, and in our own tradition. Building on the insights of John Calvin, Abraham Kuyper developed a theology of "common grace" which gave to man a redemptive role in nature.

The key to Kuyper's understanding of the role of the human in creation is evident in his declaration, at the founding of the Free University of Amsterdam, that "there is not an inch of the whole area of human existence of which Christ, the sovereign of all, does not cry, 'It is mine.'" Christ is "sovereign of all"—Christ is king. That kingship extends, of course, not only through the sphere of human existence, but through the whole realm of creation. All creation, according to Kuyper, is to give God honor. That it does so is the result of "common grace." And common grace is available to the world at large through Christ, the mediator of creation, in Whom all things exist.

Yet, though this common grace was sufficient to keep the world from destruction because of sin, it is not sufficient to keep it from ultimate destruction. It is here that special grace intervenes. Through Christ's sacrifice, all men are redeemed. They are "re-created." And creation in general shares, through man, in that recreation. Ultimately, then, the whole creation will not be destroyed, but redeemed.

Though the redemption of creation is made perfect only through the elect, it is begun through the workings of common grace on humanity as a whole. Thus, as Henry Van Til puts it:

Due to the fall of man, the seed of Adam lost its kingship over nature on which culture is basically posited . . . but through common grace this power over nature is restored in the advances of science, whereby the effects of the curse are diminished. Hereby the glory of the image of God in mankind is exhibited, of which the fruits shall enter into the eternal kingdom.

It is not, then, a stripped and barren earth which the meek will inherit, but an earth rich in its created diversity, enhanced by the labor of man as co-worker with God. Because of God's special grace, the sparing of creation which began in common grace will culminate in a heaven and earth which is *this* heaven and earth, but from which sin and its fruits have been purged.

We have considered three occurrences in Christian thought of an idea implicit in the Gospel: that man is not saved out of the world, but that the world is saved through him. Though man, like God, stands out from nature, if he is to follow the example given him in Christ, he will exercise his transcendence by using it to re-enter, and to care for the creation he transcends.

This is not an easy ideal for humans to enact. Our tendency has been to develop our transcendence, to increase our legitimate God-given powers of knowing and shaping the earth— thus the enormous concern in our time with science, which promises to approach *omni*-science, and with technology: the collection of skills by which we exert our power over the earth. Such knowledge and power are appropriate; yet we have seldom used either our knowledge or our power to "redeem" the earth, as the Gospel suggests, and as these three traditions from within the history of Christendom have affirmed. It is time that Christians began the task of "redeeming the earth."

Questions

1. Summarize the debate over whether humans are a part of or apart from nature. Can you add other supporting arguments to either side?
2. How does man's creation from "the dust of the ground" support the argument that humans are a part of nature? What Hebrew words illustrate this link?
3. Define man's *transcendence* and his *immanence* in the context of his relation to nature. How does the "job description" of human beings differ according to these two views?
4. Describe how the idea of man as redeemer was developed in the thought of (a) Eastern Orthodoxy, (b) St. Francis, and (c) Abraham Kuyper.

The Theology of Ecology

John R. Claypool

The selection is a sermon preached by John R. Claypool, a well-known pastor and author. He says that the Church has a responsibility to help relieve ecological problems. Just knowing the facts won't be enough for most people to make the necessary changes. They have to want to change. It is especially hard because the changes will have to come from individual lifestyle decisions.

Scripture Reference: Romans 8:18-23

Two years ago I am not even sure I had heard the word "ecology," and I certainly did not realize the gigantic proportion of the problems this word stands for. Since then, however, we have all been inundated about what may happen very shortly to this planet earth; and whether we like it or not, we have to make some kind of response to all of this. It is part of the mission of the church that she should be involved with you in such an endeavor, which is why we are offering this particular emphasis at this time. It is appropriate both to our spiritual and historical lives, and in this sermon I would like to set the stage for what is to follow by trying to put the issue in as clear a perspective as possible.

The ecological problem, as I see it, is basically one of man's relationship to the various support systems of the world on which he depends for his life; specifically, the air, the earth, and the water. Both in quantity and in quality, this relationship is in trouble, which is why the dire threats of suffocation and starvation in the immediate future are being made. Perhaps we can grasp it more readily if I try to scale it down and illustrate it by something I once personally witnessed happening.

It occurred to a farmer in middle Tennessee who fixed up

a dwelling on his place to house the tenant who was to work for him. This farmer went far beyond what many did in that area, for he saw to it that the house was not only wired amply for electricity, but he also installed a water system at no little expense that included a large cistern and inside plumbing. He "made a trade" as they put it in that community, and the new employee moved in, and right away my friend had his first misgivings, for the man turned out to have more children and relatives living with him than the farmer expected, and from the first, the five-room house was badly overcrowded. Two days after they moved, the owner was called and told that the water system had stopped working, only to find that the tenants had let the faucets run indiscriminately, and the whole cistern had been used up. Three nights later the house burned to the ground, and it was subsequently discovered that the electrical system had been overloaded by too many appliances. I remember standing in front of the remains of that house with the farmer as he expressed both his frustration and anger. "This was a decent place to live—a workable set-up—and look what they have gone and done. With a little judgment and insight, a family could have lived here for decades."

That scene comes to my mind when I hear of ecological problems, for here in tiny microcosm were some of the same dynamics. For example, part of the difficulty in this situation was a quantitative one—there were simply too many people trying to live in too small a space and off too few resources. No wonder that the water system and the energy system gave way. And of course, this same factor is basic to so many of our environmental problems today. There are simply too many people trying to inhabit this spaceship called earth. The medical revolution that has made it possible for more people to be born and survive and live longer now threatens to turn on itself and destroy all life. The population explosion, unless somehow brought under control, will cause every problem we have so to escalate that they will be unmanageable. The quantity question, then—to my farmer friend and to the world—is basic.

But there was also a qualitative dimension to this little tragedy that cannot be ignored. This tenant family did not try to understand the support systems which made that house the livable unit it was, and out of such understanding to collaborate with them. Rather, they arrogantly acted as if their desires were the only factor to be considered. They never thought of a cistern that held only so much water or wires that could carry only so much electricity. It was as if these things were looked on as so much "stuff" to be treated any way they pleased, and thus the problem. They found out too late that these support systems had a life and structure of their own, and that they could strike back when abused. The same thing can be said about our treatment of the universe and its many support systems. We have related to the air and the earth and the water pretty much like those tenants related to the cistern and the electric wires, and this is why the whole thing is starting to collapse all around us. The quality of our relation here—that is, thinking we were all that mattered and that the universe has no life or structure of its own—has been our undoing.

To talk like this is to take a page straight out of the Bible, for if you look at the early chapters of Genesis, this is exactly the perspective you will encounter there. This world is pictured as being fashioned by a joyful Creator, and—to use a modern slang expression—this Creator really knew how "to put it all together." While what we have in Genesis are not scientific essays but religious poems, nonetheless they depict how masterfully everything fits together and works hand-in-hand with all else. There is an incredible balance between the various aspects of nature. For example, we humans need oxygen to survive, and we inhale this from the atmosphere and exhale carbon dioxide. However, many forms of plant life need carbon dioxide to live, and they inhale it and exhale oxygen. This is but one example of the fantastic balance built into the way God put it all together, and Genesis indicates that man's place was to be a knowing partner in this finely balanced process. He was called on to name the animals; that is, to understand their structures and penetrate the mystery of their lives, and then to collaborate with them in a reciprocity that flowed back and forth. Man was part of the animals' and plants' support system, just as they were part of his, and so life was to be.

However, Genesis records that a breakdown occurred in all this, and it pinpoints the problem with man and his refusal to be himself and to plan the part he was meant to play. Instead of being an insightful collaborator with all these support systems, man decided to assume the stance of an arrogant manipulator. Just like those mindless tenants, he refused to learn the "names" of what supported him, and chose rather to treat them any way he wanted to. As a result, all creation was thrown out of kilter, and instead of being collaborators together, everything assumed an adversary role—man began to have to battle his mate and brother and the animals and the earth and everything. The root cause here is this quality of relation we have spoken of earlier, and it is the poison spring that contaminated all else.

This attitude of mindless arrogance toward the physical universe is why we have come to such an ecological impasse. By not realizing that the air and the earth and the water have lives and structures of their own and cannot be treated any way we please, we have seriously disrupted the balance of life and imperiled our survival. For example, by wiping out vast areas of plant life and covering them with inert concrete, or defoliating large segments of greenery so we can kill the enemy better, we have threatened the oxygen-carbon dioxide balance and could well wind up suffocating. Or again, by dumping indiscriminate amounts of waste into our rivers and oceans we have unsettled the vital processes there. Lake Erie is today like a tank of poisonous chemicals, and many say it is a prophecy of what all our bodies of water will become.

On and on I could go, but the evidence is clear. We are in big trouble with our environment—bigger trouble than we have known—and the problem is our human relation to the support systems of the air and the earth and the water on which our survival depends. In terms of quantity and quality, we are in trouble, and the question arises: what are we going to do about it? In light of this apocalyptic sword of Damocles hanging over our future, what response are we going to make?

Some people with great faith in man's rational power say: *get out the facts.* Tell people the situation! The problem, they feel, is basically one of ignorance, and if man can just be apprised of the situation and how he got into these straits and what the consequences are, then he surely will adapt and find ways to solve the problems. And I, for one, would not want to underestimate what this approach can accomplish. After all, our Lord himself recognized that much of the evil of life is rooted in blindness as well as in badness, and thus prayed from the cross: "Father, forgive them, for they know not what they do." Surely it is important that the alarm be sounded and that the facts be disseminated, for we would not even be as aware as we are now of this threat were it not for heralds of truth like Rachel Carson and many others.

Yet having said that, I must confess a real doubt of my own that information alone is going to be our salvation here. The problem is that man is not just a rational creature for whom knowing is the same as doing. He is, in fact, a complex creature of many facets, like, for example, emotions, fears, defenses, habits and other things. And for this reason getting men to change radically, even when their own self-interest is at stake, can be extraordinarily difficult. The way most people have responded to the link-up between tobacco and lung cancer is a revealing case in point. The evidence is now overwhelming that excessive smoking, particularly of cigarettes, is hazardous to health. Yet I know many people who do not contest this fact at all, but go right on smoking and intend to do so even if it means cancer and a shorter life.

And this is a side of the problem we have to face in terms of the ecological situation. It is not just a question of information or education for the simple reason that man is more than a mind. There is a darkness deeper down in us than that of not knowing. It is the darkness of not wanting to be, of not wanting to live, of not wanting to grapple with existence as it is given to us in freedom and responsibility.

I am deeply impressed by the question Jesus asked the lame man who had lain helpless for thirty-eight years by the pool of Bethesda: "Do you want to be healed?" (John 5:6). On the surface that may sound like a ridiculous question, for we naively assume that everyone wants to be well and never sick. But Jesus realized it was not that simple. You see, paradoxical as it may sound, sickness has its own strange consolations. To be sick is to be exempt from responsibility and complex decision-making. It is to be taken care of instead of having to care for another. And after a while, it can become a habit, a way of life. Take this man by the pool for example. Thirty-eight years is a long time, and having grown accustomed to certain routines, a change, even back to health, would have involved costly adjustments. This is why Jesus was so right in asking the question: "Do you really want to be healed?" He meant by this: are you prepared to change and accept the new challenges of health? Are you willing to pay the price that must be paid if healing becomes a reality?

I contend this is the question facing all of us as far as ecology is concerned. Do we really want to be healed? That is what we have to ponder, and we need to think about what it involves. A simplistic "yes" may not truly represent the way we really feel about this matter.

For example, wanting to be healed means admitting openly and honestly that there is a problem and that we are sick and are partly at fault. Some of the hardest words a human being ever has to utter are: "I am wrong. I have sinned. I have made a mistake." And our capacities for denial and evasion here are massive. In fact, I know many people right now who refuse to believe there is an ecological crisis, and dismiss it as another Communist plot or a fad that is soon to pass again. Our ability to choose fantasy over actuality and accept only what we want to be true runs very deep, and this is part of what has to be faced in wanting to be healed. We have to have reality-perception enough and courage enough to admit: we are sick. We are ecological sinners. We are at fault.

Another facet of being healed is a willingness to become involved in the cure and not expect it to be done for us without any cost or effort. There is a childishness that likes to sit and wait and have some super-power solve all his problems for him. In religious terms, this is called "quietism," and can be seen in the people who say: "God must do it all. We are to wait, sit passively, and let Him intervene." While there are probably millions like this, there are even more whom I would call "secular quietists"; that is, they do not expect God to intervene, but they do expect our vaunted technology to come up with some innovation that will solve all of this without any pain. You have heard people talk of the mythical "they"— "they" will come up with this or that, and pretty soon all will be well. And as a result we do not have to change a thing, but can go right on as we are. Really wanting to be healed is putting aside this kind of childishness and recognizing that because we are the ones who are sick and have made ourselves sick, we must be involved painfully in any cure. A theme that runs through all the Bible is the assertion that "without the shedding of blood there is no remission of sin," and this means that salvation or healing always involves suffering or it never happens.

And right here is where I have my greatest uneasiness about all of us and this question of healing the ecological wound that runs so deep. What is going to have to change is our style of life, the way we have become accustomed to living and consuming and acting. Are we willing to adapt at the level? The Good Life—however vaguely it may be defined— has most of us securely in its clutches, and this glut of affluence is one of the main culprits to our environment. Do you realize that in 1969 our country alone produced 48 billion cans and 28 billion bottles to be disposed of, to say nothing of the 7 million cars that had to be junked and the 142 billion tons of pollution we emptied into the air? It is estimated that the average American is anywhere from 25 to 500 times as destructive of his environment as the average Indian peasant, which is why the ecological night of total extinction may well come to

America first. These are the apocalyptic facts, and Jesus' question is the real issue: "Do we want to be healed?" Which means, are we willing to undergo the radical alteration of life style that will be called for if the balance of man and air and earth and water is to be restored? Nothing less than this will really touch the depths of the problem. Yet, nothing could be harder than to get people to change what they have grown accustomed to having and spending and consuming.

I must admit that I fluctuate between pessimism and optimism at this point. At times I have very little hope, for I realize how deeply ingrained our habits are and that nothing is harder to alter than habit. As the *Three-penny Opera* puts it:

For even saintly folk will act like sinners
Unless they have their customary dinners.

And this is not just other people's problems, this is a problem for me personally. In preparing this sermon, I was forced to ask: what real change have you made in your life style since learning of the ecological crisis? We have changed soap powder, take shorter showers and try to buy lead-free gas, but I still have two eight-cylinder cars, have done nothing to work for mass transit systems, still buy plastic milk cartons, and have yet to write that first public official in either support or disagreement. If I am to do my part in the healing, one hundred times more radicality than I have shown thus far is going to be called for. And while a few are doing more, I do not see many people aroused, and thus my pessimism. Are we willing to pay the price?

But then I pick up the Bible and read in Romans how "the whole creation waits in eager longing for the revealing of the sons of God . . ."; how "all creation is groaning in travail together" until at last it is "freed from the bondage of decay" and "obtains the glorious liberty of the children of God." And then some optimism rises in me, for I realize that God is on the side of health and wholeness and is at work for good in all this as he always has been. This does not mean he is going to do everything for us so that without any pain or effort what is crooked will come straight. Even for God, "without the shedding of blood there is no remission of sin." But it does mean that we are not alone in our efforts. The promise of God applies to ecology: if we will confess our sin, he will do something in faithfulness and justice to forgive us our sins and cleanse us from all unrighteousness. If we will just be sons of God with all the responsibility and freedom that implies, things could be different.

There is hope, then, but it is not automatic. We do not *have to be* saved in this area or in any other. It is the ultimate dignity of man to decide finally whether he wants to be healed or not healed, or more profoundly, whether he wants to live or to die. I talk occasionally with people who are threatening suicide, and while I do everything in my power to persuade them against it, I remind them that the choice finally is theirs. To live or not to live, and how one shall live, these are decisions no one can make for another. Which is where the question of ecology finally leads. I am convinced we can be healed and save both the earth and ourselves, but in order for this to happen, we have to want to be healed and to be willing to undergo the treatment that this involves. And to want to be healed means you must want to live and not die.

So the question is: do we want to live? Deuteronomy pictures Moses as standing before Israel for the last time and saying: "I call heaven and earth to witness this day, that I have set before you life and death, the blessing and curse. Therefore, choose life" (30:19). This remains the challenge to every generation, and to us.

Well?

Questions

1. Why is Claypool's story of the destruction of the tenant house a good illustration of the ecological issue? What did you learn from that story?
2. Why is information alone not enough to get people to do something about ecological problems?

3. Why is the question "Do you want to be healed?" at the heart of the ecology issue? What does it imply about human beings? What factors hinder us from truly wanting healing?

Our World Belongs to God

This selection is excerpted from "Our World Belongs to God: A Contemporary Testimony." This is a statement of faith adopted by the Christian Reformed Church to help its members and friends better understand how Christians are to live in the world.

Our world belongs to God—
not to us or earthly powers,
not to demons, fate, or chance.
The earth is the Lord's!

As God's creatures we are made in his image
to represent him on earth,
and to live in loving communion with him.
By sovereign appointment we are
earthkeepers and caretakers:
loving our neighbor,
tending the creation,
and meeting our needs.
God uses our skills
in the unfolding and well-being of his world.

Grateful for the advances
in science and technology,
we make careful use of their products,
on guard against idolatry
and harmful research,
and careful to use them in ways that answer
to God's commands
to love our neighbor
and to care for the earth and its creatures.

Questions

1. To whom does our world belong? To whom does it not belong? Why is that distinction important?
2. Why are humans made in God's image? What "job" has God given to people on earth? How does God use our skills?
3. What two divine commands are Christians to answer to?

Endangered Wildness

Philip Yancey

Philip Yancey is a writer and regular columnist for the mag-azine Christianity Today. *This selection first appeared in that magazine. Here he thinks aloud about "the world as God sees it." God seems to have a special appreciation for wild animals (God, in fact, is "untamable."), and yet this wild-ness is almost totally lost as humans capture animals and display them in zoos. What do we lose when we lose a sense of the wild?*

In what she later called "the most transporting pleasure of my life on the farm," Isak Dinesen went flying across the unspoiled plains of Africa with her friend Denys Finch-Hat-ton. In the film version of *Out of Africa*, the character playing Denys offers to show "the world as God sees it," and indeed, the next few minutes of cinematography come close to pre-senting exactly that. As the frail Moth airplane soars beyond the escarpment marking the beginning of Kenya's Rift Valley, the ground falls abruptly away and the camera captures a glimpse of Eden in the grasslands just below.

Great herds of zebras scatter at the sound of the motor, each group wheeling in unison, as if a single mind controlled the bits of modern art dashing across the plain. Huge giraffes—they seemed so gangly and awkward when standing still—lope away with exquisite gracefulness. Spry gazelles, bounding past the larger animals, fill in the edges of the scene.

The world as God sees it—does that phrase merely express some foamy Romantic notion or does it contain truth? The Bible gives intriguing hints. Proverbs tells of the act of Creation when Wisdom "was the craftsman at his [God's] side . . . filled with delight day after day . . . rejoicing in his whole world." The seraphs in Isaiah's vision who declared "the whole earth is full of his glory" could hardly have been referring to human beings—not if the rest of the book of Isaiah is to be believed. At least God had the glory of Nature then, during that dark period when Israel faced extinction and Judah slid toward idolatry.

God makes most plain how he feels about the animal kingdom in his longest single speech, a magnificent address found at the end of Job. Look closely and you will notice a common thread in the specimens he holds up for Job's edification:

- A lioness hunting her prey.
- A mountain goat giving birth in the wilds.
- A rogue donkey roaming the salt flats.
- An ostrich flapping her useless wings with joy.
- A stallion leaping high to paw the air.
- A hawk, an eagle, and a raven building their nests on the rocky crags.

That's a mere warmup—Zoology 101 in Job's education. From there God advances to the behemoth, a hippo-like creature no one can tame, and the mighty, dragonish leviathan. "Can you make a pet of him like a bird or put him on a leash for your girls?" God asks with a touch of sarcasm. "The mere sight of him is overpowering. No one is fierce enough to rouse him. Who then is able to stand against me?"

Wildness is God's underlying message to Job, the one trait his menagerie all share. God is celebrating those members of his created world who will never be domesticated by human beings. Evidently, wild animals serve an essential function in "the world as God sees it." They bring us down a notch, reminding us of something we'd prefer to forget: our creatureliness. And they also announce to our senses the splendor of an invisible, untameable God.

Several times a week I run among such wild animals, unmolested, for I run through the Lincoln Park Zoo in downtown Chicago. I have gotten to know them well, as charming neighbors, but I always make a mental effort to project them into their natural states.

Three rock-hopper penguins neurotically pace back and forth on a piece of concrete sprayed to look like ice. I envision them free, hopping from ice floe to ice floe in Antarctica, surrounded by millions of their comic-faced cousins.

An ancient elephant stands against a wall, keeping time three ways: his body sways from side to side to one beat, his tail marks a different rhythm entirely, and his trunk moves up and down to yet a third. I struggle to imagine this sluggish giant exciting terror in an African forest.

And the paunchy cheetah flopped across a rock shelf—could this animal possibly belong to the species that can, on a short course, out-accelerate a Porsche?

It requires a huge mental leap for me to place the penguin, elephant, and cheetah back where they belong, where they came from. Somehow God's stirring message about wildness evaporates among the moats and bars and plastic educational placards of the zoo. Yet, I am fortunate to live near the zoo. Otherwise, Chicago would offer up only squirrels, pigeons, cockroaches, rats, and a stray songbird. Is this what God had in mind when he granted Adam dominion?

It is hard to avoid a sermonic tone when writing about wild animals, for our sins against them are very great. The elephant population alone has decreased by 800,000 in the last two decades, mostly due to poachers and rambunctious soldiers with machine guns. And every year we are destroying an area of rain forest—and all its animal residents—equal in size to the state of California. *California!*

Most wildlife writing focuses on these vanishing animals themselves, but I find myself wondering about the ultimate impact on us. What else, besides that innate appreciation for wildness, have we lost? Could distaste for authority, or even a loss of God-awareness, derive in part from this atrophied sense? God's mere mention of the animals struck a chord of awe in Job; what about us, who grow up tossing peanuts across the moat to the behemoths and leviathans?

Naturalist John Muir, who never lost a vision for "the

world as God sees it," concluded sadly, "it is a great comfort . . . that vast multitudes of creatures, great and small and infinite in number, lived and had a good time in God's love before man was created."

The heavens declare the glory of God; and so do breaching whales and pronking springboks. Fortunately, in some corners of the world vast multitudes of creatures can still live and have a good time in God's love. The least we could do is make room for them—for our sakes as well as theirs.

Questions

1. What do you think Yancey means by the phrase "the world as God sees it"? What does this say about our view of the world?
2. How do the wild animals remind us of our creatureliness? How do they remind us of the untamability of God?
3. What does the quote by John Muir suggest about the creation prior to the appearance of human beings? Is his observation biblically sound?

Wealth/Poverty

Shame

Dick Gregory

*Dick Gregory is a popular black comedian who travels wide-
ly, speaking to school and community groups on issues related to poverty and racial injustice. This selection, taken from
Gregory's autobiography,* Nigger, *reveals the circumstances
surrounding his first experience of shame.*

I never learned hate at home, or shame. I had to go to
school for that. I was about seven years old when I got my first
big lesson. I was in love with a little girl named Helene Tucker,
a light-complexioned little girl with pigtails and nice manners.
She was always clean and she was smart in school. I think I
went to school then mostly to look at her. I brushed my hair
and even got me a little old handkerchief. It was a lady's handkerchief, but I didn't want Helene to see me wipe my nose on
my hand. The pipes were frozen again, there was no water in
the house, but I washed my socks and shirt every night. I'd get
a pot, and go over to Mister Ben's grocery store, and stick my

pot down into his soda machine. Scoop out some chopped ice. By evening the ice melted to water for washing. I got sick a lot that winter because the fire would go out at night before the clothes were dry. In the morning I'd put them on, wet or dry, because they were the only clothes I had.

Everybody's got a Helene Tucker, a symbol of everything you want. I loved her for her goodness, her cleanness, her popularity. She'd walk down my street and my brothers and sisters would yell, "Here comes Helene," and I'd rub my tennis sneakers on the back of my pants and wish my hair wasn't so nappy and the white folks' shirt fit me better. I'd run out on the street. If I knew my place and didn't come too close, she'd wink at me and say hello. That was a good feeling. Sometimes I'd follow her all the way home, and shovel the snow off her walk and try to make friends with her Momma and her aunts. I'd drop money on her stoop late at night on my way back from shining shoes in the taverns. And she had a Daddy, and he had a good job. He was a paper hanger.

I guess I would have gotten over Helene by summertime, but something happened in that classroom that made her face hang in front of me for the next twenty-two years. When I played the drums in high school it was for Helene and when I broke track records in college it was for Helene and when I started standing behind microphones and heard applause I wished Helene could hear it, too. It wasn't until I was twenty-nine years old and married and making money that I finally got her out of my system. Helene was sitting in that classroom when I learned to be ashamed of myself.

It was on a Thursday. I was sitting in the back of the room, in a seat with a chalk circle drawn around it. The idiot's seat, the troublemaker's seat.

The teacher thought I was stupid. Couldn't spell, couldn't read, couldn't do arithmetic. Just stupid. Teachers were never interested in finding out that you couldn't concentrate because you were so hungry, because you hadn't had any breakfast. All you could think about was noontime, would it ever come? Maybe you could sneak into the cloakroom and steal a bite of some kid's lunch out of a coat pocket. A bite of something. Paste. You can't really make a meal of paste, or put it on bread for a sandwich, but sometimes I'd scoop a few spoonfuls out of the paste jar in the back of the room. Pregnant people get strange tastes. I was pregnant with poverty. Pregnant with dirt and pregnant with smells that made people turn away, pregnant with cold and pregnant with shoes that were never bought for me, pregnant with five other people in my bed and no Daddy in the next room, and pregnant with hunger. Paste doesn't taste too bad when you're hungry.

The teacher thought I was a troublemaker. All she saw from the front of the room was a little black boy who squirmed in his idiot's seat and made noises and poked the kids around him. I guess she couldn't see a kid who made noises because he wanted someone to know he was there.

It was on a Thursday, the day before the Negro payday. The eagle always flew on Friday. The teacher was asking each student how much his father would give to the Community Chest. On Friday night, each kid would get the money from his father, and on Monday he would bring it to the school. I decided I was going to buy me a Daddy right then. I had money in my pocket from shining shoes and selling papers, and whatever Helene Tucker pledged for her Daddy I was going to top it. And I'd hand the money right in. I wasn't going to wait until Monday to buy me a Daddy.

I was shaking, scared to death. The teacher opened her book and started calling out names alphabetically.

"Helene Tucker?"

"My daddy said he'd give two dollars and fifty cents."

"That's very nice, Helene. Very, very nice indeed."

That made me feel pretty good. It wouldn't take too much to top that. I had almost three dollars in dimes and quarters in my pocket. I stuck my hand in my pocket and held onto the money, waiting for her to call my name. But the teacher closed her book after she called everybody else in the class.

I stood up and raised my hand.

"What is it now?"

"You forgot me."

She turned toward the blackboard. "I don't have time to be playing with you, Richard."

"My Daddy said he'd . . ."

"Sit down, Richard, you're disturbing the class."

"My Daddy said he'd give . . . fifteen dollars."

She turned around and looked mad. "We are collecting this money for you and your kind, Richard Gregory. If your Daddy can give fifteen dollars you have no business being on relief."

"I got it right now, I got it right now, my Daddy gave it to me to turn in today, my Daddy said . . ."

"And furthermore," she said, looking right at me, her nostrils getting big and her lips getting thin and her eyes opening wide, "we know you don't have a Daddy."

Helene Tucker turned around, her eyes full of tears. She felt sorry for me. Then I couldn't see her too well because I was crying, too.

"Sit down, Richard."

And I always thought the teacher kind of liked me. She always picked me to wash the blackboard on Friday, after school. That was a big thrill, it made me feel important. If I didn't wash it, come Monday the school might not function right.

"Where are you going, Richard?"

I walked out of school that day, and for a long time I didn't go back very often. There was shame there.

Now there was shame everywhere. It seemed like the whole world had been inside that classroom, everyone had heard what the teacher had said, everyone had turned around and felt sorry for me. There was shame in going to the Worthy Boys Annual Christmas Dinner for you and your kind, because everybody knew what a worthy boy was. Why couldn't they just call it the Boys Annual Dinner; why'd they have to give it a name? There was shame in wearing the brown and orange and white plaid mackinaw the welfare gave to three thousand boys. Why'd it have to be the same for everybody so when you walked down the street the people could see you were on relief? It was a nice warm mackinaw and it had a hood, and my Momma beat me and called me a little rat when she found out I stuffed it in the bottom of a pail full of garbage way over on Cottage Street. There was shame in running over to Mister Ben's at the end of the day and asking for his rotten peaches, there was shame in asking Mrs. Simmons for a spoonful of sugar, there was shame in running out to meet the relief truck. I hated that truck, full of food for you and your kind. I ran into the house and hid when it came. And then I started to sneak through alleys, to take the long way home so the people going into White's Eat Shop wouldn't see me. Yeah, the whole world heard the teacher that day, we all know you don't have a Daddy.

Questions

1. Describe the role that Helene Tucker played in Gregory's early life.
2. Why did the teacher think Gregory was stupid and a troublemaker? Do you think she really cared about Gregory?
3. Why was Gregory's not having a Daddy a source of shame for him?
4. How did Gregory try to "buy a Daddy"?
5. Why did Gregory feel shame everywhere after the incident in school?
6. Do you think his shame was justified?

Voices of Homeless Teens

Lois Stavsky and I.E. Mozeson

These selections are excerpted from a book called The Place I Call Home. *It is a collection of stories and photos of young teens who live in urban poverty. These selections describe the very serious conditions which face these young people every day. And yet, despite their poverty, these young people have not given up on finding a place they can call home.*

Delores Sanchez, 16 years old

I grew up in a big apartment on the Grand Concourse in the Bronx. But as the years went by, the building began to deteriorate. The landlord never made repairs, and we'd go for weeks at a time with no hot water or heat. My mother tried to organize the tenants. She even took the landlord to court, and she urged the other tenants not to pay their rent. But she could never rally more than three other tenants, and eventually the landlord evicted us.

In the meantime, while we were still living in the Bronx, my little brother was born prematurely. He spent most of the first year of his life in and out of hospitals. We didn't know if he'd survive. The lack of hot water and heat made life very difficult for my mom and her new baby. Then, at the same time we were evicted from our building, my stepfather, and the only father I'd ever known and loved, died of a heart attack.

After we were forced out of our apartment in the Bronx, we tried to live with relatives. We stayed with our cousins for a while, but that didn't work out. Whenever anything was missing there'd be a big fight, and my mother was blamed. Then we went to my uncle's house. But he and I used to get into arguments all the time, and he decided that I couldn't live there any more.

At that point we went to the EAU, and we were assigned to a shelter in the Bronx. The shelter had a terrible reputation and was known as a haven for AIDS victims. My mother refused to accept the assignment. After my mother turned down a number of other assignments, we were finally sent to Jamaica Arms in Queens. We spent six months there. We had our own apartment and I went to a local junior high school in the neighborhood. Most of the other kids lived in private houses. I went to their homes, but I never invited them to mine. None of them knew my living situation.

What I remember most about that year, though, is all the time my mother spent with my brother in the hospital. He was forever throwing up, running high fevers, and being rushed to the emergency room. My mother never wanted to leave him alone in the hospital. So I didn't see much of my mother that year at the Jamaica Arms.

One of the social workers there helped us find our current apartment on the F.D.R. Drive. We were so happy to have our own place, but shortly after we moved in, my mother suffered a nervous breakdown. She was too depressed to do anything. It was so frightening to me. My mother was admitted to Mount Sinai Hospital. I was left alone with my brother who was three at the time. I was thirteen. I prayed for my mother's recovery, because I knew that if she didn't get well quickly, my brother and I would be placed in a home. Luckily, my mom was released a month later. I did miss a lot of school, and I've had a lot of making up to do.

I'm very happy to be living where I am. We never have problems with heat or hot water, and I don't miss the Bronx of my childhood at all.

Eric Johnson, 15 years old

I grew up in the Park Slope section of Brooklyn. Everything was cool until five years ago. That's when my brother was arrested for rape. He was innocent. He never raped anyone. It was a set up. He had been having trouble with some of the white boys in the neighborhood. A white lady was paid off to say that my brother raped her. The cops forced him to confess to something he didn't do. He was seventeen at the time. He was sent to a juvenile detention center upstate and then the following year he was put in prison. He's never gotten into any fights with anyone, but he was denied parole after three years. He's supposed to be coming out this June. At first he was all my mother talked about. Now she tries not to even think about him.

After the trouble with my brother, we left Park Slope. My mother and I moved into my aunt's apartment in Coney Island. I liked it there. I was in P.S. 145 and went to school every day. I was a pretty good student. But then one day I came home from school to find out that we had been evicted. It seems that my aunt hadn't been paying her rent. My mom was working at a video store and she would have helped my aunt out. But my mom didn't know that my aunt hadn't been paying her rent. By the time my mom found out, it was too late to do anything about it.

After we were evicted, we spent six months in Forbell, a shelter on the border between Brooklyn and Queens. I remember our first night there. My mom and I were real nervous. Forbell consists of three levels with about one hundred beds on each level. What bothered me the most about Forbell was the lack of privacy. Also, I had no independence. It was like being in jail. I couldn't leave without my mom's permission. My mom was working in the video store at the time so, except for the hours I spent in school, I was stuck in the shelter with nothing to do. And the food was terrible. Everything they served us tasted funny.

Then we were transferred to Traveler's. Traveler's is a hotel in Queens. We were so happy to have our own room there. We even had our own hot plate so my mom was able to prepare her own food. But there were problems at Traveler's. The ladies there were always getting into fights. They fought over everything. Also, we weren't allowed to have any guests over. So the ladies used to sneak in their boyfriends, and the only friends I had were the other hotel kids. That's when I got into playing hooky. The kids never wanted to go to school.

Instead, we hung out and drank beer.

We lived in Traveler's for two years. Then we had to leave. My mother's welfare payments had stopped, and we couldn't afford to live in a hotel. I'm not sure why she wasn't eligible for welfare anymore. Then my mom and I had to split up. She went to live with her sister in Brooklyn, and I went to live with my grandmother in Staten Island. I lived with my grandmother for one year.

Now my mom and I are back together at the shelter on Catherine Street. There's a new policy at Catherine Street with two families sharing one room. So me and my mother are together with another lady and her fourteen year old son. What I don't like about Catherine is all the drugs. About 75 percent of the people are doing one drug or another. The most popular drug here is crack which is sold in $10 vials. Drugs are sold outside the shelter—mainly by teenage boys—but there are also people inside selling them. I also don't like when the guards mess with the ladies. I feel that they are taking advantage of them.

We hope to be out of Catherine by the end of this month. My mom is waiting for an apartment anywhere. But all I want is my own place in Brooklyn. I don't want to have to live with anyone, including my own mother.

Pamela Watkins, 15 years old

I know that the Prince George Hotel has a terrible reputation, but to me it is home. I have lived here for two years, and it's the best home I ever had.

I grew up in a dreary apartment in Crown Heights. I never felt safe there. Just walking through the streets to get home from the closest subway station was like walking through a war zone. About three years ago, the landlord died. The building was sold, and my mother couldn't afford the new rent. So we moved in with my grandmother. But things didn't work out. My grandmother has high blood pressure, and it was too much for her to have my mother, my sister and me living with her. After six months of staying with my grandmother, my mother went to the EAU and we were assigned to a shelter on Catherine Street.

I didn't like the shelter. It was too crowded, and I didn't have any privacy. Here in the Prince George we have our own room. What I like most about living in the Prince George Hotel is its location. I am right near mid-town. There is always something to do. In Crown Heights, there was never anything happening, just muggings and shoot-outs. I don't miss anything about my old neighborhood.

The only problem I have here is dealing with my mother's constant worrying. About 95 percent of the teenagers here deal drugs. Just about every one I know sells $5 vials of crack. And my mother is afraid that me and my sister will start using drugs. But she really doesn't have to worry. I'm not interested in that life, and neither is my sister. The other thing my mother worries about is my getting pregnant. About half the teenagers who are here have babies with them. They are living here because their mothers threw them out of their houses. But I'm not about to bring home any babies. I'm a baby myself.

School is the only problem I've had since we lost our apartment in Brooklyn. I used to go to school every day. But last year, I cut a lot. Most of the teenagers here don't go to school. They just hang out instead. My cousin influences me not to go to school, and now missing school is my worst habit.

There is talk now of closing down this hotel. My mother wants to move back to Brooklyn, and our social worker is helping us find an apartment in some projects near our old neighborhood. But I don't ever want to leave Manhattan. I like it here. It is the place I call home.

Questions

1. Describe three or four of the problems common to each of these teens. How are they dealing with the problems?
2. What is "home" for these teens? Why is it important for them to find the place they can call home? What factors make it difficult for them to find that place?

Heartbreak Hotel

Jonathan Kozol

Jonathan Kozol is a writer and teacher who has long been concerned for the care and education of children. This selection is taken from his important book Rachel and Her Children: Homeless Families in America. *He describes the story of Laura, a homeless mother living in a welfare hotel in New York City, who finally yields to the empty promises of prostitution in her desperate search for a better life.*

Laura is so fragile that I find it hard to start conversation. Before I do, she asks if I will read to her a letter from the hospital. Her oldest son has been ill for several weeks. He was tested in November for lead poisoning.

The letter tells her that the child has a dangerous lead level. She's told to bring him back for treatment. She received the letter some weeks ago. It's been buried in a pile of other documents she cannot understand.

Although she cannot read, she knows enough to understand the darker implications of this information. The crumbling plaster in the Martinique Hotel is covered with sweet-tasting chips of paint that children eat or chew as it flakes off the walls. Infants may be paralyzed or undergo convulsions. Some grow blind. The consequences may be temporary or long lasting. They may appear at once or not for several years. This final point is what instills so much uneasiness; even months of observation cannot still a parent's fear about the future.

This, then, is her first concern; but there are others. The bathroom plumbing has overflowed and left a pool of sewage on the floor. A radiator valve is broken. It releases a spray of scalding steam at the eye level of a child.

Impending Danger

The crib provided by the hotel appears to be unstable. It may be that it was damaged by another resident or perhaps by one of Laura's children. One of the screws is missing. When I test it with my hand, it starts to sway.

The beds in the room are dangerous too. They are made of metal frames with unprotected corners; the mattresses do not fit the frames. At one corner or another, metal is exposed. If a child has the energy or playfulness to jump or do a somersault or wrestle with a friend, and if he falls and strikes his head against the metal ridge, the consequences can be serious. Laura knows of a child on the fourteenth floor, for instance, who fell in just this way only the week before. He cut his forehead and required stitches.

Most of these matters have been brought to the attention of the hotel management. In Laura's case, complaints have brought no visible results.

The room is lighted by fluorescent tubes fixed high above us on the ceiling. They cast a stark light on four walls of greenish paint smeared over with some sort of sludge that drains from someone's toilet on the floor above.

There are no table lamps to soften the fluorescent glare, no books, no Christmas tree, no decorations. She tells me that her father is of Panamanian birth but that she went to school in New York City. Spanish is her first language. I don't speak Spanish well. We do the interview in English.

"I cannot read," she says. "I buy the *New York Post* to read the pictures. In the grocery I know what to buy because I see the pictures."

What of no-name products, the generic brands that have no pictures but could save her a great deal of money?

"If there are no pictures, I don't buy it. I want to buy pancakes, I ask the lady: 'Where's the pancakes?' So they tell me."

She points to the boys: "He's two. He's five. Matthew's seven. My daughter is four months. She has this rash." She shows me: ugly skin eruptions on the baby's neck and jaw.

"The carpets, they was filthy from the stuff, the leaks that come down on the wall. All my kids have rashes but the worst she has it. There was pus all over.

"Somewhere here I have a letter from the nurse." She shuffles around but cannot find the letter. "She got something underneath the skin. Something that bites. The only way you can get rid of it is with a cream."

She finds the letter. The little girl has scabies.

"I been living here two years. Before I came here I was in a house we had to leave. There was rats. Big ones—they crawl on us. The rats, they come at night. They come into our house, run over my son's legs. The windows were broken. It was winter. Snow, it used to come inside.

"My mother lived with us before. Now she's staying at my grandma's house. My grandma's dying in the bed. She's sixty-five. My mother comes here once a week to do the groceries. Tomorrow she comes. Then she goes back to help my grandma.

"I know my name and I can write my name, my children's names. To read I cannot do it. Medicines: I don't know the instructions.

"I can read baby books—like that, a little bit. If I could read, I would read newspapers. I would like to know what's going on. My son, he tells me I am stupid. 'You can't read.' You know, because he wants to read. He don't understand what something is. I tell him: I don't know it. I don't understand. People laugh. You feel embarrassed. On the street. Or in the store."

More Unthinkable Conditions

"I sign papers. Somebody could come and take my children. They could come. 'Sign this. Sign that.' I don't know what it says. Adoption papers I don't know.

"I get $173, restaurant allowance. With that money I buy clothes. Food stamps: I get $200. That's for groceries. Subway tokens I take out $10. Washing machine, I go downstairs. Twenty-five dollars to dry and wash. Five dollars to buy soap. Thirty dollars twice a month."

I ask Laura who stays with the children when she does her chores.

"My mother keeps the children when I do the wash. If she can't, I ask somebody on the floor. 'Give me three dollars. I watch your kids.' For free? Nothing. Everything for money. Everybody's poor.

"This is the radiator. Something's wrong." She shows me where the steam sprays out. I test it with my hand. "Sometimes it stops. The children get too close. Then it starts—like that! Leak is coming from upstairs down." I see the dark muck on the wall.

"The window is broke. Lights broke." She points to the fluorescent tubes. They flicker on and off. "I ask them: 'Please, why don't you give me ordinary lights?' They don't do nothing.

"So it been two weeks. I go downstairs. They say they coming up. They never come. So I complain again. Mr. Tucelli said to come there to his office. Desks and decorations and a lot of pictures.

"So he says: 'You people bring us trouble.' I said: 'Why you give my son lead poison and you didn't care? My child is lead poisoned.' He said: 'I don't want to hear of this again.'

"What I answer him is this: 'Listen. You live in a nice apartment. You got a home. You got TV. You got a family. You got children in a school that learn them. They don't got lead poison.'

"How I know about the lead is this: Matthew sits there, and he reach his fingers in the plaster, and he put it in his mouth. So I ask him: 'Was you eating it?' He says: 'Don't hit me. Yes, I was.'

"So then I took him to the clinic and they took the blood. I don't know if something happen to him later on. I don't know if it affects him. When he's older . . ."

I ask her why she goes to church.

"I figure: Go to church. Pray God. Ask him to help. I go on my knees. I ask him from my heart: 'Jesus Christ, come help me, please. Why do you leave me here?'

"When I'm lying down at night I ask: Why people got to live like this? On the street, the people stare at you when you go out of the hotel. People look. They think: 'I wonder how they live in there?' "

I ask her if the older children are enrolled in school.

"This one doesn't go to school. He's five. I need to call tomorrow. Get a quarter. Then you get some papers. Then you got to sign those papers. Then he can start school.

"For this room I pay $1,500 for two weeks. I don't pay. The welfare pays. I got to go and get it." The room, because it is divided, is regarded as a two-room suite. "They send me this. I'm s'pose to sign. I don't know what it is. Lots of things you s'pose to sign. I sign it, but I don't know what it is."

While we speak, Matthew comes in. A dark-eyed boy, he sits beside his mother. He lowers his eyes when we shake hands.

"Looking for a house, I got to do it. I can't read so I can't use the paper. I get dressed. I put my make-up on. If I go like this they look afraid. They say: 'They going to destroy the house!' You got to dress the children and look nice.

"Owners don't want homeless. Don't want welfare. Don't want kids. What I think? If they pay one thousand and five hundred dollars every two week, why not pay five hundred dollar for a good apartment?"

She hands me another paper. "Can you tell me what is this?"

It's a second letter from the hospital, telling her to bring her son for treatment.

"Every day my son this week, last week, was vomiting. Every time he eat his food he throw it right back out. I got to take him to the clinic. . . ."

Paltry, Impossible Dreams

In the window there's a spindly geranium plant. It has no flowers but some of the leaves are green. Before I leave we stand beside the window. Snow falling slantwise hits the panes and blurs the dirt.

"Some of the rooms high up—they got a view. You see the Empire State."

I've noticed this, seen it from a window. It towers high above the Martinique.

"I talk to this plant. I tell him: 'Grow! Give me one flower!' He don't do it." Then, in an afterthought: "No pets. Goldfish, no. You don't got. Animals, they don't allow."

It occurs to me that this is one of the few places I have been, except a hospital or a reform school, where there are 1,400 children and no pets. A few people keep cats illegally.

"I wish I had a dog," she says. "Brown dog . . . Something to hug."

There's little joy in Laura's life, no sign of indulgence. Anything like luxury or fun is not simply absent from this bleak existence. It's as far away as daisies—or a brown dog—on a hillside in New Hampshire.

Her longings are so dreadfully austere. She wishes she had a room where she could see the symbol of New York that mocks her pitiful existence. She'd like to see that plant do what a plant is supposed to do—give her one flower.

She wants to read. She feels ashamed to go out to the store. "I would like to know what's going on," she said. She doesn't have the least idea.

Several months later, one night in March, I wait in the lobby for Kim, the woman who first introduced me to Laura. She has to sign me in. As soon as we're on the stairs, she tells me: "Something terrible has happened. Laura's gone."

As soon as we are in her room, Kim lights a cigarette and tells me this: "Everyone sees her as a simple person, plain and dull, nobody of interest, even to a man.

"Well, I could have told you what would happen. Somebody finally told her she was pretty. He bought her some clothes and took her out. She put on make-up.

"I had never thought of her as glamorous. Neither did she. She saw herself as someone colorless and drab.

"Now a man likes her, buys her a dress. He gives the kids a TV and some toys.

"Two days later, Laura's gone. Things happen fast. He was a pimp. He gave her drugs. Nobody's seen her since.

"Her mother came to the hotel. She's staying with the kids."

I go down to visit with her mother. Her father's there too—a man in his fifties. Her mother tells me that she's forty-five.

"When I was called, they told me she was taking men to a hotel. I asked what was she wearing. They said she was wearing a red coat.

"I went out to look for her. I went to the bars. I went in the hotels. I spent the night on Forty-second Street. Times Square. All over. I can't find her.

"Then somebody says he saw her on Fifth Avenue—a place where women take the men to a hotel. I went to the hotel. The man in the hotel, he asked me who she was. I said that she's the one in the red jacket and he said: 'Oh yeah! She's here.' She was upstairs."

The Fruits Of Deprivation

"She came downstairs to speak with me. I told her I had come to bring her home. She said: 'I have a better life here now. I have these things. This jacket. See?' I couldn't get her to come home."

So Laura's mother is staying here to take care of the kids until she figures out a way to find a home for them. Her own mother has a place in Flushing but is near the point of death and cannot take them in. Laura's father walks with a cane; he's permanently disabled. They've applied for custody of Laura's children.

"The baby's sick. She has a fever. Matthew has an ear infection. I'll take them to the hospital tomorrow. I'm responsible. It's in my hands."

March 21: I'm visiting with Kim. A woman I have never seen bangs at the door. She's come upstairs from Laura's room to ask for help.

When Kim and I arrive, the mother's kneeling on the floor. She's in a state of near hysteria.

As she explains it, this is what took place: She had noticed that the crib was swaying and was worried that it might collapse. She had therefore lifted the baby out and placed her on the bed. A moment later, as she turned to warm some milk, the baby somehow toppled over, striking her head against the metal frame.

"I put her here. I told her. 'Do you want some milk?' I went to warm the milk. I turned around, and she was bleeding. Her head was swelling up, like this. Her eyes are getting big. She's changing colors. I said: 'She is dying.'"

The child was taken to the hospital. Her grandfather is with her, waiting there for the report. The other children sit nearby, not understanding.

On a shelf above the crib there is a lion, a stuffed panda and a bear. A small pink elephant lies with his four feet in the air beside the metal bed. There is a color photo of the baby on the door.

The child survives the night. Her future is unclear. A few days later, Laura's mother is served papers—charged with child neglect. No charges, to my knowledge, have been brought against the Martinique Hotel.

Questions

1. List five adjectives to describe Laura's lifestyle.
2. Describe the health and safety dangers present in her room.
3. How does poverty affect her children?
4. How does Laura overcome her illiteracy?
5. How large of a role does extended family play in her life? Do you think that is typical of families living in poverty? Why or why not?

Facing the Dilemma

William W. Wells

In this selection from the book The Agony of Affluence
*author William W. Wells describes the dilemma of living
with personal prosperity in a world of need. There are many
choices that must be made. Christians have a responsibility
to make wise choices. Wells calls it "the agony of affluence."*

"There is no way out," Kent Hartford concluded. "No matter how I resolve this, someone is going to disapprove."
The land was not the problem. That was an inheritance from an uncle. Getting the money was not the problem. Kent was a partner in a prosperous law firm. The problem was nothing as relatively straightforward as money or land. The problem was this: In a world where one billion people go to bed hungry each night, did Kent, a Christian, have a right to build a vacation home for his family?
Kent's pastor had taken a strong stance on the matter. Christians should not, he argued, spend their money on luxuries while there were still people in the world going hungry. Sarah Downs, a Christian colleague in his law firm, disagreed vehemently; she considered Kent's scruples unjustified in light of his clear commitment to both the church and the work of the kingdom of God. For example, their law firm allowed them to spend up to ten percent of their time on "charity" cases for which there would be no income. Out of concern for the poor, Kent regularly used his quota of time. Furthermore, he consistently and generously supported the work of his church with both his time and his money.
Kent's wife understood both sides clearly and had concluded that they should build a vacation home. Kent's profession placed him under a great deal of pressure and stress, and

limited his time with the children. She believed that building a place where Kent could unwind on the weekends and where they could spend their vacations together as a family was an appropriate use of a portion of their money. But she had assured Kent that she did not want to begin building unless he felt right about it. So the final decision rested on his shoulders and conscience.

Living with personal prosperity, yet wanting to please God by making responsible and moral economic decisions in a world full of human need: that is the agony of affluence. But what do I mean by affluence?

Do I mean men in perfectly coordinated Ralph Lauren shirts and slacks working their golf handicaps down at a posh resort? Or perhaps diamond-ringed, gracefully aging women flitting between their spas, club luncheons, and theater openings? Certainly these are some of the images of affluence in our culture. Yet in a worldwide context and by any reasonable standard, you and I are wealthy. We are both educated; I am able to write, and you are able to read. We both have leisure time to pursue these and other activities.

Or let's look at our wealth in another way. Suppose the word *wealthy* means that you have more than your *fair* share. Again, measured by the average income worldwide, we both probably have more than our share. You may think that definition is too broad, and I agree. It tends to destroy the concept of a middle class, making everyone either wealthy or poor. So let's modify the standard somewhat and say that the *wealthy* are those who have annual incomes in the top 20 percent worldwide. Again, on a worldwide standard, we are probably both wealthy.

Then, let's see ourselves honestly in relation to the rest of the world and admit that we are affluent; and let's admit that this affluence raises two sets of questions that could create some agonizing dilemmas for us.

First of all, why do we have this wealth? Where did it come from? Is it ethical to possess this wealth? Is there an inevitable link between wealth and oppression? These questions focus on a search for truth, and we will need to draw information from both Scripture and economics in order to answer them.

Second, what should we do with our wealth? Some biblical passages seem to suggest that God expects us to give it away. Does he expect us to give *all* our wealth away? Or can we keep some? Can we save some for our retirement? At what point does our appreciation of the good things God has given us become materialism? How can we recognize when we have accepted the moral and ethical standards of our culture? Is a "Christian capitalist" a contradiction in terms?

Some evangelical writers assert: "If you are wealthy, you are guilty of injustice. You should, therefore, give it all away now." Other Christians point to the Old Testament promises of wealth and prosperity to the faithful, claiming that we can enjoy the wealth of this world.

Most evangelicals find themselves somewhere in the middle, dissatisfied with both extremes, yet lacking the biblical or intellectual framework that would provide an alternative.

Questions

1. Describe Kent's dilemma. How would you counsel him?
2. How had Kent's wife resolved the issue in her own mind? What did she tell her husband? Do you agree with her reasoning for desiring to build the vacation home?
3. Are you wealthy? How does your standard of living measure up with others in your neighborhood? In your city? In other parts of the world? How do you feel about your standard of living?

Business: Is There a Christian Perspective?

Richard C. Chewning, John W. Eby, Shirley J. Roels

This selection is taken from the book Business Through the Eyes of Faith, *published by the Christian College Coalition. The authors say that there are biblical principles that can guide Christians in business, although making ethical decisions does not always guarantee success. The selection is concluded with a listing of biblical principles of economics.*

Corporate Goals

Computer Management and Development Services (CMDS), in Harrisonburg, Virginia, develops, markets, and supports administrative management computer software for colleges, universities, and health care organizations. In 1987 it was listed by *Inc.* magazine as one of the fastest-growing privately held companies in North America. Its top management and many of its more than fifty employees are committed Christians. CMDS has adopted the following corporate goals.

To Honor God

We believe that our Christianity is something that is a part of all we do. Therefore, we commit ourselves to operate CMDS within our understanding of Christian ethical and moral beliefs. We believe Christ should be honored by all that we do and say.

To Develop People

We believe that people employed by CMDS are our most important asset. We commit ourselves to pay fairly, treat one another honestly, and promote development of the individual. We believe that people we work for are also important and commit ourselves to training them in the operation of the system, treating them honestly, and assisting in the development of the individual in any way we can.

To Pursue Excellence in Service

Service is our most important product. We recognize the importance of service to our customers and commit ourselves to responding promptly to requests and/or problems. We will continue to refine and improve our products. Only by providing an important service to our customers will we continue to exist as a company. We commit ourselves to excellence.

To Make a Profit

We recognize the need to make a profit in order to operate a viable business. We are nonetheless committed to meet goals one, two, and three and will sacrifice a larger profit in order to meet these goals.

Business from a Biblical Perspective

A certain amount of tension between business and Christianity seems always to have existed. St. Jerome said, "A merchant can seldom if ever please God." St. Augustine, a fifth-century Christian bishop, wrote, "Business is in itself evil."

Most Christians today, however, would disagree. All around the world, in a wide variety of political and economic systems, Christians are involved in business. Some see business merely as a way to make a living. Others, like those at CMDS, see it as an integral part of God's plan for meeting the needs of people. If you agree with Augustine, you can stop reading now. If, instead, you think that business is one setting in which Christians can live out God's call, keep going. The statements by St. Augustine and St. Jerome are provocative, and they are quoted here to catch your attention. Many people think it is easy to be a Christian in business. It is not easy, but it is possible.

This book tackles some of the really important issues Christians face in business. It suggests that Christians approach business as part of God's work in the world. It argues that it is possible to be both ethical and successful, but that being ethical and Christian will not necessarily guarantee success.

A Christian approach to business is not a cookbook of simplistic recipes for resolving complex business problems. Certainly CMDS cannot expect the Bible to explicitly answer its questions about which new computer software-products to develop, or which of several qualified employees to hire. The president of CMDS does not look to the Bible to find his business plan. Yet CMDS can employ a number of biblical principles, recurring scriptural themes, that provide sound and helpful guidelines for facing real business issues in the real world.

This in no way implies that biblical principles, such as "We are stewards and God is the ultimate titleholder," are easy to apply. Nor does it imply that every Christian will apply the principles the same way. For example, some Christians might use an unusually large profit from a successful year's operations to modernize capital equipment. Others might pay out an extra dividend to investors or share the profit with employees. God is concerned about workers, customers, and other stakeholders; but the responsibility for determining what is fair and what achieves business objectives in the light of biblical principles requires hard thinking, creative problem solving, and careful implementation.

The business environment is filled with uncertainty. Even though decision makers have the best intentions, the results are not always what they would want. This happened recently in a small community in eastern Pennsylvania. A firm there had been operated as a closely held corporation for two generations by committed Christians. They took very seriously their responsibility to run their business in a way that served the community, the employees, and customers who related to it. It had grown rapidly and had developed a good reputation among its employees and customers. The local newspaper did an article praising the founder for his humble Christian spirit. During the last several years the business faced economic difficulty that required it to seek a friendly merger with a larger firm with needed capital. This firm shared the values of the owners of the smaller firm, so the merger seemed like a good idea.

The larger firm, however, was traded on the open market. Soon after the merger, it was the target of a successful unfriendly takeover by a firm with very different values. The company changed dramatically. Many employees lost their jobs. Profit, not service, became the highest objective. The original owners were sadly disappointed. They had made the best decisions they knew how to make, but the results were not at all what they wanted. Uncertainties can sometimes alter the outcome of decisions so that there is little resemblance between the original intention and the actual result.

Making decisions in business is not a simple function of running anticipated actions through a formula or process. Decisions rest upon a vast array of judgments that require the integration of perceived facts and beliefs concerning technology, resources, markets, individuals, society, moral perceptions, and a host of other components. To function in a godly manner in the marketplace, we need all the wisdom that is available.

We are called to be like Christ and to think like he would think (Philippians 2:1-8). Christians know that this is made possible by the presence and inner work of the Holy Spirit, not by our efforts alone. We are called not only to know the will of God, but to do it.

Business Life from a Different Viewpoint

The Christian worldview is, at its very core, reality seen through the eyes of faith. Some people believe that faith is a mask that covers up a fundamental weakness. To them it symbolizes a deficiency, and they may even scoff at it. Faith from this perspective is blind. The truth, however, is that we are all compelled by our finite nature to walk by faith. The issue is not whether we live by faith, but in whom or in what we place our faith.

Our decisions always embody faith in something. We will ultimately make all decisions according to our faith. Those who do not seek Christ's will in business might develop their faith around highly personal independence, competition, material possessions, social status, or leisure. A Christian's faith, however, would place special value on the love and nurture of the family, the love of service, the health and well-being of the socially and economically disadvantaged, and the need to be kind and considerate of human differences. The Lord's day is also special to Christians, while many others see it only as another day to pursue commercial profits. This does not mean all Christians emphasize the same things, perceive the same risks, or respond to circumstances in the same way. We may have different priorities, emphases, and methods.

Those who do not love God do not associate going into business with fulfilling God's will for them. Christians, on the other hand, have an opportunity to see God's good intentions for them in a business career. Business is, after all, an institutionalization of God's intention for us to work and to serve each other. People form business organizations for a variety of personal, managerial, financial, legal, and other reasons; but Christians can see a much larger purpose in business. Business is a legal structuring of work where we express our dominion over creation. It affords us opportunities to plan, organize, lead, follow, and develop skills in a number of areas—all mirroring godly qualities.

Our culture alternates between applauding and condemning business. Many current public opinion polls reveal that corporate executives are not esteemed as highly today as they were some years ago. Some business people do not place moral principles very high in their decision criteria. Christians have a particular opportunity to be salt and light to the business world, and thereby demonstrate what it means to be ethical and moral.

Our way of life also places a strong emphasis on personal autonomy. Scripture affirms the value of the individual, but simultaneously calls each of us to understand that we are part of Christ's body. We are called to see ourselves as servants and stewards of something greater than ourselves. In this humble capacity we minister to others, while we are simultaneously ministered to. From a biblical perspective we are dependent, independent, and interdependent all at the same time.

The belief that God created us to be servants and stewards over his creation gives us a radically different view of business. If we have genuine faith in such understandings, we should exhibit our faith through our collective organizational behavior. The directors and managers of CMDS certainly took a faith position and expected it to influence their operations.

Some people would say that Christian faith is a "pie in the sky" view of reality and that it does not work in a world dominated by tough competition and selfish people. The faith described here, however, is neither wishful thinking nor abstract philosophy. And it certainly is not blind. Biblical faith is grounded on substantive, evidential facts: "Faith is the assurance [substance] of things hoped for, the conviction [evidence, proof] of things not seen" (Hebrews 11:1 NASB). God acts at specific times in history to communicate, demonstrate, and illustrate the way people are to live. The most relevant illustration is Jesus. He lived faithfully in a very tough situation.

This book emphasizes the faith characteristic of Christian life in business for a very good reason: because those of us who follow Christ are called upon to be different and act differently from those who have another object of faith. The distinctive character of Christian business professionals can come only through a commitment to Christ that is solidly grounded in an unshakable faith—an evidential faith.

Is Capitalism Christian?

"How is it possible for a person in America to be in business and still be a Christian?" That question was asked recently by a Soviet Christian to a visiting delegation of Canadian business-people. One was the president of a large furniture manufacturing firm. Another was a builder with a contract from the Soviet government to build a hotel in Leningrad. Another was the former president of a large real estate firm. All are deeply committed Christians active in local congregations and international Christian organizations. The Soviets found it difficult to see how a person in a capitalistic system—which emphasizes individual initiative, private ownership, competition, risk taking, and personal profit—could be a Christian. The Canadians were surprised because they couldn't understand how it was possible to be a Christian in a system that claimed to be atheist, emphasized government ownership of property, and limited personal freedoms.

Because business life is shaped by its political and economic environment, it is important to ask whether one economic system is more Christian than others. Both the Soviet Christian and the Canadian Christians assumed their system was best, and that it was easier to be a Christian in their system than in the other one.

The Bible was not written as a text outlining the best economic system, yet it does set criteria by which all systems should be judged. The following statements suggest some of the criteria that can be used to evaluate how well a given economic system serves the purposes God intended. Although these points do not relate directly to specific biblical passages, they do reflect the perspective of the Scripture taken as a whole.

1. The system should produce an adequate supply of products and services to enhance the quality of life.
2. The system should provide for the basic needs of marginal and disadvantaged people.
3. The system should respond to and allow for individual differences and needs. There should be fair and equitable means of resolving conflicts.
4. The system should reward and encourage initiative and hard work.
5. The system should provide meaningful work for all people and provide opportunities for them to contribute to the welfare of society.
6. The system should use natural and human resources efficiently and carefully.
7. The system should respect and care for other countries; it

should not exploit them or rob future generations.

8. Power and access to power should be spread equitably among sectors of society and special interest groups.
9. The benefits of the system and the costs of providing them should be spread equitably throughout the system.
10. Human rights should be protected.
11. Individuals should be valued and given opportunity to grow and develop.

Christians can and should make judgments about the strengths and weaknesses of every economic system. However, in doing so, we must avoid labeling them as either Christian or non-Christian in any absolute sense. Every system has both positive and negative aspects. Systems work better at some times than at others. We should not become so attached to any one economic system that we overlook its weaknesses. No economic system is perfect. All need to be measured by the principles of Scripture.

No matter what economic system we participate in, we need to stop occasionally and marvel at the grace God has poured out upon all people in their business relationships. God blesses all of us with an orderly creation that can be developed for our benefit. The Holy Spirit regularly exercises moral influence to restrain sin and chaos in the economic arena. God endows all who bear his image with intellect and creative capacities. The talents associated with the work of a skilled machinist, competent truck driver, accurate accountant, reliable engineer, hard-working janitor, honest salesperson, discerning manager, or wise board member should be recognized as God's gifts to us. It is God's grace that gives gifts such as these even to those who do not acknowledge him as Lord.

Questions

1. Define what it means to do business from a Christian point of view.

2. Is capitalism more or less Christian than communism? Why? Is there a Christian economic system?
3. Why do you think the communist economic system weakened so dramatically under *perestroika* in the Soviet Union in the late 1980s. Do you think capitalism could be weakened in the same way?

Consuming and Investing

Shirley J. Roels

Shirley J. Roels teaches economics and business at Calvin College, Grand Rapids, Michigan. In this selection, excerpted from her booklet Christians and Economic Life, *she offers biblical guidelines for making sound financial decisions about buying and investing.*

What should we buy?

Biblical injunctions about consumption would be easy to handle if we were poor. By historical world standards, however, most of us are incredibly rich. As John Kenneth Galbraith so aptly pointed out in his book *The Age of Affluence* almost three decades ago, society now has far more buying capacity than previous generations. Many, if not most of us, have adequate food, clothing, shelter, and transportation. We may wish our food were more gourmet, clothing more fashionable, shelter more spacious, and cars more sporty, but what we have functions effectively. We have benefited from the wealth generated by almost two centuries of capitalism. Most of the time we can buy more than we need. The question for Christians is, should we?

Christians hold different opinions on the relationship between happiness and consumption. Some of us believe what we own **does** make us happy. New clothes, dishwashers, power tools, computer games, and cottages do satisfy us. Others of us are persuaded that true contentment is found only in the **absence** of things. We advocate a spartan lifestyle; we back the principle that Christians should buy only to satisfy needs, not wants. We then spend our time deliberating over whether some purchase answers a need or satisfies just a want. Or we simply make our purchase and rationalize that we really needed it anyway.

Most of us do not find either of these two positions particularly helpful as we make choices. Basing contentment on what we own is futile. It is part of our human makeup to constantly raise our standards for economic well-being. We also tend to make upward comparisons and believe ourselves to be deserving. These human characteristics always result in a sense of relative economic deprivation. Buying, to our chagrin, does not enhance our happiness. Self-reported happiness levels are not much different than they were 30 years ago, despite our greater consumption of goods and services.

Yet we also want to escape the need/want trap. The dichotomy between needs and wants is a false one. Instead of dividing all goods between needs and wants, we should think of all possible purchases as being arranged on a continuum. At one end of the continuum are basic items required for sheer physiological survival. We need to eat. Many of us need winter coats. We need some kind of shelter from the cold, the rain, wind, and sun. At the other end of the continuum are non-essentials. Nobody really needed a pet rock or an automatic egg scrambler during the 1970s. Most of us do not need clothes from Paris fashion houses. Even if we can afford them, few of us would argue that diamond earrings or a 65-foot cabin cruiser are essentials.

Most goods and services, however, fall along the continuum **between** these two extremes. A more spacious home, a minivan, designer jeans for teens, Nintendo, better seats at the symphony, a condominium at the shore, or the latest in educational toys for our youngsters are each purchases that can be justified. We "need" more space. We "need" higher-quality leisure. We "need" to develop psychologically healthy children in a competitive peer culture. Should we feel guilty for making such purchases? What are our Christian standards?

Let me suggest three guidelines based on Scripture that may aid our decision-making:

1. **It is not wrong to buy goods and services that go beyond our basic survival needs.** God expected his creatures to do

more than simply survive. He expects his image-bearers to grow, to flourish, and to find delight in his creation. Purchases which improve the quality of our lives are not inherently evil. If buying a dishwasher or a microwave oven leaves parents with more time for backyard baseball with their children, that could improve the quality of family life. Purchasing a car that breaks down less often and has adequate space no doubt improves one's disposition. A week in Florida may do wonders for one's attitude toward work. A pleasing watercolor painting may add many minutes of quiet aesthetic pleasure to a week.

We should thank God for purchases which add to the quality of our lives as creatures. They are gifts to humankind created by his inventors for our enjoyment. We are not compelled to draw a distinction between needs and wants and then buy only what we need. As God's new creatures, he sets us free to enjoy all good aspects of his developing world.

2. **Though much of what we buy can be good, it does not follow that we should buy all good purchases.** The Bible places important constraints on what we buy. These constraints should be based less on whether we need an item than with the **effect** of our purchase on our own relationships with God, with our local community, with others worldwide, and with the natural environment.

a. **We must be careful that what we buy does not pull us away from our relationship to God.** Any purchase can become an idol when it directs our choice of vocation away from God's will for us. We become enslaved when work becomes only a means to buy more things. Sometimes we choose jobs only because they pay more, and because we can buy more, not because they are avenues of honest service in God's kingdom.

Things also become idols when we mistakenly suppose that they are the source of our happiness and security. Believing that "I know I'll be happy when we finally buy

_____" is a trap. The source of true satisfaction for Christians is in living daily before God's face and for his purposes. We should never buy so many things that we begin to deceive ourselves about our true source of contentment and goals.

Finally, our purchases can break down our relationship to God when the time they take is excessive. It is not wrong to own a boat. But if use and care of that boat interfere with attendance at regular worship services, opportunities to teach our children about faith, or responsibilities in our community, the boat should be put up for sale! The time we devote to our purchases must always be constrained by the time God expects of us in worship, family life, and work which serves others.

b. The second constraint on what we buy is the effect our purchases will have on our neighbors and fellow church members. Let me illustrate. Several years ago our family bought a 15-year-old Mercedes-Benz. The exterior was in mint condition. The car looked brand new. For us it had been a decent bargain because of its age. Our neighbors and friends at church, however, saw that car from a different perspective. Some seemed a bit miffed that they could not afford a similarly upscale auto. Others began to believe we were really quite a wealthy family, well outside their "class." In subtle ways, some acquaintances seemed to distance themselves from us. Still others probably used our car to justify their own transportation trade-up. They mused, "If they can own a Mercedes, there's nothing wrong with me buying a _____" (Corvette, Miata, Legend, Scorpio—you fill in the blank!).

Within a year we sold that car. Granted, it was too expensive to maintain easily. But in addition we were uncomfortable with the reactions the car had generated among people we knew. It seemed to encourage envy and acquisitiveness. It also appeared to chip away at a healthy sense of church community. We were concerned that the car had become a stumbling block to others.

Before we buy, we should consider the effect our purchases will have on those around us. Our purchases will trigger economic status comparisons by others. If a purchase will cause undue envy, encourage acquisitiveness, or break down our community, we should re-evaluate it. We may have to avoid some purchases for the good of others.

c. The third constraint on what we buy is the unmet needs of other people worldwide. Poverty is a complex issue. Sometimes we cause it directly. Sometimes we do not. Even when we are not directly involved, however, Scripture still implores us to hear the cry of those who weep. James writes that "Religion that God our Father accepts as pure and faultless is this: to look after orphans and widows in their distress . . . " (James 1:27). Those receiving James' letter may not have caused the death of these parents and spouses, but they still were expected to respond to their needs.

How we respond to the needs of the poor goes far beyond the scope of this booklet. However, the point is that our buying always must be limited by our sharing with those in need. In a recent promotion, the Christian Reformed World Relief Committee suggested that for every dollar we budget for vacations we should set aside one cent for donations to world relief and development. The formula could be altered, but the idea is a good one. We should constrain our personal spending budgets by simultaneously committing ourselves to spending for the disadvantaged of our world. The needy should receive as we spend our dollars, not out of our leftover change.

Often because of housing locations and choice of work and

friends, we are isolated from those in need. That lowers our level of pain and raises our comfort index. The result, unfortunately, is that too often we do not give enough, because the suffering of the needy is removed from our daily experience. Only when we actively feel the pain of the needy in our churches, our communities, and our world will this concern inhibit our consumption. We should open ourselves to empathizing with the needy in order to prompt our giving.

d. The fourth constraint on what we buy is the effect of our purchases on the natural environment. When our purchases result in more pollution—water, air, ground, or noise pollution—we should reconsider them. Although specific examples will step on somebody's toes, let me suggest that items like ATVs and jetskis might be problems for Christians. ATVs erode soil and damage landscaping. Jetskis are far noisier than any typical motorboat. When purchases needlessly damage God's world, we should avoid them.

Of course, many other purchases have more subtle effects on the environment, of which we are unaware. We should do what we can to understand the effect of these products on the natural world as well. As God's trustees, we must care for, not undercut, the balance and beauty of the earth.

3. **Finally, we should be very careful in judging the purchases of others.** Many of us too eagerly misinterpret other people's reasons for what they buy. We don't take the time to understand their circumstances. I suspect we are particularly miffed by spending among those with more money than we have.

An acquaintance of mine, who is an executive in an energy services company, recently bought an expensive home in the Washington, D.C. area. Many of his Christian friends did not understand that, as an officer in the corporation, he was expected to entertain other executives and government officials in his home regularly. He needed several "public rooms" in his house, while still having enough private space for his children. His friends also did not understand the high cost of housing in the nation's capital; nor did they know that he and his wife had quietly established a foundation by which they could better organize giving to their church and other charities.

The example is a more dramatic one than most of us encounter. But it illustrates the care we should have in judging the purchases of others. We do not always know the circumstances or motivation behind the outward symbols. We should not be discontented because others spend more for homes, cars, or other possessions.

What can we say by way of summary about our lives as buyers? God permits, even expects us, to enjoy the good gifts of his developing world. Often these come in the form of goods and services we buy. Our purchasing patterns, however, should always be moderated by a right relationship with God, by their effects on friends and churchmates, by the unmet needs of the world's people, and by our desire to care for the natural environment. Paul wrote in I Tim. 6:17-19: "Command those who are rich in this present world not to be arrogant nor to put their hope in wealth, which is so uncertain, but to put their hope in God, who richly provides us with everything for our enjoyment. Command them to do good, to be rich in good deeds, and to be generous and willing to share. In this way they will lay up treasure for themselves as a firm foundation for the coming age, so that they may take hold of the life that is truly life." May our patterns of buying fit these instructions.

How should we invest?

Most of us do not spend all of our income immediately. We try to save at least part of each paycheck to provide for the future. We anticipate the need to replace our car, to fund our children's education, or to provide for our retirement years.

Some Christians believe we should not plan for our financial futures. They point to Matthew 6, which warns against storing up treasures on earth and counsels us not to worry about food and clothing. The passage explicitly tells us to ". . . seek first his kingdom and his righteousness, and all these things will be given to you as well" (Matt. 6:33). These believers tell us to "trust God and he will provide."

While their counsel to trust God is sound, let me suggest that there is a difference between **worrying** about our material life and simply **planning** for it. Worrying suggests that in the end we do not trust God to take care of our daily needs. Therefore, we trust only our own saving and investing.

By comparison, planning for our financial future does not necessarily imply a lack of trust in God. It simply means we are being good stewards of the resources God has personally entrusted to us. Planning means that we devise sound strategies for using our assets effectively in God's service. Doing so may help us to be less reliant on exorbitant interest charges, government aid, or the financial help of the Christian community. It can also allow us to consider financial-giving opportunities such as bequests and life insurance policies, which greatly benefit charitable organizations. Planning does not imply worrying. In fact, good planning may eliminate worrying and encourage us to recognize that we still depend on God for our futures.

Assuming that financial planning is a good thing for Christians, there is still a large, unanswered question. In **what** should we, as Christians, invest?

For our grandparents, that question had a simpler answer. They usually bought a home over time and put any small amounts of extra funds into a passbook savings account, some promissory notes from a local Christian organization, some government treasury bonds, or all three. Few children continued education after high school. Shorter lifespans entailed less need for income to fund retirement and years of extensive health care.

The issues and the options have changed dramatically in a few decades. The financial costs of dependent children are much higher. The years of retirement are much longer. The investment choices are much broader.

A dazzling array of investment options present themselves: interest-bearing accounts; bonds that are labeled **discounted**, *coupon*, or *junk*; stocks of the blue chip, over-the-counter, and penny variety; mutual funds that are no load or front load; limited partnerships for real estate, oil wells, business takeovers, and mass media. Collectibles such as antiques, art, and even baseball cards are considered to be investments. There is trading in gold, silver, the yen, and the mark. One can buy a future's option on the expected value of beef or pork. One can even buy a future's contract based on expectations about the price movements of a selected group of stocks as measured by an index!

Are any of these types of investments more Christian than others? Let me suggest that there are basic differences among the categories of potential investment. Some types of investments use our personal resources to support projects of real economic value. Money put in savings and loans institutions helps others own a home. The purchase of a new stock or bond issue can provide financing to a business whose products serve people and whose growth creates new jobs. Mutual funds and secondary stock and bond markets diversify risks, and thus encourage needed investments in businesses. Limited partnerships can package economic resources so that needed buildings are constructed, more natural resources are discovered, and businesses are improved. In all such cases, we can be acting as God's trustees to see that economic resources are well-directed and effectively used. We naturally are concerned about the return on our investments, but as Christians we also can invest carefully in such products and services because they truly benefit society.

By comparison, we should avoid investments in organizations whose output is obviously harmful. It seems hard to imagine a Christian justification for investing in companies that make semi-automatic assault weapons or even cigarettes. We should carefully scrutinize our direct investments and our mutual funds to ensure they are directed toward products and services which add value to God's world.

There is, furthermore, a difference between responsible investing and speculation. Speculation is characterized by high financial risk and the promise of high return not associated with real earnings and dividends. Usually these returns are simply based on market fluctuations. Often there is little underlying economic benefit to society. Speculative investments rarely improve products or create jobs.

Suppose, for example, that you bought an option on the index of the stocks listed on the New York Stock Exchange. If the aggregate value of those stocks goes above that stipulated on your option, you win and collect the gain. If the aggregate value of those stocks goes below the amount stipulated in your option, you lose. An investment manager, protecting an organization's stock portfolio, may have good reasons for hedging risk in this way. An individual speculator in this situation, however, may simply be gambling on the numbers. For the individual investor, such a transaction may be far removed from direct stewardship of financial or productive resources. Speculation in commodities, currencies, collectibles, and junk bonds may have similar drawbacks for Christians.

As Christians, we also must recognize that investors have responsibilities. Whether we own stock in IBM or a local venture, we have an obligation to be aware of the company's policies and decisions. We should pay attention to proxy votes and stockholder reports. Bond ownership and partnerships demand similar attention. When we invest, we have become an indirect trustee of that organization. Although we may legitimately expect effective returns on our funds, we also have taken on some responsibility for that organization's customers and employees.

The point for us as Christians is that our investment opportunities should reflect our responsibility as God's economic trustees. When we invest, we must ask whether as individuals we are truly making a stewardly contribution to the development of God's plan for his creation. These developments may be managed by non-Christians as well as Christians, but they should contribute positively to unfolding God's kingdom in this world. In our investing as well as our buying, we must be God's stewards.

Deciding as Christians what to buy and how to invest is no easy task. Our choices are more complex than those of our grandparents. Therefore, we must work harder to scrutinize these decisions. Yet if we do our best, with God's grace, we can be the camels who go through the eye of the needle.

Questions

1. What three principles does Roels suggest to guide our decision making about buying?
2. Roels says that when we make purchases we should be concerned about how our decision will affect our relationship to God, to other people, and to the environment. Do you agree? Why or why not?
3. What guidelines does Roels offer to guide investment decisions?
4. Why do you think Roels and other writers in this section have insisted on taking a biblical view of wealth? What difference does it make whether a Christian looks to the Bible to guide his or her financial and business decisions?

Both Justice and Freedom

Ronald J. Sider

Ronald J. Sider is a writer and teacher who is deeply concerned about issues of equality and justice. This selection is from his book Completely Pro-Life. *He says that God cares about economic issues and so should we. He then outlines some of the central themes of Scripture which bear on the economic realm.*

The needs of the poor take priority over the desires of the rich; the rights of workers over the maximization of profits; the preservation of the environment over uncontrolled industrial expansion; production to meet social needs over production for military purposes.

John Paul II

Millions today die needlessly from starvation and malnutrition. A billion lie trapped in grinding poverty. Part of their tragedy is due to economic structures that are unfair. One crucial test of the integrity of the pro-life movement will be its attitude toward public policies that ignore the poverty of a billion troubled neighbors.

That God cares about economics is clear to anyone who reads the Bible carefully. It is probably the second most frequent topic in the Scriptures. This chapter contains a brief outline of some of the central biblical themes that relate to shalom and the economic realm: the importance and purpose of work; God's special concern for the poor; the rejection of great extremes of wealth and poverty; and the importance of and limitations on private property.

The Glory of Work

To be human is to work. God created men and women to

be co-shapers of history. As we respectfully till the garden which God has entrusted to our care, we accept this divine invitation and experience an important part of the fullness of life intended by the Creator.

The summons to work is intimately connected with the fact that we are created in the divine image. The Genesis story portrays God at work for six vigorous days before he rests from his labor on the sabbath. When God becomes flesh, we see him sawing and pounding year after year at the carpenter's bench.

Work, at its best, is the way each person expresses his or her uniqueness and individuality. When working conditions squelch or prevent this purpose of work, they obstruct God's intention.

Work is also the way we obey the divine command to care for ourselves and our families (2 Thess 3:12; 1 Tim 5:8). Even some elements of Israelite relief efforts (for example, gleaning in the fields after the harvesters) required personal initiative, responsibility and work on the part of those helped. Those who, because of laziness, refuse the summons to work despise both the example and command of the Creator.

Finally, work is the way we demonstrate our love for neighbor. Created to live in community in interdependence on others, we work to help shape a world where the labor of each enriches the life of all.

The U.S. Catholic bishops rightly conclude that this biblical perspective on work has clear implications for the shape of a just economic order: "It should enable persons to find a significant measure of self-realization in their labor; it should permit persons to fulfill their material needs through adequate remuneration; and it should make possible the enhancement of unity and solidarity within the family, the nation and the world community."

God and the Poor

God reveals a special concern for the poor in every part of the Scriptures—both Old Testament and New, prophetic writings and wisdom literature, the Gospels and Epistles. Constantly the Scriptures insist that this special concern for the poor and oppressed is central to the very nature of God (Ps 146). "He who is kind to the poor lends to the LORD" (Prov 19:17). "The LORD . . . executes justice for the needy" (Ps 140:12). Jesus' preaching to the poor is central to his Messianic mission and evidence that he is the Messiah (Lk 4:16-21 and 7:18-23). God warns the rich to weep and howl because of impending divine punishment for their neglect and mistreatment of the poor (Jas 5:1-5).

In some basic sense God is on the side of the poor. Also, in a sense, God is not on the side of the rich. That is not to say God is biased; Scripture explicitly denies divine bias (Job 34:8-19; Deut 10:17-19). God cares equally about everyone and demands economic justice for all. The overwhelming majority of rich and powerful folk in all societies past and present, however, care much more for their own well-being than for that of the poor. Corrupted by the Fall, they use the levels of power in society for their own selfish advantage. God, by contrast, is truly unbiased and thus cares equally about everyone. Hence in comparison to the actions of the rich and powerful, God appears to have a powerful bias toward the poor. God sides with the poor precisely in the sense that because he is unbiased he demands economic justice for all.

But why are people poor? Some people offer the simplistic answer that all poverty results from economic oppression by the rich. That is nonsense. The Bible is realistic. Some poverty results from laziness, or sinful choices about drugs or alcohol (Prov 6:6-11; 19:15; 20:13). Some poverty results from religious systems that do not encourage initiative, work and creativity. Obviously evangelism, repentance and conversion are central to the solution of such poverty.

Many people, on the other hand, rationalize their own affluence in the face of widespread poverty by blaming the poor for their own misery. Laziness, sinful choices or a failure to take advantage of available technology is used to allegedly explain most poverty. This is not the biblical perspective.

Although the Scriptures occasionally blame the poor for their poverty, far more often they attribute it to oppression by the rich and powerful:

The LORD enters into judgment with the elders and princes of his people: "It is you who have devoured the vineyard, the spoil of the poor is in your houses" (Is 3:14).

Or Jeremiah 5:27:

Like a basket full of birds, their houses are full of treachery; therefore, they have become great and rich, they have grown fat and sleek.

God's attitude toward such rich folk is very clear and explicit. God abhors their oppression and pulls down their houses and societies (Is 3:14-25; Jer 22:13-19; Is 10:1-3). And he hates their worship (Amos 5:21-24; Is 58:3-8).

The Scriptures even raise the most serious doubt about whether such people even know or love God at all (Jer 22:16; 1 Jn 3:17-18). Precisely because God cares equally for all, he punishes individuals and societies that oppress the poor.

Any approach to the whole area of economics that fails to emphasize God's overwhelming concern for economic justice for the poor is simply unbiblical.

Extremes of Wealth and Poverty

Another important clue about the nature of economic justice comes from the biblical teaching that God condemns extremes of wealth and poverty. Sinful people may well selfishly develop greater and greater extremes between rich and poor. Among the redeemed, however, God demands transformed economic relationships.

After Israel entered Canaan, the land was divided more or less equally (Num 26:52-56). God wanted tribes and families to have enough to earn their own way. Then God added the provision for a Jubilee every fifty years (Lev 25). Every fiftieth year all land was to return to the original owners—without compensation and without questions asked about possible failures on the part of the poor folk who had lost their land. Deuteronomy 15 added the demand that every seven years all debts must be forgiven. Both measures were divinely willed societal mechanisms to prevent ever greater extremes between the wealthy and the poor and to move society in the direction of equality of economic opportunity.

It is important to see that the Jubilee passage also teaches personal responsibility. Those who make wrong decisions and lose their land do not get it back immediately—in fact, in many cases they would not get it back during their lifetime! They must live with the consequences of their actions until the next Jubilee. On the other hand, the restoration of land every fifty years works against an ever-increasing centralization of wealth. It fosters a basic equality of economic opportunity for all, at least to the degree that all have the means to earn the basic necessities of life.

This concern for redeemed economic relationships among the people of God did not end with the Old Testament. Jesus talked frequently about the way his followers would share with the poor (Mt 25:31-40). Filled with the Holy Spirit, the first church obeyed Christ's teachings so dramatically and shared so thoroughly that "there was not a needy person among them" (Acts 4:34). And the apostle Paul, the great missionary to the Gentiles, considered economic fellowship in the body of Christ so important that he devoted hours and hours of potential preaching time to an interracial, intercontinental offering. He collected donations from Greek-speaking European Christians for Aramaic-speaking Asian Christians (2 Cor 8-9).

> I do not mean that others should be eased and you burdened, but that as a matter of equality your abundance at the present time should supply their want, so that their abundance may supply your want, that there may be equality (2 Cor 8:13-14).

Neither the Jubilee provisions or the Pauline teaching on intercontinental sharing mean that God demands some wooden, absolutely egalitarian equality of consumption. But surely the texts demonstrate beyond any doubt that God desires an end to extremes of wealth and poverty among his people.

Nor does the principle apply only in the church. God did

not impose arbitrary demands in the Bible. God's revealed norms were designed to guarantee social wholeness among the people of God. To the extent that any society implements the biblical principles disclosed by God to Israel and the church, greater wholeness will result.

Two important elements of economic justice, therefore, are the absence of extremes of wealth and poverty and the presence of equality of economic opportunity (at least with reference to the basic necessities of life). The doctrine of sin underlines why these principles are so important. Wealth is power. And power is dangerous. Because of the Fall, power tends to corrupt and absolute power tends to corrupt absolutely. Sinful, selfish people cannot be trusted to use great economic power for the common good rather than for themselves. Therefore, if freedom and economic justice for all are important goals, we will structure society to exhibit and overcome extremes of wealth and poverty.

That does not mean that economics is a zero-sum game where increasing my wealth automatically means that someone else loses. Hard work and technological invention can create new wealth for all. Not all differences in income result from sin, selfishness and greed. The biblical teaching on work and humanity's dominion over the earth affirms the goodness and importance of the creation of wealth.

Private Property

Scripture also supports the notion of private property. Both implicitly and explicitly, the Ten Commandments sanction private ownership (Ex 10:15, 17). Jesus apparently assumed its legitimacy—otherwise, his commands to give to the poor and loan to the needy would make no sense (Mt 6:2-4; 5:42; Lk 6:34-35).

Although the Bible affirms the validity of private property, it totally rejects any notion of absolute private ownership. God is the only absolute owner. As Lord of all, God possesses unconditional property rights to every thing. "Whatever is under the whole heaven is mine" (Job 41:11; see also Ps 50:12; Deut 26:10). Because God alone is absolute owner, God can insist that the right of everyone to have land (so as to earn a living) is a higher right than some notion of unlimited, absolute private ownership. Hence we have God's demand that Israel practice Jubilee every fifty years: "The land shall not be sold in perpetuity, for the land is mine; for you are strangers and sojourners with me" (Lev 25:23).

Leviticus 25:25-28 contains another striking limitation on the rights of private ownership. Between the years of Jubilee, the land can be sold. However, if a poor person sells some land and then recovers financial solvency, the new owner must sell back the land even if he prefers to keep it. The original family's right to have their property in order to be able to earn their own way is a higher right than the new owner's right to maximize profits.

The Bible challenges any person or system devoted to absolutizing property rights. It also rejects any notion of state ownership of the major means of production. Leviticus 25 does not suggest either a vast permanent welfare system (which runs the great danger of promoting dependency) or state ownership (which leads to totalitarianism). In order to promote strong families able to earn their own way, Jubilee called for regular redistribution of the land. Since land was the basic capital in early Israel, that mechanism, if followed, would have promoted a decentralized form of limited private ownership where everyone had the economic resources to shape their own life and earn their own way. The Jubilee principle, someone has suggested, "esteems private property more highly than capitalism does, for it insists that no family be permanently without it."

Decentralized, private ownership (understood as stewardship) rather than state ownership as in socialism and communism is important for both a positive and a negative reason. Positively, the biblical doctrine of creation summons each person to be a co-worker with God. God wants us to exercise dominion over the earth, shape history and genuinely influence the decisions that affect our lives. If economic power is centralized in state ownership, persons and families become cogs in complex economic machines. They are denied the freedom to shape the crucial decisions that affect their lives.

Negatively, as we have already noted, power tends to corrupt and absolute power tends to corrupt absolutely. Therefore, the centralization of economic power and political power in the same hands is exceedingly dangerous in a fallen world. As the highly repressive Communist society of the USSR demonstrates, this kind of centralization almost guarantees a totalitarianism that tramples on religious and political freedom. Decentralization of power is essential if liberty is to thrive.

It is astonishing, however, to see how inconsistently many people apply this principle about the danger of centralized economic power. Some denounce the danger in the case of totalitarian Communist societies and then fail to apply the same principle to Western societies where huge multinational corporations exercise immense economic and therefore enormous political influence. (For others, alas, the blindness is reversed!) So vast is the economic power of the five hundred largest corporations (and the few thousand people who control them) that genuine democracy is significantly undermined in North America and Western Europe. A biblically informed fear of concentrated power will demand changes in both East and West.

The preceding discussion has focused on several crucial components of a biblical perspective on economics:

First, work is essential to the nature of persons.

Second, God's special concern for justice for the poor must also be a central concern for God's people.

Third, reducing or preventing extremes of wealth and poverty and moving in the direction of equality of economic opportunity are essential for economic justice. Therefore, redistribution of resources so everyone can stand on their own feet and earn their own way is important.

Fourth, the creation of wealth is good and important, but it dare not become the ultimate goal or highest value.

Fifth, limited private ownership is good when understood as stewardship under God who is the only absolute owner. Centralized economic power, whether controlled by the state or by vast corporations, is dangerous and almost inevitably evil. We should therefore promote decentralized, private ownership, since this enables persons and families to earn their own way and be co-workers with God in the shaping of history.

Sixth, personal responsibility in the economic realm is also a biblical summons and people must live with the consequences of wrong economic decisions.

Finally, there is a significant connection between decentralized economic ownership and political and religious liberty. The biblical doctrine of sin explains the historical fact that centralized state ownership of most resources almost guarantees totalitarianism.

Tragically, we are all tempted to stress some of these principles and neglect others. But that leads to biblical one-sidedness. The Bible affirms both economic redistribution and the creation of wealth, both communal sharing and individual responsibility, both freedom and justice, both decentralized private ownership and social limitations on individual greed.

Questions

1. What is the root cause of poverty? What is God's attitude to the poor?
2. Read Leviticus 25 and explain why God instituted the year of Jubilee. What was God's primary concern?
3. Why is limited private ownership of property preferable to centralized ownership?

Racism/Bigotry

Rebirth in a Barbershop
by Charles H. King, Jr.

Charles H. King, Jr., describes a harrowing encounter with a "scrawny, rednecked white man" in this selection, "Rebirth in a Barbershop." Racism against blacks ran deep throughout the U.S. in the mid-1950s, and Evansville, Indiana, where this incident took place, was no exception. This selection illustrates the depth of hatred and bigotry which a few years later fueled the fires of the civil rights movement.

It happened in a white barbershop called Emory's. Three chairs, one bootblack stand; three white barbers, one black bootblack. Sit-ins had not yet engulfed America, the nation had not yet heard of Martin Luther King, Jr., and the back of the bus was still the place for blacks throughout the South. Rosa Parks was still riding the buses in Montgomery, Alabama, consenting to be degraded, not yet too tired to sit down. I had no role models to imitate; I was just a Baptist preacher in a sleepy little city, burning with a desire to help and comfort my people. The bootblack in that shop was an occasional visitor to the Liberty Baptist Church. He had been paroled from prison the year before and had visited my office seeking employment. Without employment he would be sent back to prison to serve out the rest of his term. His problem was just one of the thousands that exist in every city in the nation.

As I walked by, I didn't really see the barbershop. I was not interested in getting a haircut; and even if I needed one, white barbers were not trained to cut black people's hair. But I did see in that shop a black man who was reluctant to come to church, struggling to survive, and smiling at me as I walked by. I stopped, smiled back, went in, and shook his hand. We conversed. Yes, he was doing all right; yes, he would begin attending church. Mission accomplished. I glanced at my shoes, and they were dirty. So I climbed onto the shoeshine stand.

"Get out of that chair!" It was the voice of the shop owner, Mr. Emory. I was shocked not only by the command but by the tone of the voice: it was high-pitched and threatening.

"Why?" I asked, controlling my voice. "All I want is a shoeshine."

"Not in here! We don't shine Negroes' shoes in this shop." The fact that he said "Negro" instead of "nigger" surprised me, because his drawl and tone were of the deep South. He was poor white, poorly educated; the contrast to my background, education, and grooming was a ludicrous one.

"But I want a shoeshine," I objected, "and this is a public place."

"Not for you, it ain't. And if you're not out of that chair in ten seconds, by God, an ambulance will be here to haul you away."

Through the years, as I look back on that scene, I realize that it was really the first time I stared death in the face. Because as Emory spoke, he pulled out a drawer and put his hand inside as if to draw out a gun. The shoeshine man ran out onto the sidewalk. But I sat frozen to my seat because there was no strength in my legs; they were stiff with fright. Emory's eyes were like pits of fire, and his hand outside the drawer was trembling. The other two barbers, as I remember, were looking at Emory in shock.

Each second that I sat there, my manhood, pride, and self-concept were draining away. I tried to find something to say, but nothing would come out of my mouth. I foolishly began to wonder how I would look dead, who would come to my funeral, and why I had to die in a shoeshine stand. Who was this white man before me? What had blacks done to him in the past? Did I remind him of the failures in his life, the lost opportunities to achieve success like millions of whites before him? I had spent seven days on bread and water for hitting a white man who had called me a "nigger," but that was when I was in my teens, when nonviolence was not yet in vogue and not yet a working theological concept within me. In those few seconds Emory was deciding my future; it was a magic moment to decide what I was to do in the future, a moment to decide the end of me or, worse yet, the end of my manhood.

> Once to every man and nation,
> Comes the moment to decide,
> In the struggle for the future,
> For the good or evil side.

I now thank God for Mr. Emory, that scrawny, rednecked white man in Evansville. He, more than any other person, conceptualized my growth and stoked up the fire that had been flickering in my bones for years. I was coming to grips in that chair with the noble meaning of a shoeshine, of how one's spilled blood could become a process of conquering evil. This thought comes now only as a reflection after the fact; it certainly did not come then, for in the space between Emory's words and my eventual decision, time stood still. No philosophy was in play—only a draining, hollow emptiness, like a gas tank with no station in sight. I made a decision. It was not to be a hero, for heroes do not emerge from shoeshine stands but from the heat of battle where the stakes are high. Heroes are made by the masses, who admire their courage and their sacrificed offerings for others, not for a pair of dirty shoes. It would have made better sense and public press if, instead, I would have sat down in Mr. Emory's barber chair and commanded him to deal with my person, rather than asking his "boy" to shine my shoes. I would have then entered his shop with sense of purpose, a defiant mission that would have earned me a fitting epitaph on my plaque in the black hall of fame.

"To thine own self be true" I had learned from Shakespeare in a white English class. Mr. Emory did not know it, but he was facing down a black man who had studied all of Shakespeare's works, taught to him by a bigoted white teacher at Kansas Wesleyan University in 1951. My thoughts went back to that year, the year I married Annese; it was she who had held my book and checked out my meaning. As the only black in that class, I was determined to memorize pages of Shakespeare, to quote his plays and sonnets as if I were an Oxford scholar. The white students at that university marveled at my ability to memorize, but Dean Stanley Trickett (later to become president of Kansas Wesleyan) reluctantly awarded me first place in the school's annual oratorical contest, and my teacher's final reward for my class efforts was a grade of "C." And now the orator was to die over a shoeshine.

"And it must follow as night the day, thou canst not then be false to any man." That day in Emory's barbershop I knew who I was, that I had allowed myself to be false to white people. I had learned how to skillfully compromise my blackness, to smile quaintly at racial jokes as long as they came from whites engaged in "better relations." It was the tacit acceptance of white liberals as the best you could get out of the white race. They were the ones who would later denounce Emory's threat on my life, only later to inquire of me privately why I had gone into a place like that—an unmasking of their own subtle white racism. I speak of these things now for I can look back at that chair with a crystal gaze. I can milk my thoughts for all the implications that that moment gave me, the steadfast determination from that moment onward to free the fire locked up in my bones. My decision of that moment has been washed away by the tide of black protestation that would soon sweep the nation. Individual acts of protest were multiplied all across the nation, but the white press buried them under the indicting title of "disorderly conduct." The liberal press in those days was not advocating justice but "better relations," while the barbershops, hotels, buses, drinking fountains, voting booths, and five-and-dime stores were rejecting black people.

My decision was to remain in that shoeshine chair. I had to remain. The black man who was witnessing my human debasement deserved to witness the stiffening of a black backbone. This was his moment also. I was doing what he would never be able to do; he was out of prison but still in chains. His opportunities to become somebody had been erased.

So I sat. I had called Emory's bluff. I stared at him almost hoping that he would shoot me—perhaps in the shoulder for I did not want to die. Something within me told me he would not shoot, but I could not completely trust that something.

Shoot if you must this old grey head,
But spare your country's flag, she said.

The works of Barbara Fritchie marched into my thoughts from out of white history. A white woman, so full of love for her flag, had invited death for the sake of saving the old rag from burning during the Revolution. "How stupid!" I thought. "I only regret that I have but one life to give for my country," said the patriot Nathan Hale.

"I'm going to sit here until I either get a shoeshine or an ambulance hauls me away," I found myself saying to Mr. Emory. As I look back, if I would have been shot, it would not have been to save a flag or even Nathan Hale's country. If I had died, those dirty old black shoes would at last have shined, stained red by my blood.

Emory called the police. Two burly cops, Evansville's finest, came to take me away. A crowd had gathered outside, summoned by the flashing red lights and the blaring siren. Emory had reported that a black man was being disorderly in his shop. The cops came in with nightsticks in hand, ready to crush a black skull. It would not have been the first. I had politely complained to Mayor Vance Hartke about the brutality of the Evansville Police, but he had done nothing to stop it. Some of the officers—the ones whose beat ran through the ghetto—were worse than others. Acting as policemen, judges, jury, and executioners combined, and seeking to devour, these men meted out justice on behalf of the entire judicial system. Operating out of a "them versus us" mentality, they drew guns more quickly, their trigger fingers were itchier, and their nightsticks were more ready against blacks than against whites. I was later to learn that every major civil disorder that was to occur in the 1960s was a consequence of the interaction between blacks and white policemen, working in pairs, like the two officers who were now ordering me out of Emory's barbershop.

Just like a tree,
Planted by the waters,
I shall not be moved.

The refrain from the old Negro spiritual ran through my mind as I refused the order to disembark from the shoeshine chair.

"I have a right to be here, officer; this is a public place, and the Indiana statutes protect my right to be served," I stated, quoting the appropriate law. But my knowledge of the law was to no avail in the face of these "officers of the law." After declaring me a "f—-ing smart ass," they seized me—veteran of ten years' service in Uncle Sam's Navy, Army, and Air Force, the pastor of the Liberty Baptist Church, and almost elected vice president of the Evansville Ministerial Association—by both legs and arms and carried me out through the crowd and thrust me headfirst into the back seat of the patrol car.

It was my first civil rights jailing. In the years to come I would become accustomed to the dirty cells with crawling roaches, the clanging of steel doors, the dispassionate look on the faces of white jailors, and the perpetual question of jail drunks and criminals-in-residence: "What are you here for?" But in the late 1950s jail had not yet become honorable for an honorable black man. It was soon to receive the stamp of approval of Martin Luther King, Jr.; but at the time of my first arrest, my mentor was still studying about Gandhi at Crozier Theological Seminary.

What bothered me the most was that my name would appear in the morning paper, and what I had been charged with was not only a lie, but lies heaped on lies.

DRUNK!
DISORDERLY!
CAUSING A PUBLIC NUISANCE!
RESISTING ARREST!

Sweet Jesus, what had I done to deserve this? The truth, the real story—please God!—let it be known. I sat in the corner of that urine-stinking cell weeping copious tears that only innocent men can shed. Those damnable shoes! I thought of the many things I could have done—should have done—that might have saved me from this disgrace. I envisioned my church disowning me, my white friends deserting me. It was a strange feeling, this first jailing. I certainly was not proud of my actions now that it had come to this.

However, the black grapevine was at work, and the news spread quickly. My people, my beautiful people, bailed me out. A mass meeting was held that next night, and the church was full. Black people—angry black people—came in droves.

Questions

1. Why did Mr. Emory threaten Rev. King's life? How does Rev. King describe Mr. Emory's emotions during the encounter? How did Rev. King respond to the threat on his life?
2. Do you think Rev. King expected to be shot? Why?

3. How did recalling lines from Shakespeare give Rev. King a proper perspective on the incident?
4. What factors do you think kept the press from accurately covering the early days of civil rights protests?
5. How did the incident affect Rev. King's church? Why do you think his parishioners supported him?

What's a Bigot?
Who's a Racist?

Kathlyn Gay

*Kathlyn Gay is a writer who is concerned about the way peo-
ple get along with each other. Gay writes about bigotry and
racism in this essay. She defines and gives examples of prejudice, bigotry, stereotyping, scapegoating, and racism. Since
racism continues to be a problem in Western society, Gay's
final question is important: "Can anything be done to stop
it?"*

In our neighborhood there are mostly white people, except
for a family from India. But last week a young black couple
was looking at a house for rent across the street from us. I
thought my dad would go crazy. He went right out to talk
to some of our neighbors, trying to get them all worked up
so they'd protest to the owner about renting to black people. Look. I love my dad, but he was wrong to do what he
did. How could he know what that couple is like? None of
us will know because they didn't rent the house. I hope it
wasn't because of my dad or our neighbors, but I have a
feeling it was.

C.S., Elkhart, Indiana

A bunch of us went into this video store the other day. We
were just going to rent a movie. But this old guy who owns
the place kept glaring at us and started following us
around. We got pissed and left. What is it about old people? Do they think all kids steal or what?

Brad, Denver, Colorado

I thought I was prepared when I went to this new high

school. I know that other people think I'm strange, with my short arms and legs, but I've learned to accept my "problem." It's called achondroplasia—or dwarfism. Over the years I've gotten used to nicknames like Shrimp and Small Fry, but this boy really threw me. He came up to me in the hall and asked, "When you going to join the circus?" I was upset all day. Just because I'm different doesn't mean I'm a freak!

J.M., Waukegan, Illinois

I volunteered to do this project, but the morning I was supposed to go to class all dressed up like a "bag lady" I got scared. Like my stomach was all jumpy and I didn't know if I wanted to go through with it. The social studies teacher had asked for someone to come to school looking very different from everyone else. Then the rest of the class was supposed to tell what they thought of the person. Well, I knew everybody would have a lot of bad things to say. They wouldn't really be talking about me, but, well, I was inside the clothes and, I don't know, it made me feel out of place!

Nissa, Ventura, California

At first it was just teasing—kids are into that, so it didn't bother me too much. But then it became a daily thing. When my younger sister goes to school with me, I always hold her hand so the kids call us "lezzies." It hurts because my sister is blind. Most of the time she does very well on her own, but sometimes she needs my help. Why don't other people understand that? Why do they have to be so mean?

Betterae, South Bend, Indiana

That last question is one that is often raised by people who have been victims of others' prejudices, or prejudgments. *Prejudice* literally means "judging beforehand without knowledge or examination of the facts," or strongly holding a preconceived notion, idea, or attitude.

However, prejudgment does not necessarily mean that a person forms an adverse or negative opinion about something or someone. It is possible to have a prejudice, or bias, *for* something—such as a certain type of food or make of car. Many people, for example, have preconceived ideas that democracy is valuable and that democratic rule is a fair form of government. More often, though, . . . *prejudice* is used to mean unfavorably prejudging others without reason and with misinformation.

Prejudiced people are likely to act in ways that can harm those they judge in a negative manner, as the brief comments at the beginning of this chapter point out. In fact, many prejudiced people might also be called bigots. According to one simple definition, a bigot is a person who is stubbornly and unreasonably attached to an opinion or belief. You might, for example, hear a bigot argue, "The world is flat—that's what I was taught and that's what I believe. Period." You could pull out maps and globes and call attention to geographic explanations about the shape of the earth. But scientific information would not convince someone attached to a flat-earth theory to change her or his mind.

Usually, acting on prejudiced notions, bigoted people are intolerant of those who differ from them in color or national ancestry, or in religious or political beliefs. In the popular TV show of the 1960s *All in the Family*, the not-too-bright character Archie Bunker was the prime example of a bigoted person. Not only was he stubbornly attached to the "rightness" of his point of view whatever that might be. He also acted out his intolerance by insulting people who had political or religious affiliations different from his own. Or he expressed his dislike for and even hatred of those who were not part of his in-group.

Many of Archie Bunker's antics were considered humorous because his bigotry was depicted as absurd, if not downright silly. At the time it seemed that Archie's actions did not seriously hurt anyone but him. However, critics of the show have argued that this portrayal of Archie Bunker made it seem "normal" or acceptable to be a bigot, glossing over the fact that bigotry frequently has an ugly and virulent side.

Bigotry and prejudice quite often lead to stereotypes, or fixed ideas about a particular group. People are seen as part of a group rather than being recognized as individuals. Those who accept stereotypes about groups different from them might express those attitudes in statements like these:

Older people are crotchety.
Young people are selfish.
Boys are mean.
Girls are silly.
Asians are sneaky.
Native Americans are alcoholics.
Blacks are lazy.
Arabs are terrorists.
Hispanics are hot-tempered.
Lawyers are greedy.
Artists are unreliable.

Many stereotypes are fabrications, made up to show a group in an unfavorable way. Some stereotypes are based on an element of truth that is exaggerated. In other words, a few people in a group may have certain traits that are considered negative. But those selected traits certainly do not describe all people in a group and do not give a full picture of any one person in a group. Stereotypes, in short, ignore variations in people. So, if you have a stereotype idea about a group of people, you easily can overlook and never get to know what individuals within a group are really like.

Stereotypes are often the basis for discrimination, in which people who are members of a stereotyped group are excluded from jobs, housing, schools, and other institutions. In a recent case, a young black woman involved in a University of Georgia on-the-job training program was hired to be a pharmacist's assistant in a Tifton, Georgia, drugstore. But the white owner of the store fired the young woman because he said "customers complained" about being waited on by a black person.

Many Tifton residents denied this was true, but the pharmacist believed his customers would not accept the black woman as an individual but would see her only as part of a group that had been judged "inferior." The pharmacist may have been acting on his own stereotypical view, passing judgment based on preconceived notions.

Victims of stereotypes may also become scapegoats, or targets for blame. American Arabs, for example, have been subjected to hostile attacks. Attackers blame all Middle East problems on people of Arab ancestry.

Scapegoating frequently involves bigoted rhetoric such as that used by Louis Farrakhan, a Black Muslim leader. Farrakhan continually blames all whites ("devils" he calls them) for problems blacks face, spouting a particular hatred for Jews who Farrakhan falsely claims have "a stranglehold on the government of the United States." In 1985, Farrakhan drew 25,000 people to New York's Madison Square Garden to bellow his bigoted belief that "Farrakhan is hated by the Jews! . . . But if you rise up to try to kill me, then Allah promises you that he will bring on this generation the blood of the righteous. All of you will be killed outright. . . . God [will] put you in the oven."

Along with verbal attacks, scapegoating may lead to vandalizing buildings and other structures. In Springfield, Illinois, insulting statements about blacks and slogans such as "white power" and "white power rules" were painted on the tomb of Abraham Lincoln. Vandals used similar tactics to deface synagogues in many cities across the nation scrawling anti-Semitic (anti-Jewish) statements on the buildings.

People exhibit their prejudices and bigotry in a variety of ways. In one incident, an Amish family, members of a religious group that shuns modern conveniences, were riding in a horse-drawn buggy along an Indiana highway where they were jeered and stoned by a gang of young people out "joy-riding" in a car. One member of the Amish family was injured. But the only comment afterward from a parent of one of the joy-riders was "boys will be boys."

Another incident took place in Los Angeles, where an

inter-racial couple was forced to leave their $135,000 home in a predominantly white neighborhood. Shortly after moving in, the couple, a black man and a white woman, received racist leaflets and hate mail saying "blacks are trash" and "the zoo wants you." Continued harassment drove the couple out.

In Yonkers, New York, several city council members refused to obey a federal court order to build low-income housing units in predominantly white neighborhoods. The U.S. district judge fined the city and its officials and noted that for forty years Yonkers officials had deliberately placed federally subsidized apartments in black neighborhoods only. Since many blacks and other minorities have lower incomes than whites, the assumption was that only minorities would use subsidized housing. By keeping low-income housing out of white neighborhoods, segregated housing patterns have been maintained not only in Yonkers, but also in many other U.S. cities. Certainly there are integrated communities across the nation, but race often determines whether a person can get a home mortgage, and real estate agents tend to steer black or other minority buyers away from white neighborhoods.

In a suburb of New Orleans, Sheriff Harry Lee ordered his deputies to routinely stop blacks who happened to be driving through white neighborhoods. His orders were part of a plan to cut down on home burglaries, and he reportedly said that blacks traveling through all-white neighborhoods were "up to no good." Lee's remarks and actions brought sharp criticism from the president of the New Orleans chapter of the National Association for the Advancement of Colored People (NAACP), and Lee publicly apologized to the black community. Lee, of Chinese ancestry, denied he is prejudiced, saying he has often been the victim of prejudice himself.

In Philadelphia, Boston, Washington, D.C., Los Angeles and many other U.S. cities, Asian immigrants—Vietnamese, Koreans, Cambodians, Laotians—have been insulted, attacked, and had their property vandalized by blacks and whites who resent their presence. Gangs in New Jersey, who brag that they are "dot busters," have attacked people from

India, labeling them "dot heads" because of the red markings women wear on their foreheads.

In Howard Beach, a white ethnic neighborhood of Queens, New York, a gang of youths attacked several black men, chasing them from the area with the cry "Niggers, get out!" One black man was beaten with a tire iron and broom handles. The black youth was chased onto a highway, where he was struck by a car and killed. Three of the white youths were convicted of manslaughter.

Not long after the Howard Beach incident, a gang of youths in Brooklyn, New York, attacked a white youth out for a walk with two friends. The gang of young blacks apparently wanted to retaliate for "white racism."

Although most scientists today reject the idea of categorizing people according to race—that is, creating terms for subspecies of *Homo sapiens*—race is used to define people in social terms. *Racism,* then, refers to a form of prejudice in which members of a group (determined by physical characteristics) believe they are superior to all other groups of people.

On a national scale, racism can be institutionalized. In other words, the majority of people in a nation may feel it is "right" or acceptable to have unfavorable stereotypes of and prejudice against certain groups, particularly religious and racial or, more correctly, ethnic groups (those who share a culture different from the majority way of life). When those unfavorable opinions become institutionalized, widespread discrimination results.

During World War II for example, American citizens of Japanese descent who lived on the west coast of the United States were herded up and sent to inland relocation camps. Why? Because Japan had just bombed Pearl Harbor, an American military base in the Pacific. Secretary of War Henry L. Stimson wrote in a memorandum to the president, "The Japanese race is an enemy race and while many second and third generation Japanese born on United States soil, possessed of United States citizenship, have become 'Americanized,' the racial strains are undiluted." Thus, the secretary of war assumed that American citizens of Japanese ancestry would "turn against this nation when the final test of loyalty comes." He acknowledged that there had been no acts of disloyalty but, he wrote, "The very fact that no sabotage has taken place is a disturbing and confirming indication that such action will be taken."

Such twisted reasoning—shared by many Americans at that time—convinced President Franklin D. Roosevelt to issue an executive order that authorized the secretary of war to set up military camps to hold people of Japanese ancestry. Clearly, this was a discriminatory act. The United States was also at war with Germany and Italy. Hundreds of thousands of people of German and Italian descent lived in every part of the nation. But Americans of German and Italian ancestry were not singled out as "enemies" simply because of their heritage.

In spite of proven dedication to their country in the U.S. military and in civilian life, thousands of U.S. citizens of Japanese descent lost their land, businesses, homes, and personal property. They were "tagged" like so much baggage and sent to camps surrounded by barbed wire and guarded by the military. After the war, the federal government made some payments to American Japanese who lost property, but many claims were denied on the grounds that the military had acted out of necessity (which was later proven false).

Thirty-four years later, President Gerald Ford said, "We know now what we should have known then. . . . Japanese Americans were and are loyal Americans" both in battle and at home. In 1976, Ford terminated Roosevelt's executive order, which had never been formally rescinded, against American citizens of Japanese descent.

Finally, in September 1987 Congress approved a bill that provided for a token payment—a symbolic gesture, as it was called—of $20,000 each to more than 60,000 survivors of the relocation camps. Congress also set up a fund to be used to educate the public about the internment and included an apology in the bill, which stated that "a grave injustice was done to both citizens and permanent resident aliens of Japanese ancestry by the evacuation, relocation and internment of civilians during World War II. On behalf of the Nation, the Congress apologizes."

Yet other racist and bigoted acts continued to occur. Victims of bigotry have included not only racial and religious groups but also homosexuals, the poor, handicapped people and women. New victims of prejudice may appear at any time. For example, widespread fear about the AIDS epidemic has prompted people to bar children who are AIDS victims from schools or to harass and discriminate against adults with AIDS.

Can anything be done to stop harassment and violence against people simply because of their physical handicaps, color, national background, religious preference, economic status, gender, or sexual orientation? Can prejudice be reduced? How can you counter stereotypes?

There are no simple answers. But the questions represent problems in human relations that many individuals and groups have been struggling with for decades.

Questions

1. What is "prejudice"? Can it be good? When is it wrong?
2. What is a bigot? Do you know any bigoted people? TV's Archie Bunker was a bigot. What are some of his characteristics?
3. Why were American-born Japanese sent to military camps during World War II? How can you explain the reasoning behind the presidential decision to detain them for long periods of time?
4. Who are some of the new victims of prejudice? Do you think North America is becoming less prejudiced against groups of people or more? Why?

"Just Who Am I?"

Leanne Wiens as told to Chris Lutes

Leanne Wiens is the offspring of a Vietnamese prostitute and a black soldier. She was adopted as an infant by white Canadian missionaries. She has multiracial siblings. This story is an account of her struggle to understand her racial identity.

My family is an international version of the old *Brady Bunch* TV show. Two of my brothers are from Kenya, Africa. I have two sisters who are Canadian-Indian. One brother, who was born in Canada, is "homemade." And there's me. I'm half-black and half-Vietnamese. My parents themselves are an interesting mixture. My dad, who was born in Paraguay, is of German Mennonite descent. My mom is from a Russian Mennonite background. My parents are missionaries for the Mennonite church. We are a very multi-cultural Christian family.

My parents adopted me when I was a little over 3 years old. You might say I was a product of the war. While many kids my age don't seem to know much about Vietnam, I was born in the middle of it—and because of it. My real mother was a prostitute, as far as I know, and my real father was a black American G.I.

When I was adopted, I moved into my parents' home in Canada. But that only lasted about a year. My parents became missionaries in Zambia, Africa, until I was about 8 years old. It was in Zambia that I started to become aware of my skin color. The black Africans there were fascinated by the lightness of my skin. While they thought that being white was cool, they were awed by me because I was a light-skinned black. To them I was something really special. Everybody admired my fair complexion.

Then it came time for us to go home to Canada. Before leaving the continent, however, Dad decided to take us all for a short visit to South Africa. For me, that trip became more than just a little vacation. It was the second time in my life I realized my skin color meant something. But this time it wasn't something good. In South Africa, I no longer felt like the special little girl whom my parents took so much pride in; in South Africa, no one was awed by the light-skinned black girl.

Everywhere we went, people looked at our entire family like we were a disease. I couldn't understand why South African people didn't like me. I thought it was something I'd done. One time my mother and I went into a "whites only" washroom. This black washroom attendant came in and started shouting, "She can't be in here! Can't you read the sign?" My mother responded, "She's my daughter!" The black woman yelled back, "I don't care! She can't be in here!" I couldn't understand what was going on. I mean, it was just a tiny little bathroom—not the prime minister's home. I was really upset. And scared.

A Time of Denial

Back in Canada I became increasingly aware that I was different. Not that Canadian people treated me badly or anything, but they did stare a lot. I felt like they were looking at me and my parents and thinking, *What's that black girl doing with those people? Didn't she just call that white woman "Mommy"?* My feelings about all this started to affect the way I related to my family.

One time we were walking down Fountain Street in Waterloo, and I dropped back several feet behind my mom and dad. I felt ashamed to be with them because they were white and I wasn't. That was the first of many times I would fall back or run ahead to avoid being seen with them. I remember those walks so clearly. I would shove my hands in my pockets and look down at my feet as I walked, so I wouldn't have to look into people's eyes. I'm sure I was trying to conceal my body, cover up my blackness.

For a while I prayed to God: "Why can't I have black parents?" Yet before long, my feelings went in the opposite direction, and I came to despise black Americans. I didn't know how to deal with my anger. Being adopted carries its own special hurt—you feel abandoned by your real parents. But being born simply because a black G.I. had sex with a Vietnamese prostitute made me feel like a nobody. I felt very much alone. My birth—my nationality (or lack of nationality)—became a big blank in my life.

My negative images of black Americans were reinforced by American television shows. Most of the shows portrayed blacks as just dumb people. By seventh grade, the bitterness was very deep. I'd do everything to avoid being identified with the stereotypical, American black image. I wouldn't ever listen to rap or soul music. I even became a metal-head, because that was white man's music.

My seventh- and eighth-grade years were very tough. I remember a literature teacher asking the class to write one of those "Tell Everything about Yourself" papers. When it came to describing my appearance, I just wrote that I had black hair and brown eyes. I refused to say that I was even half black.

I did everything to deny my blackness. In classes when they talked about blacks, I felt like I was being singled out; like the teacher was thinking *We're doing this for Leanne*. I admit a good bit of paranoia during this time.

I began to work very hard in school. In doing so, I thought I could escape who I was. I became a representative to the student council. I was in volleyball, basketball, broomball, and hockey. I worked hard at sports and won some awards. I wanted to be a number one player.

I also studied hard. Since I was black, I felt I had to work twice as hard as the average white person. I was determined not to be characterized by the stereotypical dumb, lazy black person. I was going to be real smart. I was going to be on the honor roll. I desperately sought to be noticed for what I did, and not for who I was. I thought achievements would hide the fact that I had black skin.

Almost Real Life

Then there was this church play. It should not have been any big deal. I was just one kid trying to act a part, yet it affected me profoundly. The name of the play was *Skin Deep*. It revolved around the story of Martin Luther King Jr. and racism in the early '60s.

My part became more than just a role; I really felt I was re-creating my black character. Play practice became an intense experience for all involved. In one scene we re-created the Rosa Parks' incident. The character playing Rosa took her seat in the "white section" of the make-believe bus. The white characters were saying things like, "Get off the bus, Nigger!" I remember not liking the guy who was playing the bus driver; he was acting so harsh. Actually my feelings were stronger than that. More like hatred. It was scary to feel hatred toward somebody. I felt like I wasn't acting; it felt like real life. That's what scared me the most. It felt so much like real life.

After play practice, the cast would often have a potluck dinner together. During this one dinner I was sitting there eating potato salad, and I heard a joke from one of the "white characters." All the white kids were keyed into it and laughed. None of the blacks joined in. It was then I realized that all of the blacks were on one side of the table; all of the whites were on the other. We were so into our characters that we didn't know when to drop the roles. We had unconsciously segregated ourselves.

Somewhere to Go

I don't know where those newfound feelings would have gone if it hadn't been for Audrey, another one of the play's black characters. During the play, we became very close. Herself a Jamaican black, she introduced me to the black culture in Waterloo.

She took me to my first black party; it was so weird to be in a room with all blacks. I never realized till then that there were so many blacks in my hometown. My parents made it a point to teach me about other cultures, but never before had I *personally experienced* a black culture.

I finally realized that I couldn't deny it anymore. My black race was a part of me. I also realized that I could treat my background as a handicap or I could use it to my advantage. That's when I started really liking myself. That year will stand in my mind until the day I die. The feeling was so strong. I remember eating supper at Audrey's house and there were only black people at the table. I felt an incredible sense of unity with these people. And I hardly knew them.

I find it really hard to explain the feelings I had when I got together with those Jamaican blacks. It's like you identify with each other's struggles and hardships. Without even talking, you can sense a unity. It's like in a soccer game. Your team is down one goal and there is a minute to play. Your team must unite, work together. You experience this unexplainable energy that drives you to pull together and make that final goal. It's like the life comes back to you.

Yet with all the positives, there was a painful and somewhat negative side to this. After a while I felt really sad because I could only experience that unity with Jamaicans. I often asked myself, *Why can't I experience that with white people? With my own family?* It was all very confusing.

An American Experience

Most recently another experience added to the confusion. My dad took a year's sabbatical from pastoring a church to attend seminary in northern Indiana. So I spent last year going to Central High School, an inner-city school in a middle-sized city.

The first morning of school I got on the bus, and the blacks were all on one side, and the whites were all on the other. At school I soon discovered that the blacks lined up in the lunch line as a group, apart from white kids. Then after lunch, the blacks gathered in the gym, with maybe one or two whites present (and those white kids had rejected their white culture). It was a sub-conscious segregation, a lot like my experience during that play potluck. But here the feelings ran deeper than a play. This was real life.

I felt like an alien around the blacks at Central. It seemed strange that in a school where about one half of the student body is black, I should feel like a minority. Yet that's how I felt. I couldn't relate to their culture, their music, their dress or their lifestyles.

Some Lessons, Some Dreams

While I still struggle with some very deep feelings about who I am, I have discovered a few things about myself recently. First off, there are no easy answers. My personal struggle has been the struggle of minorities in North America for decades. I now realize that it's a long-term struggle. My attitudes and feelings, formed over several years of experience, are slow to change. And so are everybody else's. But I must not give up—nobody must give up. Positive things can happen if we keep trying.

Next, I have discovered something about my family. Even though I am adopted, I have come to realize that I am deeply loved by my mom and dad. Time and again my parents have told me that I am special. They also believed in my potential as a person. They have never discouraged me from trying anything. At one time I wanted to be in the North American Soccer League. I wanted to be the first woman in the league. My parents never said, "No way." They said, "Go for it." I always felt that they had this attitude: "If you want to become the prime minister of Canada—go for it!"

Finally, I'm discovering that I do like myself for who I am. Not long ago, I took a good look at my life and said, "Listen, Leanne, you're 5-feet tall; medium weight; you're a good athlete; you're not gorgeous or anything, but you're kind of cute-looking; you're really outgoing. You are also a mixture of black and oriental—there's nothing you can do about it. You can never change it." And right now I don't really care to.

All in all, it's been tough working through these feelings. But I feel like a stronger person because of everything. I feel like a survivor. I know that there is a purpose in life for me now. I know that God has a purpose for my life.

Questions

1. Why did Leanne feel racially separate from her parents? What factors led her to feel uncomfortable about her race?
2. Why did Leanne have a particularly difficult time on her family's visit to South Africa?
3. How did her part in the church play make Leanne feel? Why?
4. Why did Leanne not feel a part of the black students at Central High?
5. What lessons from Leanne's struggles can you learn about your own racial identity and your relationships with those of different races?

Our Unconscious Racism

Jane Dickie

Jane Dickie did not consider herself a racist because she avoided many overt racial actions and attitudes. She failed to realize, though, that racism involves more than conscious, individual attitudes and behavior. There is an "unconscious racism" which has infected our society and "innocently" perpetuates a system of injustice.

There was a time when I believed that because I personally didn't light flaming crosses on lawns and I didn't feel racial hatred, racism had nothing to do with me. In fact, the presence of blatant racist actions around me gave me a smugness about my own purity. I could distance myself from racism because, as an individual, I didn't believe that "white is right" or that blacks were genetically inferior. I didn't use racial slurs, nor did I disapprove of busing children to equalize educational experiences.

What I failed to understand was that racism involved more than conscious, individual attitudes and behavior. Racism can be unconscious, and it can involve institutions as well as individuals.

Racism is a belief that human races have distinctive characteristics that determine their respective cultures, usually involving the idea that one's own race is superior and has the right to rule others.

Prejudice and racism are different; racism is prejudice plus power. In order to see if racism exists, one must look at who has the power to control government and society. Who has the power in the United States and in Canada?—whites. Only whites, by virtue of their control of government, business, the church, and other institutions, have the power to be racist—to determine the rules of the game. Given that power structure, people of color may be prejudiced, but they cannot be racist. Our attitudes and actions may unconsciously perpetuate white privilege and superiority. It is then that racism creeps in.

Racism creeps in when we assume that minority staff can meet only the needs of minority people, but that white staff can meet the needs of everyone. For example, black and Hispanic seminary students go primarily to black and Hispanic congregations. It seems that few congregations recognize that these gifted people of God could serve whites too.

Racism creeps in when institutions consider only whites' experiences and needs in developing products, programs, or services. For example, when schools and colleges teach world literature that is really white European or American literature, or history which excludes black or Hispanic or native American perspectives, it is racism. None of this is conscious. It occurs at an institutional level, but it affects us all in damaging ways.

Racism also creeps in when we believe that our country is a melting pot. When white norms, values, and perspectives are considered American or Canadian, other views take on an alien air. We are saying, "We can all be united if you become just like us."

Racism creeps in when we deny racism. "I don't see black people. I don't see color. People are people." The good intention is obvious. But does this mean, at an unconscious level, that we don't see a heritage or culture separate from the dominant white one? That we don't see the beauty of rich brown skin or curly dark hair?

Racism creeps in when we believe that in the United States and Canada all are treated equally. This denies white privilege, which is still very real. It may be illegal to discriminate in jobs or housing, but a recent study has shown that it is still very common. Being born white in this country increases the probability of better housing, better schooling, a better job and income, and better medical care.

Often our unconscious behavior supports white privilege and undermines our Christian love for all of God's people.

These actions are not blatant, their intent is not to do harm, but the effect perpetuates a system of injustice.

Racism creeps in when we tell and laugh at racist jokes.

Racism creeps in when we conduct business with companies that discriminate. Who repairs our church buildings? Who constructs our sidewalks and parking lots? What accountants and lawyers do we hire? Do we check to be sure these are equal opportunity employers? Do we ask how many minority employees they have and in what capacities? We should.

Racism creeps in when we use pro-white, anti-black language. Perhaps this is part of the reason that Jesse Jackson and others have called for the term "African American" to replace "black." What do we mean when we say our choice is "black and white"? Are we unconsciously equating white with good and black with evil?

We must combat racism because it is a lie and it is a sin. Racism robs us of seeing God in all creation, in all people. It prevents us from doing God's will on earth.

The first step is to acknowledge that we are racist. Then prayerfully and humbly we must learn to act against white privilege. We cannot do it alone. In a Christian community, we must lovingly criticize one another. We must be ready to create structures which challenge unconscious racist actions and behavior. Finally and most importantly, we can pray for God's guidance. For the love of God, for the love of our neighbor, let us continue the struggle against racism.

Questions

1. What does Dickie mean by "unconscious racism." Can you suggest an example from your own life?
2. What steps does Dickie suggest to combat racism?

Medical Ethics

Should Treatment Be Terminated?

Clifford E. Bajema

Clifford E. Bajema is a Christian Reformed pastor in Madison, Wisconsin. This selection, which was originally published in The Banner, *deals with the variety of circumstances where the removal of life-support systems may be considered. He discusses euthanasia, mercy killing, and benemortasia.*

The recent case of Infant Doe, in Bloomington, Indiana, is an apt illustration of where the moral revolution and the drift to humanism, with its growing disrespect for human life, is bringing us. Infant Doe was born with Down's syndrome. The degree of retardation could not be determined at first, but the child also had an esophageal obstruction requiring surgery. When the parents refused to authorize surgery or to authorize any number of other eager couples to become legal guardians of the child, the case came into the Indiana courts. Incredibly, the Indiana Supreme Court refused to order surgery and thus sanctioned homicide by starvation. George Will, *Washington Post* Writers Group columnist, and himself a parent of a ten-year-old boy with Down's syndrome, had this to say after Infant Doe's death:

"There is no reason—none—to doubt that if the baby had not had Down's syndrome the operation would have been ordered without hesitation, almost certainly, by the parents, or, if not by them, by the courts. Therefore the baby was killed because it was retarded."

The broader issue raised by a case like that of Infant Doe is that of when to terminate medical treatment. This incredibly complex issue eludes precise definition or arbitration. Yet, as the life-saving technologies multiply, unquestionably it becomes even more incumbent upon Christian ethicists to spell out guidelines in this important area of moral problematics.

The difficulties surrounding the discussion of decisions to terminate treatment begin already with a confusion about the meaning of the term *euthanasia*. The literal, etymological meaning of euthanasia (from the Greek *eu* [well] + *thanatos* [death]) is "good death." This definition says nothing about any *action* that brings about a happy death. It is simply a descriptive term and may as such be equated with "death with dignity."

In Cases Involving Definite Prognosis of Imminent Death. A second-level definition of euthanasia, involving an action I favor, would be this: any action of withholding life-support mechanisms or life-extending procedures (sometimes called "heroic" or "extraordinary" means of life support) in cases where there is terminal, incurable illness/injury resulting in a definite prognosis of imminent death. I am even in favor of withholding the same if there is a definite diagnosis of a complete and irreversible loss of the functioning of the entire brain. Without an alive brain, the dynamic equilibrium of the body's systems cannot be indefinitely maintained. Sometimes this second-level definition has been called *passive*, or *negative, euthanasia*. However, it is not yet mercy killing at this level.

Action on this second level, in my view, must be taken with the intention of permitting the terminally ill person to die with dignity and of allowing death to come naturally to the dying person.

In the extraordinary case of a person diagnosed as subject to the complete and irreversible loss of the function of the entire brain, and yet whose vital functions of respiration and circulation are maintained mechanically, this action not only ensures that the terminal person can die naturally and with dignity, but it also protects the living from the inappropriate expectation to perform heroic duties of care.

In Cases of Serious Brain Injury. A third-level definition of euthanasia, involving an action I definitely do not favor, would be this: any action of withholding or withdrawing life-support mechanisms or life-extending procedures from patients who are not definitely prognosed as faced with imminent death or definitely diagnosed as subject to a complete and irreversible loss of the functioning of the entire brain. Such an action, if done for reason of serious brain injury (perhaps resulting in coma), severe retardation, painful disease, or advanced senility, is obviously taken with the intention of hastening the death of a person whose life is considered meaningless, no longer worth living. The way to help people whose lives lack sufficient "quality of life" is, in this view, to give them "death with dignity."

Here dignity is mistakenly understood to reside in the rational capacity to willfully regulate life and death. Here personhood is separated from bodiliness and is associated exclusively with self-consciousness, sentient life, and intelligent purposefulness. Although this third-level definition would also have to be classified as passive or negative euthanasia, the *motivation* here has changed, the Judeo-Christian view of personhood has been altered, and the result is indirect mercy killing.

It is especially on this third level that the decision to terminate treatment becomes extremely problematic. I think, for example, of Ernie's brother.

Ernie asked me to go visit his brother in the hospital. I didn't know the man, but went anyway, for Ernie's sake. Ernie's brother had had a serious stroke, had lain in the intensive care unit for three weeks, and was now recovering, but still suffering partial paralysis.

I said, "Hello, I'm Cliff. Ernie sent me. May I visit with you for a few minutes?"

"Yes, yes of course."

We shared a few moments of get-acquainted small talk, when, without warning, Ernie's brother suffered another massive stroke. His rolled-up eyes and bluish-white face sent me rushing to the nurses' station for help.

The hospital "code-blue squad" was prompt and efficient with all their gadgetry of survival, but still it seemed far too many minutes before Ernie's brother had pulse and respiration again, with the help of a breathing apparatus.

Back at the intensive care unit I waited for the alarmed family to come out after their conference with the doctor. Their reddened eyes revealed the gravity of the situation. They said the doctor felt that their unconscious loved one was almost surely a vegetable now. He probably had been without oxygen too long. What did the family think about pulling the plug? the doctor inquired.

"What do you think?" they asked me pleadingly.

"I think it best to wait a while," was all I could say at the moment. "And pray for God's leading and help in this situation."

We prayed for healing, we asked for guidance, and we waited.

The next morning, to the amazement of everyone, Ernie's brother regained consciousness and spoke a few words. He was rational!

"What if we had pulled the plug?" I thought.

Several weeks later, Ernie's brother suffered still a third attack and died. But during the weeks before his death, he talked with me much about God and, I believe, found his spiritual peace. The last time death came knocking, Ernie's brother was ready to open the door.

But how close he came to having the door opened for him—too soon. And not because he was considered terminal, but because he probably had become a vegetable.

In Cases of Terminal Illness. A fourth-level definition of euthanasia, involving action to which I am most strongly opposed, would be the following: any action of quickly and painlessly putting to death persons suffering from terminal illnesses, from distressing diseases, or from debilitating conditions (such as severe retardation, senility in old age, prolonged unconsciousness etc.) which have rendered their lives "meaningless." Here, obviously, "meaningless life" is tied in with a deficient "quality of life" which then calls for "death with dignity." This fourth-level definition of euthanasia can be classified as *active*, or *positive, euthanasia*, with the end result being direct mercy killing.

Because *euthanasia* is a term used in so many different ways by so many different people (much to the satisfaction of mercy-killing proponents), it would seem best to avoid calling levels one and two euthanasia and to limit its meaning to levels three and four. Thus *euthanasia* and *mercy killing* become interchangeable terms. This, incidently, is the way most modern dictionaries now handle the term.

For levels one and two, I much prefer to use a descriptive Latin term, coined by Arthur Dyck, *benemortasia* from *bene* (good) and *mors* (death). In the ethic of benemortasia, the idea of "mercy" is separated from the idea of "killing," such that "it is merciful not to kill," and "it is merciful to provide care for the dying and irremediably handicapped where consent is obtained without coercion." In instances where consent is impossible, as with those who are severely brain-damaged or unalterably comatose, ordinary life-support measures should be continued to the end and extraordinary measures used until all reasonable hope of sustaining life is virtually gone. "The difference," says Arthur Dyck, "between beneficient euthanasia and our ethic of benemortasia is that, whereas the former would deliberately induce death, the latter, as a last resort after making every effort to save and repair life, mercifully retreats in the face of death's inevitability."

I do not pretend to have given the definitive word on this complex issue, nor to have resolved all potential dilemmas. Also, it should be remembered that I write as an ethicist, not as a legislator or attorney. The guidelines I suggest are precisely and only that, moral guidelines, not prescriptions for the wording of legal statutes. The book by Germain Grisez and Joseph M. Boyle, Jr., *Life and Death with Liberty and Justice*, may be the best treatment available of the jurisprudential issues. Thomas C. Oden in *Should Treatment Be Terminated?* has also done a brilliant job of bringing light to this subject.

Questions

1. What is euthanasia? What is the difference between active and passive euthanasia?
2. Describe the circumstances where euthanasia would become mercy killing.
3. What defines personhood? Has a patient in a deep coma lost his or her personhood? Who decides?

Brave New Harvest

Andrew Simons

In "Brave New Harvest" Andrew Simons addresses the issue of fetal cell research and implants. Several ethical questions arise: Is the fetus a cadaver or a victim? Do fetal cell researchers "play God"? Do the benefits of fetal cell implantation justify the procedure? What role is the Church called to exercise in the shaping of public opinion?

Wednesday and Thursday mornings, medical technician Lisa Norris drives from her job at the University of Colorado Health Sciences Center in Denver to a local abortion clinic and dissects the remains of aborted fetuses. She is looking for the pancreas, the gland that produces insulin. After "harvesting" pancreases from a number of fetuses, she takes them back to her lab at the university, which has become the national hub for fetal-tissue research. There, she minces the tissue and further prepares it for surgery.

In surgery, doctors tuck this insulin producing tissue beneath the surface of the kidney in a patient suffering from diabetes. If the graft works, the cells will begin producing natural insulin, furnishing the patient with an improved ability to process and regulate sugars in her body, thereby improving her overall health. Surgeons have performed similar operations for Parkinson's disease sufferers, and researchers are currently investigating whether such implants might also help schizophrenics, Alzheimer's patients, and victims of spinal-cord injuries.

Norris, who describes herself as "prolife" and a "strong Christian," says the issues of abortion and fetal-cell implants are separate and ethically unrelated to each other. "We're trying to derive some benefit out of this situation. That's how I justify it," she says. Most ethicists agree with her. But are abortion and fetal-cell implants really separate issues? Should human suffering be a society's controlling concern in deciding whether to use new medical technologies? Are these new technologies dependent on immoral and unbiblical actions and attitudes?

Diabetes

Fetal-cell implant surgery is theoretically similar to replacing a car's wornout parts with new ones. Surgeons take cells from various organs of aborted fetuses and transplant them into adults suffering from various diseases. (Fetal tissue is preferred because it has a much higher chance of being accepted by the immune system of the receiving patient.) Surgeries differ depending on which "part" in the body has "worn out." A brief look at diabetes and Parkinson's disease will bear this out.

Diabetes strikes more than 11 million people nationally. The problem with those who suffer from diabetes is that their pancreases are unable to produce enough of the chemical insulin. The body needs insulin to process sugars and carbohydrates. Complications from diabetes can result in blindness, organ damage, loss of limbs, coma, and death. Ten percent of those who suffer from the condition have Type I diabetes, meaning that they are dependent on insulin treatments, usually self-injected with hypodermic needles. (Type II diabetes can normally be controlled by diet and exercise.) There is currently no cure for diabetes.

Greg Fujita, 36, was diagnosed with Type I diabetes when he was two years old. By age 32 he was learning to adjust to glaucoma and had undergone seven eye operations, including the removal of cataracts from both eyes and surgery on the blood vessels in his eyes, which had started to bleed. Apart from the specter of possible blindness, limb loss, or death, Fujita says it is the routine problems associated with diabetes that are frustrating: not being able to eat ice cream with friends on summer nights, or go on backpacking trips to remote areas, plus the uncontrollable mood swings that often accompany fluctuating blood-sugar levels.

In 1982 his kidneys began to fail. In early 1986 he went in for a kidney transplant and a new experimental procedure: the grafting of a small amount of fetal pancreatic tissue under his kidney. The results of the procedure performed at the University of Colorado were significant. After six months, the fetal tissue began to produce insulin, reducing Fujita's need for daily treatments by 60 percent. And he also resumed what had been an active life, full of skiing, racquetball, and running. "I don't really agree with people who are for abortion," he says, "but the operation has enabled me to live a more normal life." To date, 24 kidney-transplant patients at the university have undergone the procedure.

Parkinson's disease

Parkinson's disease, which affects about 500,000 Americans, destroys cells in the brain that manufacture dopamine, the chemical that allows smooth walking and lucid speaking. Thus, shaking of the hands, head, and feet, and general body rigidity characterize the disease. In November 1988, in the first operation of its kind in the United States, surgeons at the University of Colorado drilled a quarter-sized hole into the skull of 52-year-old Parkinson's victim Don Nelson and implanted fetal brain cells deep into his brain. (Yale University surgeons performed a similar operation one month later. To date, there have been nine implants performed in the United States for Parkinson's.)

Traditional treatments had failed Nelson, but following the surgery he reports that his "voice is much stronger, I can speak much plainer, my memory is improving and my mind is sharper and not confused. I can walk around the house or in my yard without cane or crutches." The operating surgeon, Curt Freed, a University of Colorado medical school professor, says fetal cells provide the cell growth necessary for dopamine production.

Cadaver or victim?

Citing ethical concerns, the National Institutes of Health in the last days of the Reagan administration declared a halt to the use of federal funds in fetal research. This ban effectively stopped research, except in programs like the ones at the University of Colorado and Yale, where the research is privately funded. The ban, however, has not stopped the debate among ethicists, who can basically be divided into two camps: those who support research on the grounds that the fetus is a cadaver, and those who oppose *most* research on the grounds that the fetus is a victim.

Arguing the cadaver justification, John Robertson, law professor at the University of Texas, says the fetus is essentially an organ donor, and that abortion is an ethically separate issue. "The issue is whether or not the tissue will be used or simply disposed of," he says. "What would be wrong with using it to help someone with a horrible disease?" Robertson would also allow a woman to get pregnant for the sole purpose of getting an abortion to provide tissue for her husband or child who needed it.

Arthur Caplan, director of the Center for Biomedical Ethics at the University of Minnesota, would draw the line at "creating a tragedy [abortion] for some other good" but agrees that the fetus is essentially a cadaver. And, he adds, laws regulating use of cadavers have been in place for more than 20 years.

Arguing the victim rationale, Allen Verhey, professor of religion at Hope College and coeditor of *On Moral Medicine,* says a distinction must first be made between elective abortions and nonelective abortions that happen as a result of miscarriage or are performed to save the life of the mother. Verhey agrees with Robertson and Caplan that doctors may ethically use fetal tissue from nonelective abortions in research and surgeries. But he argues that trying to separate the issue of *elective* abortion from fetal-tissue use overlooks the context and associations in which fetuses come into the world. "It comes back to 'Shall we do evil that good may come?' " concludes Vernon C. Grounds, president of Evangelicals for Social Action.

At what price?
Those who see the fetus as cadaver and those who see the

fetus as victim agree on one issue: Since abortion is currently legal, fetal tissue will be abundant for the foreseeable future. Because of this widespread availability, fetal tissue will not be sold on the market nor will couples conceive for the purpose of providing tissue to someone else. As it turns out, surgeons do not want to use genetically related tissue because of concerns that it might be carrying the same disease as the patient. It is also illegal under current federal law to buy or sell fetal tissue. But the groups' paths diverge on the central question of whether the goals, standards, and motives underlying this new technology are ethical and moral.

The goal of fetal-implant surgery is to relieve human suffering. "Society will not tolerate killing one life for another," Caplan says in arguing against the thought of getting pregnant for the purpose of providing fetal tissue for someone else. But, as he told an advisory panel to the National Institutes of Health, "Those who would adhere to principle must be willing to answer the question: At what price?"

But human suffering cannot be the trump card in evaluating new medical technologies, says Kathleen Nolan, physician and ethicist at the Hastings Center, a secular research and educational institution in New York. "There is a tendency to go in that direction," she says. "Some researchers have even wanted to take tissue from *living* fetuses, but that's been tabled."

The laudable goal of wanting to alleviate human suffering may ignore the fact that God, and not humanity, is sovereign over human suffering. "If we start with the premise that we're going to totally alleviate human suffering, we'll fail," Verhey says. "Such an attitude takes the problem of solving evil out of God's hands and puts it into human hands. The goal in suffering is not always to eliminate it but to share in it—to weep with those who weep, especially when we can solve the suffering technologically but *can't* morally."

Whose consent?

The fetus-as-cadaver argument also sets the standards by which the use of fetuses is justified. With cadaver experimentation, researchers must gain consent before proceeding. Consent comes either from the person prior to death or from the deceased's family after death.

In the case of fetal research, the fetus is a cadaver after the abortion, and the mother is the family member who grants consent. "I disapprove of car deaths and homicides," Robertson says, "but not against the use of those cadavers in research. It's the same thing with fetal cadavers. And even though it's true that you're deliberately killing the fetus, abortions are still legal."

But the consent issue is trickier than that. Verhey disputes whether a mother's consent following an elective abortion—as opposed to an abortion to save the life of the mother—is true consent. "One of the reasons we allow next-of-kin to give consent is that they're presumed to have the person's best interest at heart. But on the face of it, that is called into question by the fact that they've elected to have an abortion. The parents have, in effect, refused their parental identity over the child, and when that identity is called into question, then so is the justification behind the consent."

Playing God

The motive behind fetal-cell implants is a desire to develop more effective methods of treating debilitating diseases. But the biblical doctrine of sin suggests another important, if unstated, motive behind such research. "I think these researchers are slipping into playing God," says John White, retired psychiatrist and author. "All research arises out of a view of the universe, and secular doctors view matter as a thing in itself without reference to God. A scientist either takes the role of a magician or prophet. The prophet hears the word and obeys it. The power and authority of the prophet spring from his desire to be obedient to God.

"The magician, on the other hand, desires power in and of itself and wants God's power to do miracles. He may not call it God's power, but he lusts to play a God-like role. This magician's mentality is almost universal in scientific research."

Thus, starting points determine ending points. Those who view aborted fetuses as cadavers will usually support the goals, standards, and motives supporting most fetal research. Those who view aborted fetuses as victims will usually oppose the goals, standards, and motives cited in fetal research.

The church's response

Much of the moral strength of the prolife position comes from the fact that convenience or the unwillingness to suffer consequences prompts most abortions. According to a 1989 *Boston Globe* poll, more than 90 percent of abortions are performed because of the emotional strain or inconvenience—economic or personal—to a mother carrying a baby to term (75 to 90 percent of voters polled would oppose abortion for such reasons). But the church can hardly fault diabetics, Parkinson's victims, and others for taking hope from a new medical procedure. Nor can we discount their real affliction without, in the words of Isaiah, "hiding ourselves from our own flesh."

The church needs to formulate cohesive arguments before going out into the world. "We need some kind of dialogue between theologians . . . and researchers," says White. "It's also important that we minister to the doctors in the church who are doing this kind of research, providing them with theological guidelines."

Local churches can strive to influence the perspectives of their surrounding communities. "It is important that the church call the idolatry of technology idolatry," Verhey says. "It's also important that they shape the ethos of the community with respect to the unborn. And we can also shape the ethos by demonstrating other responses to suffering besides the technological response; i.e., we can endure and share suffering together."

Attitudes toward abortion will continue to control most of the debate over the ethics of fetal-cell implants. For those Christians opposed to elective abortion, however, the issue becomes complicated because of the laudatory goals of those trying to help persons suffering from diabetes, Parkinson's, and other diseases. The church cannot just say no to these people in regard to this procedure. It must also say yes to them in tangible ways.

Questions

1. What is fetal cell harvesting? How is this technology used for the benefit of people with debilitating diseases?
2. What is Lisa Norris's justification for fetal cell implants? What do you think of her argument?
3. Do you think a fetus is a cadaver or a victim? Why?
4. Do you think it is ever right to do something wrong in order for something good to result? Is this question always "black and white," or are there shades of gray?

Imaging God in Sickness and in Health

Hessel Bouma III, Douglas Diekema, Edward Langerak, Theodore Rottman, and Allen Verhey

This selection was excerpted from a book entitled Christian Faith, Health, and Medical Practice. *The authors deal with the issue of humans as God's image bearers in creation. They outline five broad biblical principles which guide the reader to a fuller understanding of image bearing. Because humankind bears both the imprint of God and nature, medical ethics needs to take into account God's revelation in Scripture and creation.*

What the Bible says about the image of God reveals a number of important points. First, it gives embodied human beings a special moral status, as Genesis 9:6 makes clear, by prohibiting murder because persons are imagers of God: "Whoever sheds the blood of man, by man shall his blood be shed; for God made man in his own image." Wrongfully spilling human blood is viewed as the iconoclastic desecration of God's image. In fact, even cursing persons is forbidden because it is a contradiction to praise God and curse God's image: "With [the tongue] we bless the Lord and Father, and with it we curse men, who are made in the likeness of God. . . . this ought not to be so" (Jas. 3:9-10). And the Heidelberg Catechism (Q. and A. 105) forbids insulting our neighbors in deed or in thought as well. In other words, not just certain behaviors but certain attitudes are unfitting toward other human beings. Or, to put it positively, some of the attitudes we have toward God we should have, in a derivative way, toward God's imagers. Thus, some of the same kind of fear we have toward God is also appropriate toward those who bear God's image. Experiencing the fear of God should not be reduced to being scared, but it should be associated with feelings of reverence and awe, feelings elicited by God's goodness, holiness, majesty, power, and kingship. Creatures who represent God both by mirroring God and by being God's delegates (having the authority to rule in God's name) should be valued and loved; love of God and neighbor, after all, is Jesus' basic ethic. And seeing our neighbors as bearing God's image can help us love them, even when they are otherwise unlovable. As John Calvin advises, we should ". . . look upon the image of God in them, which cancels and effaces their transgressions, and with its beauty and dignity allures us to love and embrace them" (Institutes X.vi.31). It is important to notice that Christian love is influenced by awe for the nature of its object—an imager of God. "Sanctity" is the term many religious persons use to characterize that which elicits their reverence. As Richard Stith writes, the sanctity of personal life calls for a love that has a "stand-backish" element and not just an urge to value, to nurture, or to control:

> Reverence, by contrast [to valuing], eschews domination. It steps back before the "sanctity" of that which is revered, and thus necessarily before every particular which has sanctity. A limit is given to us and to our schemes of domination. We can no longer destroy and rebuild as we wish, but must accept and accommodate being, even the being of individuals. If I revere human life, if I say it has sanctity, then rather than making and controlling it, I acknowledge and defer to it, I let it be (p. 6).

Thus, those who image God are to be loved reverentially, even deferentially, a point that will be relevant when we discuss such topics as violating a person's right to informed consent or killing a person out of love. Of course, there may also be secular reasons for reverencing the sanctity of persons and perceiving them as having a dignity beyond price (Kant, 103), but the biblical theme of being created in God's image implies that the basis of a Christian's disposition toward people is fundamentally a religious feeling and responsibility.

The second biblical point to notice is that God's decision to create human beings in itself designated their suitability for a specific role: "Let us make man in our image, after our likeness; and let them have dominion over the fish of the sea, and over the birds of the air, and over the cattle, and over all the earth, and over every creeping thing that creeps upon the earth" (Gen. 1:26). The psalmist celebrates both the human role and the special nature of those called to it: "Yet thou hast made him little less than God, and dost crown him with glory and honor. Thou hast given him dominion over the works of thy hands; thou hast put all things under his feet" (Ps. 8:5-6). The implication of these passages is that God did not arbitrarily select a species of creatures for special status, conferring on its members an "alien dignity." Rather, we human beings are specifically constituted for the role of representing God both in the sense of mirroring God as rulers and in the sense of being God's delegates and having the authority to be stewards over creation. Since our suitability for this stewardly role requires the capacity for reflective choice-making, we infer that we image God by virtue of our being givers and hearers of reasons, beings who not only make choices but also reflect on them and make choices about our choices, who not only have desires but also have desires about our desires, who not only evaluate but also evaluate our evaluations, who not only think but also think about our thinking. These capacities, in turn, require not just consciousness but self-consciousness, the sort of "reflexivity" (Van Leeuwen, 127) which provides us with the freedom and creativity that enable our choices to be more than previously determined responses to stimuli. Other organisms may, in some sense, think and choose, but the integrated functioning of the human organism provides for a referring to itself that constitutes a capacity for choosing how to choose. With this capacity comes the responsibility to exercise it in the way that our good and wise creator intended, and consciousness of this responsibility is the foundation of our moral sense. So an important part of imaging God is recognizing and accepting the exhilarating freedom and the sobering burden of making moral judgments about proper stewardship.

The third biblical point to note about the image of God is that God's imagers were created both male and female, implying both that stewardship will be exercised in community and that community will be created through human sexuality. As with other creatures, this sexuality is natural and instinctive, but in self-reflective humans it is also controllable by the very stewardly responsibilities and moral sense by virtue of which we image God. This responsibility is part of the larger responsibility that we have toward one another as communal individuals—that is, as individuals whose identities are not just those of individual atoms but are constituted by deep, caring relationships with others. We are not simply individuals who happen to have relationships with other individuals; in an important sense we *are* those relationships. Our identities can overflow into others because our relationships involve not just the capacity to sympathize, to feel *for* others, but also the capacity to empathize, to feel *with* others, to transcend ourselves and "get inside" the viewpoint of others. We are "embodied" not just as individuals in physical bodies but also as "relatives" in a moral and spiritual body of which we are members. The depth, creativity, and character of these caring relationships are in turn conditioned by our ability to symbolically interact with each other, not just to exchange signs but to communicate by infusing these signs with infinitely rich and textured meanings, meanings that can be passed on and developed into profoundly interesting and distinctive cultures. Genesis portrays Adam's naming of the creation as the beginning of his caring for it, caring that for us involves the ability to envision reality, to imagine how it might be different, and to use aesthetic and moral sensitivities to desire and create changes in it (Gaylin, "In Defense"). These characteristics enable us to converse with God, and they presumably have to do with why God wants to converse with us, although they may not entirely answer the psalmist's question " What is man that thou art mindful of him?" (Ps. 8:4).

So the Bible implies that human persons are all in a four-fold relationship: we are in relationship with God as created representatives, with the rest of his creation as stewards, with each other as community members, and with ourselves as self-reflective creatures. And these relationships interpenetrate and condition one another: it is as self-reflective, free, and responsible beings that we recognize our caring relationship with others, our stewardly relationship with creation, and our creaturely but imaging relationship with God. Losing sight of any one of these relationships or misconstruing its character will warp the rest of them, as we will suggest when discussing the covenantal ethic that flows from these relationships.

A fourth biblical point to notice is that we are imagers of God who live in a fallen condition. Our hearts—the biblical term for the center of our being, including our minds and our affections—are directed away from God and therefore away from our proper relationships with God, with ourselves, with others, and with God's creation. Idolatry and self-deification alternating with self-debasement, hatred and depersonalization alternating with deification of others, and destructive exploitation of nature alternating with pantheism (deification of creation)—these have become the dispositions of the human heart. This does not mean we have completely lost our imaging of God: neither Genesis 9:6 (which, as we saw, forbids murdering any person because that would be an iconoclastic desecration of God's image) nor Psalm 8 (which, as we saw, celebrates the ruling status of humankind) is restricted to pre-Fall persons. Many Reformed theologians distinguish here between imaging God in a broader, structural or static sense and imaging God in a narrower, functional, or dynamic sense (Hoekema, 83-85). In the former sense even fallen persons have God-like capacities, but in the latter sense fallen persons do not exercise those capacities in true knowledge, righteousness, and holiness. We fallen persons still represent God, but we do so in a perverted way, as funhouse mirrors distort images, making them recognizable but twisted. Even our instincts retain a vestige of human nature as it was created: nurturing, caring, and stewardly dispositions are common in fallen humanity, as are a sense of moral obligation and, as Calvin says, a longing for God *(sensus divinitatus)*. Ruined nobility can often be recognized—not only as ruined but also as nobility (Plantinga, 11).

The fifth biblical point to note about imaging God is not only the good news that in Jesus we have a new model for imaging God—"He reflects the glory of God and bears the very stamp of his nature . . ." (Heb. 1:3)—but also that we have in that model one whose reconciling and redeeming work can save us and restore to us the ability to image God as God intended—"And we all . . . are being changed into his likeness from one degree of glory to another" (2 Cor. 3:18). So there are in human beings not only a created and a fallen imaging but also a redeemed and, eventually, a perfected imaging of God (Hoekema, 82-95). Because Christians will be informed not only by *natural* dispositions (which, because they are distorted by the Fall, can also be called *unnatural*) but also by what the biblical story reveals about the creator's intention for those dispositions, Christian ethics, including medical ethics, should ignore neither what God has written on the hearts of all people (Rom. 2:15) nor what has been revealed in the biblical story.

Questions

1. Why is murder wrong? Why are "murderous" thoughts condemned along with murderous actions?
2. Why is it significant to image bearing that humans are created male and female?
3. What four relationships play a role in our image bearing?
4. How does the discussion of humankind as image bearer relate to this section's topic—medical ethics?

When is it OK to Tell the Doctor to Pull the Plug?

Tony Campolo

Tony Campolo is a popular speaker, author, and sociology professor at Eastern College. He is known for being very out-spoken on behalf of the urban poor and for providing oppor-tunities for teens to help the poor. In this selection, taken from his book 20 Hot Potatoes Christians Are Afraid to Touch, *Campolo explores the issue of whether it is right to "pull the plug" when a patient is critically and irreversibly ill.*

In the motion picture, *Rollerball*, one of the main characters has an accident in which his head is crushed and his brain is rendered dead. However, the rest of his body organs are still healthy. His heart is still capable of pumping blood. His lungs still have the capacity to process oxygen and expel carbon dioxide. His liver still can process bile and keep his body "clean." All the organs can function with optimum efficiency if only the body is hooked up to machines that provide the electrical energy to keep them going.

This man's best friend, his teammate in the game of Roller-ball, has more than enough money to pay the hospital what is necessary to keep the machine going indefinitely—and he decides to do it. He decides to keep the brain-dead body of his friend "alive" in spite of the enormous cost involved. He regu-larly visits the man who had been his friend, meditating as he sits for hours by the "living" biological remains of a man who once has been the dearest person in the world to him.

Is he doing what a Christian should do? I doubt it—for several reasons.

First of all, there is the obvious matter of stewardship. The money that is being used to keep this insensible body pumping and breathing might be better used. In a hospital in Haiti, children die because there is not enough money to buy basic medicines such as penicillin. In India, young men are immobilized because there is no money to pay for artificial limbs. And in affluent America, there are children with burns or birth defects who will be disfigured for the rest of their lives because they cannot afford the plastic surgery they need. How is it possible to justify huge expenditure to sustain a brain-dead body when the money could do so much for so many of the living?

The economic factors related to sustaining the bodies of persons who have been pronounced brain dead is not just a hypothetical consideration for thousands of families across this country. Recently a friend of mine had to make a life-or-death decision for her husband, who had been rendered brain dead by a disease. Maintaining his body was exhausting the limited financial resources at her disposal, resources that her husband had worked a lifetime to put together. Their hopes and dreams of a college education for her two daughters, as well as her own hopes for a decent life, were wrapped up in those resources. All of a sudden, what had seemed to be a solid basis for meeting the future needs of this family was threatened.

My friend would gladly have made any sacrifice if she had believed there was some hope that her husband might once again be conscious. But such a hope was scientifically impossible. Once the brain dies, whatever knowledge and awareness it held is gone. Brain death is like magnetically erasing the message on a cassette. Once what is there is gone, it is gone forever. When the doctor asked my friend if he should disconnect the machine that was maintaining her husband's bodily functions, she gave her consent. I believe she did the right thing.

Doctors and medical ethicists have thought long and hard about what to do in such instances. Those in the social sciences also have reflected upon the morality of "pulling the plug," as the dilemma is succinctly labeled. I think that what they have to say on this subject can provide help for Christians who have to make hard decisions when loved ones are physically alive but brain dead.

What happens in brain death is that the electronic impulses that run through the brain cells and are essential to the thinking process cease. The cessation of brain waves is registered on an electronic device. No value judgments need be made as to whether or not it happens. When the brain dies, the dial on the electroencephalograph tells us so. And once the brain dies, there is no reviving it. The deterioration of the brain cells starts immediately.

With regard to understanding what makes a person human, social scientists often contend that the conscious interaction the person has with others is of crucial significance. They argue that all those qualities which make humans distinct from other higher primates come through meaningful exchanges with those significant persons who help us to achieve humanness.

When asked to list the traits that establish the infinite qualitative differences between humans and animals, we are likely to come up with traits that are acquired through interpersonal relationships, such as symbolic thinking. We might also include having a conscience to influence our behavior. Some would say that to be human is to have an awareness of self and a consciousness of our inevitable future—which is death. The list could go on and on.

However, when all is said and done, most social scientists would claim that all such traits are taken on by the humanized homo sapien because he or she is caught up in interactive relationships with others. They would claim that individuals become human through a process which they call socialization.

If all this seems a bit too technical, suffice it to say that our humanity is a gift that comes to us from other people. This is not to say that God is not involved. Those who believe that it is God who makes us human simply contend that God does

His work of creating our humanity through the agency of the significant other persons who are part of our lives.

If this argument from social scientists is accepted, then we may easily be led to believe that our humanness is so tied up in conscious relationships with others that when those relationships are impossible, as in the case of brain death, what makes us human is gone. All of those qualities which enable us to transcend animals seem to depend upon our having an awareness of others. When this awareness is no longer possible, it may be said that a person is dead.

There are those who argue that none of this takes into consideration whether or not the vegetating body still has a soul. Those who assert this seem to think that the soul is some kind of thing that God puts into people at birth or conception. In reality, biblical scholars teach us that when the Scriptures employ the word "soul," they are referring to the totality of the human personality. A soul is all that an individual becomes in the course of a lifetime, and it is this sum total of a person's humanity, created over the years, which survives the grave. With brain death, the personhood or soul is no longer alive in the body, and it is on this basis that the plug can be pulled and bodily remains allowed to expire.

But brain death is not the only situation in which there is a question of whether or not to turn off life support systems. Even more difficult perhaps, is the situation in which a person who is fully conscious as being kept alive by artificial means and is ready to die.

Beth, the wife of a dear friend, had a disease that rendered several of her vital organs inoperative. She would have died had doctors not hooked her up to an array of machines that kept her alive. Beth was in constant pain. The drugs which were supposed to deaden the pain were no longer effective, and the doctors talked about some kind of surgery that would sever the connections of her nervous system. Beth begged that nothing more be done to her and that she be allowed to die the death that would have been hers were it not for the miracles of medical science. The doctors felt that it was their duty to prolong her life as long as possible, but Beth's husband persuaded them to let her die. He and his wife and worked through the stages of dying (see the writing of Elisabeth Kübler-Ross) and had come to accept Beth's death with grace and faith. The doctors granted her request and, in accord with her husband's agreement with her in this matter, "pulled the plug." I believe that Beth and her husband decided to do the right thing.

In this case, pulling the plug by no means brought about Beth's death. The cause of her death was the disease that had destroyed her body. All that was decided was to stop fighting what God would have allowed to happen had it not been for human interference.

I am not suggesting that interfering with the process of dying is wrong or sinful. That is what modern medicine is all about. Instead, I am suggesting that people do have the right to decide when such interference should end. When continuing life through artificial means causes horrendous pain and exorbitant expense or diminishes the dignity of a dying person, then the decision to keep that person alive seems immoral to me.

Please understand that I am *not* talking about euthanasia, or "mercy killing." Mercy killing requires actively *doing* something—such as giving a pill or injection—to bring life to an end. In Beth's case, the decision was simply to *stop doing* what was prolonging life in an unnatural manner. Mercy killing involves unnatural death. For Beth, death was a very natural thing. Nobody was playing God when the plug was pulled.

Recently a friend of mine received a phone call from someone who was close to her. The caller said he wanted to borrow eight hundred dollars in order to travel to Holland where euthanasia is legal. He has been infected with the AIDS virus and was already experiencing its painful effects. Rather than die a slow and agonizing death, this young man had opted to go to a country where it was legal to receive a painless lethal injection.

My friend, who cares deeply for this young man, turned down his request. She believes that euthanasia is a way of playing God and, therefore, should not be practiced by any of us.

I am convinced she is right. While I understand those who advocate euthanasia, I just do not approve of it. When it comes to human life, I believe the Lord gives it and that only the Lord has the right to take it away.

The church has never accepted suicide or murder, and euthanasia is only suicide or murder by another name. In all of these matters, we must heed Scripture, which says:

> I call heaven and earth to record this day against you, that I have set before you life and death, blessing and cursing: therefore choose life, that both thou and thy seed may live. (Deut. 30:19)

Questions

1. What is brain death? How is the condition determined?
2. What is the soul? Campolo says that with brain death "the soul is no longer alive in the body," and therefore the plug can be pulled. Do you agree? Why or why not?
3. What role does stewardship of resources play in this discussion? Should the financial cost of keeping a brain dead person alive be considered? Why or why not?
4. What would you say caused Beth's death—disconnecting her from life-support systems or her disease? Why?

The Abortion Wars

Tim Stafford

Tim Stafford is a Christian writer and magazine editor who has authored several books and articles on ethical and sexual issues. This selection is taken from the magazine Christianity Today. *He traces the history of the three "abortion wars" when the practice of abortion was widespread and explains how abortion came to be legalized in the United States.*

Ours is not the first abortion war. Two previous periods saw protracted contests over whether abortion would be accepted or proscribed.

The first was in the early centuries of Christianity, when faith spread within a Greco-Roman culture that considered abortion (and infanticide) routine. The second was in America during the mid-nineteenth century when abortions became widespread, freely advertised in virtually every newspaper.

The third abortion war is now approximately 25 years old and shows no sign of peace. Living in a battle zone, we can easily focus on the tactics of the moment and forget the wider context. The danger in forgetting is that when the situation suddenly shifts, as it did in 1973 with *Roe v. Wade* and again this year with *Webster,* we get thrown off. Suddenly the tactics we had honed become irrelevant, and the goals we had set are outdated.

The first war

People commonly suppose that abortion is an invention of modern, technological medicine. In fact, it was well known in Greco-Roman society. Plato's *Republic* made abortion or infanticide obligatory if the mother was over 40. In Aristotle's ideal society, abortion would be compulsory for families that exceeded a certain size.

Aristotle also made a distinction that would develop a life of its own: the "formed" versus the "unformed" fetus. Aristotle believed that human life was present in the fetus when distinct organs were formed, 40 days after conception for males and 90 for females. This was a metaphysical, not a moral, distinction; Aristotle would abort both "formed" and "unformed" fetuses. But some Christians—Augustine of Hippo and Thomas Aquinas in particular—would later adopt his distinction. It survived in various forms right down to the arbitrary trimesters of *Roe v. Wade.*

Both Plato and Aristotle believed that a child had life long before birth; it was just that the welfare of society and family were more important to them than the rights of a child. The Roman empire made the same assessment while adopting the Stoic belief that life begins only at birth. Abortion was common. As Michael Gorman puts it in *Abortion and the Early Church,* the Roman empire was paradoxically "profamily but not fundamentally antiabortion. . . . That the fetus is not a person was fundamental to Roman law. Even when born, the child was valued primarily not for itself but for its usefulness to the father, the family and especially the state."

Many Romans opposed abortion, but Gorman says, "Pagan antiabortion statements are consistently mindful of the welfare and rights of the state, the father, the family and even occasionally the woman, but never those of the fetus. . . . Christians discarded all pagan definitions of the fetus as merely part of the mother's body. To Christians, the fetus was an independent living being."

From the first, Christians were outspokenly opposed to abortion on the basis of the child's right to life. The *Didaché,* an early second-century document summarizing Christian belief and practice, declares, "Thou shalt not murder a child by abortion/destruction." Clement of Alexandria, Tertullian, Jerome, Basil the Great, Ambrose—all pronounced against abortion. Tertullian wrote eloquently in his *Apology,* aimed at non-Christians: "To hinder a birth is merely a speedier man-killing; nor does it matter whether you take away a life that is born, or destroy one that is coming to the birth. That is a man which is going to be one; you have the fruit already in the seed."

That is how Western society came to be antiabortion. Although the church's antiabortion arguments were consistent and insightful, the change in society was due more to the fact that Christians won the empire to their faith. Not long after Constantine legalized Christianity, it was made illegal for a father to kill his children. Roman abortion laws were never changed, but as the institutional church's role grew more important, ecclesiastical penalties for abortion—their severity was between those for manslaughter and murder—became meaningful legislation for the entire society.

No one can say to what extent behavior changed. What is sure is that a stable antiabortion consensus, based on Christian values, had been formed. It endured intact throughout the medieval period and into modern times.

Through Augustine, Aquinas, Luther, Calvin, and on to Barth and Bonhoeffer, Christian theologians have condemned abortion in the clearest terms. Aristotle's distinction between the formed and unformed fetus was carried on by some, for whom abortion was only murder 40 days after conception. (Yet even before then, it was a violation of developing humanity, and thus still wrong.) Therapeutic abortion, in which the life of the unborn can be sacrificed to save the life of a mother, was sometimes allowed. But the values of Greco-Roman society, in which the life of a child had meaning only as state or family granted it meaning, would not resurface for 1,500 years.

The second war

There were no written laws against the practice of abortion in colonial America; courts operated on the basis of English common law, by which abortion was illegal after "quickening," the time when a mother could feel the movement of her unborn child in the womb. The "quickening" distinction seems to have been a survival from the Aristotelian idea of a "formed" fetus, as it filtered through centuries of theological discussion.

"Quickening" might not have survived on the strength of

its history alone, though; it had practical significance as well. There were no reliable pregnancy tests, and so until quickening, no one could be certain whether a woman was actually pregnant or merely experiencing some kind of menstrual "blockage." Doctors treated a "blockage" by doing just what they would do to carry out an early abortion. Before quickening, it was impossible to say whether an abortion was intended. There was no point in outlawing behavior that could not be ascertained.

In fact, since "quickening" was generally only known to the woman involved, it was legally difficult to try any kind of abortion case. American courts steered a lenient course with the few cases that came before them. In 1803 Britain passed a strong and clear antiabortion law, but it was not until 1821 that Connecticut passed the first American antiabortion statute. By 1840 most states still had no such law, and those that did rarely enforced them.

A dramatic change began in the decades after 1840: the number of abortions shot up. American conception dropped precipitately: the average American woman bore seven children in 1800, three and a half by 1900. Estimates of abortions ranged between one-fifth and one-third of all pregnancies. Before, abortion had been the refuge of desperate, unmarried women; now most abortions were by married women, using it as birth control. Abortion operations were not regarded as particularly dangerous, and the belief in quickening made them seem innocent as well. This was a period of rapid industrialization, with growing cities and easy transportation by railroad. Along with many aspects of American life, abortion became commercialized.

In 1838 Charles and Anna Lohman, adopting the names of Dr. Mauriceau and Madame Restell, began to advertise extensively in the *New York Herald*. They were the first to seize an opportunity offered by a new kind of newspaper that sold cheaply, circulated widely, and depended on advertising revenues to make a profit. Madame Restell's business flourished; she soon opened branch offices in Boston and Philadelphia, and moved into a lavish mansion on Fifth Avenue.

Others imitated her. Soon newspaper ads offered a whole portfolio of potential abortionists. They had the political and economic influence to protect themselves; historian James Mohr notes, in one example, that "between 1849 and 1857 there were only thirty-two trials in Massachusetts [under a new, toughened law] for performing abortions and not a single conviction." Newspapers avoided the subject. Only one, the sensational *National Police Gazette*, reported on and crusaded against abortion. (Not coincidentally, it did not take abortion advertising.)

The increase in abortion, however, led to a counterreaction. The most visible group opposing abortion were "regular" doctors. The American Medical Association (AMA), formed in 1847, took up antiabortion as its cause. Though the AMA was a group with insignificant power, and the medical profession was at an all-time low in prestige, "regular" doctors did raise the issue before the legislature.

The religious establishment did not. Protestant clergy had considerable prestige and were important in other reform movements of the time—notably temperance—but to the dismay of doctors, most churches ignored the issue. No one really knows why; perhaps the topic was too delicate. Catholics, mainly immigrants, were not having abortions like Protestants, and Catholic leaders were at that time in no position to exert political influence.

The rising feminist movement was against abortion. Not even the most radical considered abortion to be an instrument of freedom for women; on the contrary, abortion was understood to be an aspect of male domination, whereby (outside marriage) men tried to conceal the results of their seduction, or (inside marriage) women behaved tragically because of the terrible conditions of a home governed by a tyrannical husband.

In 1870, under a new editor, the *New York Times* began to campaign actively against abortion. Their investigative reports were too sensational for other newspapers to let pass; soon widespread press attention forced prosecutors to act. The more they acted, the more sensational news was available to report (the bodies of young women found dismembered in trunks; numbers of babies found buried in basements). Marvin Olasky notes in *The Press and Abortion* that Madame Restell became "an object of general hatred in New York City. Occasionally, her carriage would be chased down Fifth Avenue by a volley of rocks, and by shouts of 'Madame Killer.' "In 1878 she was arrested and could not buy her freedom as she had in previous cases. The night before she was to be tried she committed suicide. The *Times* headlined the news: "End of a Criminal Life."

Gradually, through the century, laws were toughened. The quickening distinction was dropped. Under the Comstock Act of 1873, abortion advertising became illegal nationally. By the end of the century, abortion was illegal everywhere; and while veiled advertising continued (the Comstock Act was seldom enforced), observers reported that abortions greatly decreased.

The antiabortion crusade was successful despite the fact that only regular physicians publicly worked for it. They were not a particularly influential group, but they did have confident scientific knowledge on their side. Doctors had known since early in the century that the "quickening" distinction was without merit—that the development of the unborn child was gradual from the time of conception.

Some recent histories have commented on the quickening distinction as though it had preserved a right to abortion for women, but that is a classic case of imposing modern thinking on a historical situation. The law and common belief had always held that it was wrong to abort a child once it had life, after quickening. The doctors could presume that society's moral commitments would lead to the banning of abortion once enough people understood that life was at stake from the beginning.

The third war

Yet the success of the nineteenth-century crusade was short-lived. The life of an unborn child is easy to ignore—

invisible and voiceless. The *New York Times,* which had led the press crusade to stop abortions in the 1870s, suddenly stopped reporting on it at all in 1896, when Adolph Ochs assumed ownership and introduced two new slogans: "All the News That's Fit to Print" and "It Does Not Soil the Breakfast Cloth." Abortion news was apparently not fit to print, for it did soil the breakfast cloth.

The *National Police Gazette* no longer crusaded against abortion either; it now took abortion ads. Other newspapers reported occasionally on lurid abortion cases, but journalism professor Olasky notes a change. In the late nineteenth century, press coverage often referred to abortion as the killing of unborn children. Stories in the twentieth century rarely mentioned the unborn; the focus was exclusively on the dangers of abortion to women.

Doctors also lost interest. By early in the twentieth century the AMA had regulated the irregulars (whose nineteenth-century abortion practices had threatened to take away patients and income from regular doctors) out of business, and had no more need to appeal to the legislature for the control of medical business. Doctors could regulate themselves—but showed little interest in interfering with the practices of their fellow regulars.

There was, therefore, no one to show an interest in the lives of the unborn. The American clergy never had. Sexual behavior grew more promiscuous in the Roaring Twenties, and perhaps the failure of Prohibition made America less interested in moral reform. The Soviet Union legalized and promoted abortion, to the acclaim of some. Population-control groups such as Planned Parenthood began cautiously and privately to favor abortion. So did some doctors, mainly on the basis of their claim to know what was best for the welfare of their patients without governmental interference.

Contrary to popular assertions, the number of women who died from "back-alley abortionists" was small; according to the Kinsey Report, 85 percent of abortions were done by doctors, and the number of annual deaths declined steadily, to an estimated 300 by 1967. The deaths were tragic whatever the number, but far more significant in putting abortion back on the public agenda was doctors' discomfort with the rigidity of the antiabortion laws.

Perhaps the most important thing to remember about the beginning of the third abortion war was that it seemed to be about a relatively small change in the law—"abortion reform," as it was called. The "right to abortion" was not an issue, at least for women; if anyone's rights were at stake, they were the doctor's. In 1959 the prestigious American Law Institute (ALI) published a new "model code" for state legislatures. It would allow a doctor to perform abortions in cases of rape, incest, serious deformity, and whenever the doctor believed there was risk to the mental or physical health to the mother. The word *believed* was significant, because it meant a doctor was virtually immune from prosecution so long as he would claim, whatever the medical facts, that he had believed them threatening. Few imagined that such terminology could become an open door to abortion on demand.

Protestants, and even many Catholics, had historically recognized the validity of what is called therapeutic abortion. Abortion reform purported to expand the categories of those tragic decisions. Suppose that the birth of a child conceived by rape threatened to destroy the mother's mental stability; could not an abortion be considered life saving?

Such "hard cases" were real, and proabortionists could expand on them at length. They were received sympathetically in the press, and seemed, in the light of publicity, to be far more numerous than they really were. One well-publicized event brought the abortion issue into public view.

In 1962 an Arizona "Romper Room" TV hostess named Sherri Finkbine learned that a drug she had been taking during pregnancy, thalidomide, had caused numerous birth defects in Europe. She applied for a therapeutic abortion and was granted one by a committee of three doctors. But Finkbine talked to reporters before the scheduled abortion, to warn others about the dangers of thalidomide.

The hospital, wary of public scrutiny, refused to allow the abortion until an advance court judgment was made that the abortion was legal. A judge said that he could make no ruling unless someone had filed a complaint. No one was complaining, but cautious hospital officials were not willing to go ahead without official assurances. The legally complex case was presented in the press as a woman persecuted by an inhumane, hypocritical legal system. Ultimately, Finkbine traveled to Sweden to have an abortion. Her story had a strong emotional hook, enabling many Americans to identify with the plight of a woman who believed she was bearing a deformed child.

In 1967 the AMA voted in favor of legal reform. In the same year the National Organization for Women came out in favor of abortion, and feminists joined the cause. A number of states passed reforming legislation, along the ALI recommended lines, which would give physicians greater latitude in performing therapeutic abortions.

Another issue arose, adding to the apparent urgency: the "population explosion." In a few short years, experts said, the world would starve to death unless population growth could be stopped. . . . It raised a very different set of issues: not abortion as tragic choice, but abortion as crusade to save the world. The campaign for abortion-law reform began to turn into a campaign for abortion-law repeal. In 1969, the National Association for the Repeal of Abortion Laws (NARAL) was formed. Many denominations—Lutherans, Methodists, Presbyterians—supported their cause.

But the movement was beginning to outdistance its popular support. The American public was sympathetic to therapeutic abortion, but solidly against abortion on demand. In 1970 New York, Alaska, Hawaii, and Washington repealed their abortion laws; by then, 13 other states had passed some form of reform legislation. But after 1970 resistance arose, and only one more state, Florida, passed a reform bill. In several other states, reform or repeal were rebuffed. In New York, the legislature tried to reimpose abortion controls, but these were vetoed by Gov. Nelson Rockefeller.

Thus the proabortion movement shifted its energy toward the courts, a tactical shift that was to prove fateful.

Who was against?
Press accounts of the late sixties and early seventies gave a clear picture of who stood against abortion: the Roman Catholic Church. This stereotype of antiabortionists was actively encouraged by proabortionists, who believed it would paint the opposition as narrow and sectarian. Actually, in the general public, Protestants were as likely to be against abortion as Catholics. Yet there was some truth to the caricature: Catholics brought determination and national organization to the cause. The bishops could and did draw up a national plan for opposing abortion, while Protestant antiabortionists remained splintered and disorganized.

It is startling to review the change in evangelical feeling as reflected in the pages of this magazine. The November 8, 1968, issue of CHRISTIANITY TODAY carried several articles on contraception and abortion. One leading biblical scholar wrote, "Clearly, then, in contrast to the mother, the fetus is not reckoned as a soul." A theologian mentioned the ALI reform proposals favorably. The articles concluded with "A Protestant Affirmation," the consensus of 25 evangelical scholars. On abortion, it read, "Whether or not the performance of an induced abortion is sinful we are not agreed, but about the necessity of it and permissibility for it under certain circumstances we are in accord." The statement spoke of "a tragic moral choice" and endorsed the American College of Obstetricians and Gynecologists' statement favoring therapeutic abortions for the life and health of the mother, in cases of rape, incest, or deformities.

By the next year, though, red flags had begun to fly. An editorial noted that under a new Maryland law numerous abortions were being approved on the basis of mental health. "No doubt most state abortion laws need revision," the editorial stated.

Evangelist Francis Schaeffer, who had only recently

become well known, was making an impact among evangelicals with his strong warnings against abortion. Harold O. J. Brown, who would soon write strong CHRISTIANITY TODAY editorials against abortion, felt Schaeffer's influence. So did a Bible college student named Randall Terry, who would become the leading spokesperson for Operation Rescue.

By 1971 there was no more talk in CHRISTIANITY TODAY about therapeutic abortion. The direction reform was leading was clear. "Let it be no great surprise when America is subjected to severe judgment," an editorial read. In the same year, however, the Southern Baptist Convention "urged Baptists to work for legislation permitting abortion under certain conditions. These include: rape, incest, deformity, emotional health."

Roe v. Wade

Few anticipated the complete victory that *Roe v. Wade* gave to proabortionists in 1973. Though the Supreme Court claimed to offer no opinion about when human life began, it implicitly set the time at birth; and though the new law divided pregnancy into equal trimesters, allowing that the fetus might receive some protection in the last three months before birth, in practical terms—because it stipulated that abortions could be done at any time if the mother's mental health was believed to be in danger—the Court assured that an abortion could be done up until the very moment of birth.

CHRISTIANITY TODAY greeted *Roe v. Wade* with a firestorm of criticism. "Christians should accustom themselves to the thought that the American state no longer supports, in any meaningful sense, the laws of God." That was a revolutionary thought to most evangelicals.

But CT was ahead of many evangelicals. In its news report on *Roe v. Wade*, it quoted prominent Southern Baptist pastor W. A. Criswell: "I have always felt that it was only after a child was born and had life separate from its mother that it became an individual person, and it has always, therefore, seemed to me that what is best for the mother and for the future should be allowed." (He has since repudiated this position.) It would be years before such a statement from an evangelical leader would be unthinkable. According to Brown, evangelicals simply could not imagine themselves lining up with Roman Catholics, nor could they imagine that the Supreme Court of their beloved nation (which they thought of as Protestant) would support a cause directly opposed to Christian values.

Few in the press seemed to understand how radical the justices' decision had been. *Time* gave it two pages in the back of the magazine; *Newsweek* gave it one. An editorial in the *Christian Century* proclaimed that "this is a beautifully accurate balancing of individual vs. social rights. . . . It is a decision both proabortionists and antiabortionists can live with."

Roe v. Wade demonstrates that fundamental moral conflicts should not be decided by fiat. The absolute polarization we currently experience is directly traceable to the Supreme Court's decision to take abortion out of politics and declare it a settled question. Those who opposed abortion had suddenly no recourse except radical action. The discussion had been about where to draw the line among tragic choices; the justices erased the line completely and said there was no room for further discussion.

Antiabortionists may someday have reason to remember this lesson, if they gain the power to stop abortion by fiat. As we have seen, restricting abortion works best when it is based on a wider consensus about the value of life. The first centuries of the church gained this consensus through centuries of witness. They spoke passionately against abortion as a part of their faith; they also suffered for their faith. Ultimately, their faith triumphed, and legal changes followed.

By contrast, the nineteenth century, though it passed antiabortion laws, seems not to have built a strong, public consciousness of the humanity of a fetus.

Ethicist Stanley Hauerwas touches on this issue when he notes the frustration of antiabortionists who fail to convince their opponents that a fetus is a human being. He says that more than logic is needed. "Christian arguments about abortion . . . have not merely failed to convince: they have failed to suggest the kind of 'reorientation' necessary if we are to be the kind of people and society that make abortion unthinkable. . . . Even if [we succeed politically], our success may still be a form of failure if we 'win' without changing the presuppositions of the debate."

That is what Christians in the first three centuries managed to do. They changed the world, not just the law.

Questions

1. Where were the three abortion wars waged? What common characteristics do they have?
2. How did Plato view abortion? Aristotle? What was the view of the Roman state toward the unborn?
3. What role did the early Church play in the abortion controversy? Who were some key opponents?
4. What is "quickening"? What was its practical significance in colonial America?
5. What political and legal issues led to the current abortion war in the United States?
6. How did the case of Sherri Finkbine advance the abortion cause in recent decades?
7. What does the author mean when he writes, "Fundamental moral conflicts should not be decided by fiat"? Do you agree with him? Why or why not?

The Lingering Pain

*by Jenny Livingston as told to
Sandra Brooks*

*We are not given Jenny Livingston's real identity, but her
story is true. She tells of her relationship with Thomas, of her
getting pregnant, and of Thomas's insistence that she "get rid
of the baby." Jenny reluctantly goes through with the abortion. After many months of bearing the physical and emotional pain, she experiences the complete forgiveness of God.*

The professor's announcement made every nerve in my
body stand on end. Our whole class would be doing term
papers on abortion.

"I want to see in-depth research on these projects," he said.
"In addition to facts and statistics, I want case studies of people who have been faced with the abortion decision and how
the decision has affected their lives."

I trembled. How I wanted to wake up and find it was just a
bad dream. After two years of struggling to cover up the pain
and ugly memories of my abortion, the professor's words had
ripped open my wound. And though no one knew my secret, I
felt like everyone in the room was standing and pointing their
fingers at me.

When the bell rang, I snatched up my books and left quickly, ignoring my roommate's invitation to lunch.

For two weeks I also ignored my emotional state. I managed to maintain an air of composure and mechanically went
about my routine.

One afternoon, as I rushed back to my dorm to pick up a
lab notebook I'd forgotten, my cover was blown. As I ran into
our room, I froze in my tracks. Strewn about our room's floor
were dozens of anti-abortion materials my roommate had sent

for. Then, before I knew what I was doing, I reached down and picked them up. For several minutes I stared at the hideous color pictures of fully formed infants—some decapitated and dismembered—taken from abortion clinic dumpsters. And grim statistics declared that one in ten women become sterile and one in ten thousand women die from unsanitary conditions in abortion clinics. A handbill entitled "One Hundred and One Uses for a Dead Fetus" explained that tissue from abortions is used in products like fertilizer and collagen cream. Suddenly I began to feel nauseous, dropped the pamphlets and ran into the bathroom.

Afterward I locked the bedroom door and lay in bed, staring at the ceiling and wondering how, as a Christian, things had gone so wrong for me.

Thomas's and my relationship had been so beautiful in the beginning. He was the most wonderful guy I'd ever known and the first I'd ever been committed to.

At first we spent hours just sharing our hopes and dreams. And Thomas would tell me how beautiful and special I was. No one had ever told me that before. Whenever we were together, I felt as if the rest of the world didn't exist.

As we spent more and more time alone, our light kisses gave way to heavy petting. Thomas would tell me how his love for me was growing every day. "Let me show you how much I love you today," he would say as he took off my clothes. Within a few weeks, in my desire to show how much he meant to me, I had given all of myself to him.

But sex, instead of making me feel more secure about my relationship with Thomas, made me fear that I would lose him. When he would leave after one of our encounters, I hated myself for being so weak.

Each time we had sex I promised myself that it would be the last time until we were married. But as soon as I would see him again those big promises dissolved. I felt trapped in a cycle of Mount Everest highs when we were together and Death Valley lows when we were apart.

My self-esteem reached an all-time low when his summer

job separated us for several weeks. I could hardly wait to be with him. I needed reassurance that he still loved and needed me, and that he hadn't found someone else to take my place.

When he returned, I was alone at my parents' home. We melted into each other's arms, and before I knew it we had made our way into my bedroom.

Six weeks after summer vacation I began experiencing occasional dizziness, then severe nausea. At first I thought it was a virus, but it didn't go away. Once I realized I'd missed my period, I was terrified. Hoping to be reassured by a negative pregnancy test, I made an appointment with a doctor. But when I called to find out the results my worst fears were confirmed. In anger I screamed at the nurse who told me, slammed the phone down and burst into tears.

I was so embarrassed that I couldn't tell any of my friends. And I couldn't stand disappointing my parents, especially Daddy, who still thought of me as his little girl.

But I had to tell Thomas. Breaking the news to him wouldn't be easy because I knew how eager he was to finish his education. Having a baby would mean he would have to drop out of school to earn more money.

I tried to phone him all day, but couldn't get through until late in the afternoon.

"Jenny? Hi!" he said excitedly. "I was just about to call you—I have some great news!"

Trying to sound cheerful, I said, "What is it?"

"I've been recommended for a raise and promotion on my part-time job. My boss is sending me to Florida for the weekend for special training."

"When are you leaving?"

"Tonight."

My heart sank. How could I tell him about the baby now? I just couldn't bring myself to spoil his happiness and excitement, especially when he needed a clear mind for training sessions. At the same time I wondered how I could continue to carry the burden of my secret alone for one more moment.

"I wish you could go with me," he continued.

"I do, too," I answered. "You can't begin to guess how much I want to see you right now."

"Me, too. Well, guess I'd better pack. My boss is coming to take me to the airport in a few minutes. Love ya! Be sweet, and I'll see you Monday!"

"Okay," I whispered, pausing until I heard him hang up. I had never felt so alone and frightened.

By the time Thomas returned from his business trip, I had resigned myself to becoming a mother. The wonder and amazement of carrying a new life inside me had begun to take root in my heart. Being a teenage mother wouldn't be easy, but I was willing to try. That is, until I talked to Thomas.

"You can't be!" he yelled while pacing the floor like a caged tiger. "It must be a mistake!"

"It isn't," I said, feeling completely responsible for what had happened. "I wish it was."

"Do you realize how this messes me up?"

Dropping my head, I whispered, "This isn't exactly a picnic for me either."

His expression softened. Taking me into his arms, he said, "I know it isn't. It's just as hard on you as it is on me."

His support at that moment kept me from going over the edge. He held me in silence for several minutes. Then he quietly said, "There's only one thing we can do."

Snuggling in the warmth of his embrace, I closed my eyes, fully expecting Thomas to ask me to marry him.

"We've got to get rid of the baby."

"What?" I screamed as I jerked away from him. "You know I can't do that! This baby is part of you and me. I love it and I want it!"

"I'd want it, too, under different circumstances, but not under these! Don't you realize what this will do to our lives?"

"Okay, if you don't want the responsibility of a baby, I'll raise it alone. Just let me keep this part of you inside me."

"You know that wouldn't be right!" He stormed toward the front door and stopped before going out. "I've got to

think," he said between gritted teeth. "I'll call you tomorrow."
Then he left.

His last words encouraged me. Maybe he was just reacting
to the shock of the news. I had reacted the same way at first.
Maybe he'd change his mind when he had time to get used to
the idea.

He didn't.

When I talked to him the next day, he was even more
adamant about the abortion. I begged him to reconsider, but
his mind was made up.

That night I tossed and turned weighing what I should do.
How could I give up the baby? But what I kept coming back to
was my fear of losing Thomas. Although he never said so, I was
convinced Thomas would leave me if I didn't do what he wanted. And he had become the most important person in my life. I
couldn't bear the thought of not having him anymore. Besides,
an abortion would save my parents the agony and embarrassment of an illegitimate grandchild. In my deliberations I never
once gave thought to the actual abortion procedure. Abortion in
my mind simply meant not being pregnant anymore.

When I talked to Thomas the next morning, I told him I'd
have the abortion on one condition: that he promise not to
desert me when it was all over. He assured me he wouldn't
and offered to pay my expenses.

My family doctor reluctantly gave me the name of an out-
of-state physician. I called for an appointment and the receptionist told me to come in for a thorough examination the next
week. I naively thought the procedure would be no more complicated than filling a tooth.

The doctor was kind, understanding, and didn't ask any
questions, for which I was deeply grateful. But then I went
back to the front desk to schedule the surgery. "The fee must
be paid in cash and in advance," the receptionist said.

Suddenly, it all felt so ugly.

On the morning of the surgery, after Thomas and I filled
out and signed the necessary forms, a grandmotherly looking

woman came and took me to a room filled with dressing stalls and lockers. I blushed with embarrassment when she looked at me. I felt as if the word abortion was written all over my face.

"Take off all your clothing and put it into this metal basket," she said while handing me a hospital gown and paper moccasins. "I'll be back for you in a few minutes."

When she returned, she took me to a waiting room with a television. The Disney channel was featuring Mickey Mouse cartoons. The vertical button on the screen needed adjusting; the images kept flipping over and over as I sat there in a daze staring at it. *How can I just sit here watching Mickey Mouse when I'm waiting to kill my baby?* I thought. Quickly I reminded myself that Thomas and I had made the decision together and that I was going to stick by it.

Just then a nurse came and directed me to the surgical room. It was cold and sterile.

While she prepared me for surgery, I caressed my abdomen and thought, "It's not too late. My baby's heart is still beating. I could leave right now." But again I remembered all the reasons for my decision and repeated them silently to myself like a chant: "I'm doing what I have to do. I have no choice. I'm doing what I have to do. I have no choice. . . ."

Finally I mustered enough resolve to go through with it. I embraced my tummy once more and whispered, "I'm sorry, my little baby. Please forgive me for what I'm about to do. I love you and I want you, but your daddy thinks this is best. I'm doing what I have to do, not what I want to do."

The doctor came in with a cheery greeting and tried to put me at ease by talking about the weather and other trivial matters. Behind him a nurse wheeled in a stainless steel box. After explaining the procedure, he pulled the steel box—a suction machine—beside him and turned it on.

A moment later the machine's shrill noise assaulted me. As the pain in my abdomen grew worse, the noise seemed to slice into my brain. I cried out in agony.

"Just hang on a little longer, honey," the nurse said gently. "He's almost through."

It seemed like an eternity! Fifteen minutes later I felt something let go and it was over. The stomach cramps were agonizing, but infinitely worse than that, my baby was gone. I wanted to die.

Like me, I don't think Thomas realized how serious the operation was until it was over. I'll never forget how pale he got when he saw how bad I looked after the surgery. I had, in fact, developed a hemorrhage which lasted several weeks. On the way home I tried to tell him about the surgery, but he changed the subject and has refused to talk about it ever since.

The first few months after the abortion Thomas constantly was at my side, but once I was back on my feet, I rarely saw or heard from him. "Working and studying takes all my time," he'd mumble when I asked him why he didn't spend more time with me.

Thomas had promised not to desert me after the abortion, and I think he tried really hard to keep his word; but we both knew our relationship had changed. An uneasy politeness would fall between us when we saw and talked to each other. We used to be completely relaxed with each other and never ran out of things to say. Now we couldn't think of anything to say. All those dreams we used to share seemed so far away. And now, two years later, I still felt weighed down by the pain and guilt of what I had done. I sobbed bitterly, wondering if I'd be feeling this agony for the rest of my life.

"Jenny! Jenny! Are you all right?" I suddenly became aware of my roommate pounding on the bedroom door. "Please open the door. You've been locked in that room for hours. Don't you want something to eat?"

Clearing my throat and trying to sound as normal as possible, I replied, "I'm all right. I'll be out in a few minutes. I guess I must have fallen asleep."

I hated keeping the truth from her, but I just couldn't take a chance on confiding in anyone. Fear of exposure and rejection because of my secret outweighed my desperate need for comfort and support.

Later that evening when my roommate went to the library to study, I was left alone again with my guilt. Falling prostrate on my bed, I prayed with an intensity I'd never known. "Oh, Jesus, please forgive me!" I cried out as tears burned down my cheeks. But my words seemed so empty. I knew I'd have to come to terms with my past before I could do my research paper, but even more importantly, before I could have a normal, happy life.

Through my tears I saw my Bible on my bookshelf. I felt an unusual impulse to pick it up. I wiped my tears and flipped through the pages, sensing that the answer lay buried somewhere inside. If I only knew where to look! I read a few scattered verses which seemed to make no sense at all, and started to lay my Bible aside when a prayer guide given to me by a Sunday-school teacher fell from between the pages and into my lap. I opened it and found a long list of topics and Scripture passages aimed at helping people struggling with problems. Running my finger down the list, I found the word *Forgiveness*. My fingers trembled as I turned to the first reference on the list, 1 John 1:9. "If we confess our sins, he is faithful and just and will forgive us our sins and purify us from all unrighteousness."

The words seemed to leap off the page and into my heart. The knot in my stomach loosened, and I turned to the next reference in Romans 4:7-8. "Blessed are they whose transgressions are forgiven, whose sins are covered. Blessed is the man whose sin the Lord will never count against him."

Tears welled in my eyes and trickled down my face. It was as though God had written these words just for me, and had waited thousands of years for me to discover them.

The last reference said, "He does not treat us as our sins deserve or repay us according to our iniquities . . . for he knows how we are formed, he remembers that we are dust" (Psalm 103:10, 14).

I sobbed aloud. I was forgiven! All this time it wasn't God who was unwilling to forgive me, it was I who was unwilling to forgive myself. That evening, alone in my dormitory room, I burst into thanks and praise to God for the depths of his love and mercy.

When I think back on it now, I can hardly believe I went through with the abortion. At eighteen I was so insecure and immature.

Now that I'm a little older, I realize that getting pregnant wasn't my first mistake. My first mistake was giving myself to Thomas outside a marriage relationship. Too late I learned that God didn't make the rules to keep me from having fun. He made them to keep me from hurting myself.

My second mistake was aiming too low. In a sense I deified Thomas. I aimed to fulfill his every desire and need at the expense of my own legitimate desires and needs—most tragically of all, my need to keep my baby. I thought I needed Thomas to be happy. I put my trust in him rather than in God.

If only I could relive it, I'd keep my baby, no matter how embarrassing the circumstances. It would be easier than living with the memory of taking a human life. That little creature inside me had God's thumbprint on it.

It wasn't until I finished the research paper that I realized the assignment was a gift from God. He used it as therapy to draw me closer to him. It forced me to turn to him for healing and comfort, and since then my relationship with him has deepened.

Still, the emotional wounds haven't healed completely. I'm continually working through the pain and dealing with the consequences. When I typed the final draft of my research paper, I spent more time crying than typing. I even thought of ways to punish myself for what I had done, and seriously considered suicide. But I survived.

It still hurts when I see a baby or news item on abortion. My baby's due date and abortion date never pass without my reliving some of the grief. But God has shown me his mercy. No matter how ugly and unfit for life I feel, I know I can come to him without pretending. He has comforted me time and time again.

The day our research papers were returned to us, the professor called me to his desk.

"Jenny, that was an exceptional paper," he said, placing it in my hands.

"Thank you, sir."

"I was impressed with your arguments against abortion and would like to print your paper in the campus newspaper."

"I'd love for you to," I replied.

Returning to my desk, I wondered how he would react if he knew that I based most of the paper on my own experience.

As I slid back into my desk, I glanced down at my grade. But for an instant my eyes wouldn't focus. All I could see was a word that God had brought to my mind: *Forgiven*. And that meant more to me than any grade ever could.

Questions

1. Why was Jenny so shaken by the research assignment?
2. Why did she choose not to tell her friends or her parents about her pregnancy? Do you think she made the right decision to keep quiet?
3. How did Thomas react to the news of her pregnancy? What did he recommend? Why did he want Jenny to have an abortion? Was he being selfish or simply realistic about his future?
4. How did the abortion affect Jenny's and Thomas's relationship? How did it continue to affect Jenny even two years later? Why?
5. How did Jenny find peace with God and with herself?

Juli Loesch

Studs Terkel

Studs Terkel (born 1912) is a Pulitzer Prize-winning author who was made famous by his technique of interviewing common people and then compiling their stories into books. This selection is excerpted from his book The Great Divide. *Juli Loesch is a crusader for peace. She opposes war, nuclear power, and the death penalty. But in a surprising move, she changes her mind on abortion.*

Despite her crutches, she gets around with what appears to be remarkable ease. Immediately, her fervor and enthusiasm come forth: hers is a personal crusade.

She is founder of Justlife, an anti-abortion, antiwar, anti-nuclear-power group. She is opposed to the death penalty.

She is thirty-five years old. "I was born and raised in Erie, Pennsylvania. We were part of the working poor. My parents had to sacrifice considerably to send my brother and me to Catholic schools. My father was a laborer who loved books. He would go to secondhand bookstores and bring home boxes full of them. I read everything."

My aim in life was to work against war and against violence. I left Antioch College after three months because I wanted to get more involved in the antiwar movement. I was disillusioned by the so-called radicals who were more interested in smoking dope and getting laid.

I went to work for the United Farm Workers in California as a boycott organizer. I learned more about nonviolent social change from the farm workers than I did at college.

I did a lot of drifting between the ages of eighteen and twenty. In the lives of the saints, this would be the sins-of-youth period. I saw a lot of casualties in my generation: casualties of the sexual revolution, drugs, militant politics. It shook me up. I saw girls my age getting abortions, getting venereal disease, and messed up personally.

In 1972, I went back home to Erie. I worked as a waitress till I was fired because I dumped a cup of hot coffee in the lap of a half-drunk guy who was pinching my butt (laughs).

During that time, I organized organic garden groups in the neighborhoods of Erie. Heavily blue-collar. No controversy here: no one's antigarden. Naturally, I began reading environmental things and the dangers threatening the air, the water, the soil, the crops. I became aware of things outside my little garden (laughs).

I began going around giving talks against nuclear power. That was ten years ago. If there's a nuclear war, it's gonna blow up everything. Why should I plant blueberries if the world might not last two years? I mean, I was that depressed.

I started reading about prenatal development because I wanted to be able to tell people, If you care for your own children, you got to stop this stuff. That's when I began to realize that I was asking everyone to be concerned about everyone else's unborn children, while these same children were being torn to pieces by abortion.

Up to that moment, I was a pro-choice ambivalent feminist. I'm still a feminist. I even wrote a pro-choice article that said it's outrageous for a male-dominated legislature to tell us what to do with our bodies. I was even taking a pro-choice stand in the early seventies, even though I thought it was a lousy choice. I didn't think I would ever have an abortion, because I'm a peace woman and peace women don't do violent things.

There's no way to nonviolently get an abortion. If you want a baby dead when it comes out, you have to tear it to pieces. It's not a philosophical question. I know the difference between a live fetus and a dead one. In order to go from alive to dead, you've got to kill something. This is baby talk. Everyone knows this.

One day, as I was talking to a group about nuclear radiation, a woman said, "If you think it's wrong to injure these kids accidentally, don't you think it's wrong to kill them deliberately?" I said, "These are two separate issues. Nuclear radiation is a corporate crime, it's the government, it's global. Abortion is personal, it's private." This other woman kept at it: "You're tryin' to get us to feel responsible for everyone's unborn children all over the world. On the other hand, you're saying each individual pregnant woman has the choice to kill or not to kill, period." This woman was sharp. She was pointing out to me my own glaring inconsistency.

The fetus as human life is undeniable from a biological point of view. It's a living individual of our species. It's your son or your daughter. Planned Parenthood knows this, abortionists know this, they have to kill a living being every time they do an abortion. The question is, Are we going to discriminate against certain forms of human life or not? Are we going to say some humans have rights and some of them don't?

Are there no circumstances in which you'd recognize the need?

It's a real toss-up, if it's a life for a life, a genuine toss-up between the mother's life and the baby's. If it's a tubal pregnancy, that's life-threatening to the mother and the baby can't survive it either. The surgical removal of this tubal pregnancy is morally not the same as an abortion.

If the woman is raped—?

I don't believe in the death penalty for the rapist. Why should I want to kill a rapist's child? It's the woman's child, too. But the child is its own child, too. The child is not the property of one or the other, the mother or the father.

Embryologists have said—forget the theologians—that human life is transmitted to a new generation every time a child is conceived, every time fertilization occurs. You can discern an individual human life, at least, by day 12 after fertilization.

When that woman challenged me at the antinuke meeting,

I didn't jump to my feet and say, Oh, you're absolutely right, let's go join the right-to-life movement. Not at all. I didn't want to hear this stuff. The reason why it upset me is that is exactly what I was hearing from the antinuclear movement. From Helen Caldicott, from Rosalie Bertell: human life in its delicate beginnings is very precious.

I wasn't attracted to the right-to-life movement at all. They're usually promilitary, hawkish, inconsistent. This woman was concerned about the arms race. She was not rigid, uncaring, authoritarian. She was open-minded and willing to listen to the other point of view. But she wanted to be heard, too. I owed it to her.

I don't think any decent human society will allow the destruction of our youngest children. It hurts women, too. One of the fastest-growing sectors in the pro-life movement are women who have had abortions and are now anti-abortion. There's a group called WEBA, Women Exploited by Abortion. They're just like the Vietnam Veterans Against the War. They came back and said, We were there, it was terrible.

In the peace movement, I found other people that were anti-abortion, but they were keeping their mouths shut, because they felt it made them freakish.

After Three Mile Island happened, I was tearing around Erie getting people on a bus to Washington to protest nuclear power. The organizers gave me a packet of literature. In it was this pro-abortion leaflet: why we should have government-funded abortions. Because women in the Harrisburg area may have gotten contaminated. Why should they suffer the suspense and fear of possibly giving birth to a child with a defect?

I have genetic defects. I have rheumatoid arthritis. This is a disease that can be crippling and deforming, as well as painful and deadly. But I'm alive and I find it worthwhile to be alive even with a defect. We're all vulnerable, unprotected human flesh.

I began to realize that it was bigotry of the worst kind to say that it's better to be dead than to be born retarded or blind or without a limb. It's a value judgment you're making about someone's life, based on their degree of perfection. Are you perfect?

What happens to the lives of parents whose child is born a vegetable?

I guess they're challenged. It challenges you to love or reject. This is what makes us human.

Questions

1. What was Juli Loesch's aim in life? Why was she pro-choice? How did she change her view? What is her basis for being anti-abortion now?
2. What is WEBA?
3. Why does Loesch compare abortion to bigotry?

Conscience Over Duty

Cindy Barrett

This selection is a news item from Macleans, *a Canadian newsweekly. David Packer is a Toronto police officer with ten years on the force. Because of conscience, he decides he can no longer guard a certain abortion clinic, which has been the target of anti-abortion protest. Packer is called before a police tribunal where he says that "God's law is primary."*

For the past 10 years police Const. David Packer has patrolled the streets of Toronto. His superiors have called his work outstanding, and in 1985 Packer, 35, received an official commendation after pulling a woman and child from a burning building. But in April the soft-spoken father of five refused to continue guarding an abortion clinic operated by Dr. Henry Morgentaler, the target of frequent demonstrations by prolife activists. Packer—an Anglican who is converting to Roman Catholicism and who is a strong opponent of abortion—objected to what he called the "unspeakable crime" being carried out in the clinic. That refusal last week led to Packer's appearance before a police tribunal on charges of disobeying a lawful order. Declared the unrepentant officer: "God's law is primary—always has and always will be."

Packer's moral convictions have won him international attention, including a handwritten five-page letter of support this month from Mother Teresa, the Calcutta-based nun. But police department officials claim that his action was a breach of discipline. During the two-day hearing, Staff Insp. John Addison, acting as prosecutor, said that chaos would result if every police officer checked his conscience before obeying an order. Anti-abortion groups supported Packer, but many other observers backed the police department. Lawyer Jeffrey

House, a member of the Ontario Law Union, said that a police officer should not be allowed to put religious beliefs ahead of official duties. "If God is speaking to him so directly," said House, "then perhaps God should guide him toward a different line of work."

The tribunal reconvenes on Nov. 19, when presiding Supt. Bernard Nadeau will receive submissions from Addison and Toronto lawyer Harry Black, who is representing Packer. If the tribunal finds him guilty under the Ontario Police Act, Packer could be reprimanded, demoted—or fired. His wife, Anne, a devout Catholic, said that her husband might drive a taxi if he is dismissed from the force. Whatever the outcome, the constable says that he has no illusions about future promotion. Said Packer: "I know beyond the shadow of a doubt that I'll be making no advancement within the force."

Questions

1. How was David Packer rated by his superiors?
2. How did Packer's superiors react to his "breach of discipline"?
3. What did Staff Inspector Addison say about Packer's action? Do you agree with the inspector?
4. What might happen to Packer if he is found guilty? What are his options?
5. What would you have done if you were Packer? Why?

The Prolife Credibility Gap

Spencer Perkins

Spencer Perkins is a pastor at Voice of Calvary Fellowship and writes for the John Perkins Foundation for Reconciliation and Development, both in Jackson, Mississippi. This essay was first printed in Christianity Today. *Perkins says that before the black evangelical community can fully support the prolife movement, white evangelicals need to understand the importance of "justice everywhere." "A true prolife perspective must include a concern for justice in all its forms," he says.*

Abortion—and the prolife movement—present black evangelicals with a dilemma. It is not that we question the evil of abortion; Jesus clearly would have condemned it. But for me, a black man, to join your demonstrations against abortion, I would need to know that you understand God's concern for justice everywhere .

It is hard for me, for example, not to be distracted by the faces I see leading the prolife crusade. Aren't some of these the same people who 20 years ago were calling Martin Luther King, Jr., a Communist? Are they not the same people who 15 years ago moved out of the neighborhood in which I now live because too many blacks were moving in? Or aren't they the same Christians who opened private schools as soon as the courts ordered desegregation in the South in order to avoid any contact with us?

When it comes to abortion, these experiences have led to a credibility gap. Ever since I can remember, it has been almost axiomatic that if we blacks took a stand on an issue, conservative evangelical Christians would line up on the opposite side of the street, blocking our way. The gulf between us is so deep that it is hard to imagine us on the same side of an issue.

When love is costly

When I was growing up in Mississippi, we were taught that the evidence of love for Christ was love for neighbor. I always asked if that meant that I had to love white people, too. The answer was always the same: *"especially* white people." Even after my father, John Perkins, was severely tortured and beaten almost to death by angry white men blinded by hatred and prejudice, the answer was the same: *"especially* white people." Since it was increasingly obvious in the sixties that white people did not love *us,* I wondered if there were no white Christians south of the Mason-Dixon Line.

The wounds of racism and oppression still cut deep. Just how deep was made plain to me by comments made by a black single mother while she watched white antiabortion protesters on the evening news. "Do you think they would care if only black babies were being aborted?" she asked. Many of us, even now, struggle with our answer. I know this sounds callous, but such sentiment demonstrates the magnitude of the gulf between us and illustrates our desperate need for reconciliation.

The issues get even more complex. For blacks who have a huge stake in the well-being of the black neighborhood, what does the reality of "zero abortions" mean? How many more female-headed households would be created? How many more young women would be trapped in the cycle of poverty and dependence on welfare? How many more gang members would these families produce? Wouldn't the ghettos be twice as large in just a few years? Wouldn't the crime rate soar? Wouldn't the prisons overflow? Who would take care of all of these children?

Am I not right in assuming that as the ghettos became larger and more dangerous, these same antiabortionists would move farther and farther into the suburbs, taking little or no responsibility for the social consequences of the lives they helped save?

Hope for healing

These questions are real to us; before I can pick up a picket sign and join in this parade—before I can join hands with you and sing "We Shall Overcome," and certainly before I can go to jail with you—some of my fears need to be calmed. I need to feel secure that you have had a change of heart. I have heard very few Southern evangelicals admit they were on the wrong side of the race issues back in the fifties, sixties, and early seventies. I have never heard any of them say that they should have blocked the entrances to the jails where we were beaten and tortured, or taken a stand with us when we wanted equal access to "life, liberty, and the pursuit of happiness." In fact, over the past few years there have been only a few Southern, white, evangelical Christians who have asked our forgiveness and extended a hand in reconciliation. On the contrary, for every step we take in their direction, it seems that most take another step toward the suburbs.

This is the truth as we see it—the truth that needs to be heard in order for healing to take place in the Christian church, black and white. Healing will be hindered as long as Christians let their "Thus saith the Lord" on one issue be the evidence of their righteousness—at the expense of a lifestyle of justice. As Christians we are called to be "prolife," but that must have more than a narrow meaning, for life without dignity is a fate worse than death. A true prolife perspective must include a concern for justice in all its forms.

A recent incident illuminates the contradictions and frustrations surrounding the abortion issue because this broader prolife concern has not always been in evidence. One of the black women in our church was tending the nursery a few months ago while a Right to Life meeting was being held. Our church, Voice of Calvary Fellowship, is unusual for a Southern church in that the racial make-up is approximately half black and half white. Some of the white brothers and sisters of our church are passionately involved in the prolife movement, which is probably why the meeting was held at our church. One local white woman obviously did not realize our racial mix and did not prepare her children for what they would encounter. When they walked into the building, the first thing they saw was the skin color of our black children. One of the woman's boys immediately asked in disgust, "What kind of church is this?" His brother's response summed up what these young boys felt about their black brothers and sisters: "We'd better be careful what we touch here," he said, drawing his hands back as if fearing contamination.

I have to wonder at the answer these young white children are given in words and deeds when they ask the question, "Does loving my neighbor mean loving blacks too?"

Where strategies meet

Being prolife and demanding an unborn baby's "right to life" is a high calling. But I believe that God cares about a deeper principle—a "right to justice"; that is, a right to a decent *quality* of life.

It is not a simple, glib response, then, when I must counsel an unwed black teenager against an abortion, even though I believe with all my heart that abortion is morally wrong. I feel that if the love of Christ compels me to save the lives of children, that same love should compel me to take more responsibility for them once they are born. Until Christians like me are willing to offer more than counseling for prospective mothers, until the Christian church is willing to take responsibility for the quality of life of these mothers and children, whatever that may entail, then our crusade for the lives of unwanted children will continue to be perceived as lacking integrity, especially in the black community.

For me, the issue is not about abortion—whether it is wrong or right to kill unborn children. The issue for me is much deeper—whether together we will embrace a Christianity committed to justice for all, or whether we will remain apart and fight our separate battles. Perhaps the abortion controversy is the vehicle God will use to bring us together.

As for answering the question, "Where do black Christians stand on abortion?" it looks to me as if we are on the same side of a moral issue. But if, from where you stand, you insist the battle is against abortion, while we believe the battle is against injustice, our strategies must remain different. We believe your plans for an all-out war on abortion will prove to be short-sighted. When and if you win the abortion battle, the war will be over for you and you will be able to return home. Then *we* will be left to undertake the reconstruction. Therefore, our strategy must continue to be the fight against injustice—a war with many battle fronts. Where abortion will rank in our battle plan will depend on the strength of the relationship we can establish in the future and on how much your burdens and concerns, because of that relationship, can become ours.

Questions

1. Perkins speaks of a "credibility gap" between whites and blacks. What does he mean by that term?
2. Explain what Perkins means when he says, "Healing [in the black and white churches] will be hindered as long as Christians let their 'Thus saith the Lord' on one issue be the evidence of their righteousness." Can you think of examples of what he means?
3. Where does a "white" abortion victory leave the black community?

Peace

The Day the Bomb Hit: A Hiroshima A-Bomb Survivor Remembers

Akihiro Takahashi

Akihiro Takahashi was a 14-year-old student on the day in 1945 when the atomic bomb was dropped on the city of Hiroshima in Japan. Takahashi was standing about a mile from the epicenter of the explosion. His account of the day the bomb hit is a gripping story of unimaginable pain and suffering rooted in a deep sense of the wrongness of war.

It was very hot on the morning of "that day," 35 years ago. I was 14 years old and in the second grade of Hiroshima Municipal Junior High School (now called Nakahiro Junior High School, 1.4 kilometers from the point of explosion, or hypocenter). In those days of the war, I was a mobilized student working in the building evacuation program at Koamicho.

I went to school on August 6. I was in the school playground with my classmates lining up for the morning roll call when a B-29 approached over our heads, leaving a vapor trail behind it. Strangely the air-raid alerts had all been canceled. I was watching the blue sky and pointing with my classmates at the B-29.

No sooner was "Get into line!" shouted by a headboy than we were surrounded by dark brown smoke, which was accompanied by a roaring sound as if the ground had been split in two. We could not see even an inch ahead. I found myself thrown back about 10 meters and to the ground. Five minutes, maybe almost 10, passed before it became faintly light around us. Looking around, I found the schoolhouse totally flattened and my classmates lying here and there on the ground.

For a while I was not aware of anything at all; I stood absentmindedly, and then I looked at my body. The skin of my arms and legs was peeling off just like shreds of cloth, and I could see red flesh. The palms of my hands developed blisters just like the belly of a globefish; my skin had turned yellow.

Several pieces of glass fragments blown off by the blast were sticking into my arms and back. My clothing, which was called "national uniform," was totally burnt. My combat cap had been blown off, and my hair was singed. I felt terribly hot, and I thought that I could not endure the smarting on my back. Suddenly a sense of horror ran through my body.

I thought, "Nothing can be done standing here! I must jump into the river." In the refuge training program we had been instructed to jump into the river in case of an emergency, so I made up my mind to go to the River Yamate that was flowing near the school.

When I happened to turn around, my friend Yamamoto was following me crying, "Mother, Mother. I'm afraid my house in Kusatsu (about 1.5 kilometers from the hypocenter) must have been burned down. What has become of Daddy and Mommy? What will become of me, if they have died?" He was sobbing and mumbling.

Strangely enough, I kept my presence of my mind. No tears were in my eyes. I managed to find a way to the bank of the river while encouraging Yamamoto.

I shouted, "Don't cry! Let's go to the river." Every street was blocked by the ruins of fallen houses, so we went through them on all fours. Our arms and feet were badly injured because of glass fragments, small stones, wood, and nails.

As we crossed over a small wooden bridge, a raging fire started in the fallen houses along the streets we had just passed. If we had been an instant longer in leaving there, we would have been engulfed by a sea of flames.

"Oh, we are saved!" I cried in my mind, and I did not try to stop the tears falling for the first time. I was not aware that Yamamoto had disappeared.

I got to the bank of the river on the side of Yamate-cho and, exhausted, lay down on the sand. As the pain on my back was becoming unendurable, I dipped myself into the water; but each time I dipped my body, I felt an unbearable tingling pain as the sand came between the peeling skin and flesh. On the river numerous dead bodies were floating, one on top of the other.

While I was sitting on the sand, a woman came to me and applied some oily ointment to my body. She told me that there was a first-aid station built by the Army Hospital at Mitaki (about 3 kilometers from the hypocenter).

At the first-aid station, I rested after receiving medical treatment. Then a heavy black rain started to fall in large drops.

When the black rain stopped, I left on foot for Kusatsu where my home was. After walking for a while, I heard a voice calling me, "Takahashi, Takahashi!" Turning in the direction of the voice, I found my classmate Hatta squatting down along the roadside. Hatta was suffering from burns on the soles of his feet, where red flesh could be seen: "I can't walk; please take me home."

I was at a loss to know how to take him home. Then I got an idea and suggested that he crawl on all fours. Proceeding in this way we did not cover any great distance, so I let him lean on me and walk on his heels. By using these two methods alternately, we progressed towards Kusatsu at a very slow pace.

While we were resting by the roadside, I saw my great uncle and great aunt coming toward us from a Buddhist ceremony. The coincidence made me feel that an old saying had come true: "To meet Buddha in hell."

"Auntie!" I shouted to my great aunt. They were upset to see our burns. I was carried on great uncle's back and Hatta on my great aunt's. I finally reached home, being taken the last part of the way on a stretcher prepared by my grandfather who had come to meet us.

I heard later that Yamamoto and Hatta had died in great pain. I narrowly escaped death during almost one and a half year's struggle against illness, including three weeks in a coma. I have been hospitalized three times in order to have keloids, enlarged masses of scar tissue, removed and to receive treatment for a liver malfunction. Even today, I am obliged to go to the hospital to have treatment for this liver malfunction as I am designated an A-bomb disease patient.

The United States and Japan went through the unfortunate experience of war some 30 years ago. I am convinced that the hatred, the sufferings, and the grief of A-bomb survivors can be overcome. It is my understanding that your people are also still suffering from the deep scars of war, and I sincerely hope that they will be healed by efforts for peace. I would like our two peoples to join each other in speaking out against war and making a step towards the abolition of nuclear weapons.

Questions

1. Describe the scene on the playground after the bomb hit. How close to the epicenter was Takahashi?
2. How did the blast injure Takahashi physically? Where did he go first? What did he see on the way to the river?
3. How were his two friends affected by the blast?
4. Do you think it was right for the United States to take an action that killed so many innocent civilians? What other course of action do you think the U.S. government should have considered in order to save lives?

The Just-War Theory:Will It Work in the Nuclear Age?

Robert L. Spaeth

In this selection from Robert L. Spaeth's book No Easy
Answers, *the author outlines seven conditions which must
be present for a war to be considered a just war. The question
of going to war is never simple nor easy. The fact that we live
in the nuclear age compounds the difficulties of the just-war
issue.*

When the Empire of Japan attacked Pearl Harbor on
December 7, 1941, the United States responded swiftly with a
declaration of war. Little time was spent debating whether a
war against Japan and its ally, Nazi Germany, would be morally justified. America judged that moral principle allowed and
the defense of America demanded that the war be fought. This
judgment—that the war would be a just war—was shared by
an overwhelming majority of Americans; only a handful of
strict pacifists disagreed.

Had a person paused to construct a moral justification of
U.S. entry into World War II, the outline of the argument
would have been readily available. That outline is the set of
moral principles known as the just-war theory, which was
developed over many centuries by Christian philosophers and
theologians—Augustine of Hippo and Thomas Aquinas, in
particular—who wished to apply the principles of justice to
war. Justice, according to this kind of thinking, needs to be
brought to bear both in the decision of whether or not a nation
will go to war and in the decisions made during the conduct of
the war. The former application of justice to war, called *jus ad
bellum* in Latin, has seven requirements: just cause, lawful
authority, right intention, just means, reasonable hope of suc-

cess, last resort, and proportionality. All seven conditions must be met for a war to be considered just according to the theory.

These principles might have been applied to the decision by the United States to fight World War II.

1. *Just cause.* A nation's cause is most just when it is defending itself against armed aggression, equally just when it defends innocent allies who are the victims of such aggression. The theory simply recognizes one of the primary functions of the government of a sovereign nation—protection of national security. At Pearl Harbor the Japanese attacked U.S. citizens and military forces directly; since 1939, allies of the United States, including Britain and France, had been under attack by Germany. An armed defense against these aggressions readily meets the just-cause condition of the just-war theory.

2. *Lawful authority.* In 1941 the United States had been organized as a sovereign nation for 165 years, ever since the British colonies in North America declared their independence from the mother country. Ever since 1789, the nation had been governed by a single Constitution, which grants to the Congress the authority to declare war and to the President the authority to be Commander-in-Chief of the armed forces. It seems clear that the U.S. government was legitimate and that it had authority to order an armed defense of the country.

3. *Right intention.* Intentions of nations vary with their leaders, with the mood of their people, with the circumstances of the moment. Certainly the primary intention of the U.S. declaration of war in 1941 was to bring the German and Japanese aggressions to a halt and restore peace among the nations. This intention meets the requirement of right intention under the just-war theory.

4. *Just means.* The first aim of a defensive war is to immobilize or destroy the armed might of the enemy. In the twentieth century that means sinking ships, shooting down airplanes, invading military installations, and killing enemy soldiers in the process. It may also include invasion of enemy territory in order to induce the war leaders to cease their war making. All these means involve the violent killing or injuring of human

beings. Thus the justification of defensive war leads to a justification of taking lives or at least violently attacking other people in the process. Definite restrictions apply: Not all citizens of the enemy country are responsible for the aggression or are involved in it; these innocent persons must not be attacked or killed. Nor are certain methods of treating enemy soldiers—such as torture—morally acceptable. When World War II began for the United States, the conventional albeit brutal capabilities of modern warfare were available to both sides in the conflict, and the use of these means by the United States seemed then (and now) to be morally acceptable. As that conflict wore on, however, other means became available and were used—including counter-city bombing with TNT and incendiary bombs, and finally with atomic bombs. Whether the new means were immoral under the circumstances and whether, if so, the U.S. role in the war then lost its moral justification are debated to this day.

5. *Reasonable hope of success.* The United States in 1941 was an industrialized nation, capable of producing large quantities of effective weapons and other wartime equipment. Its citizens appeared quite prepared to go to war. Neither the Japanese nor the Germans seemed to possess any invulnerable offensive or defensive force. So Americans could reasonably expect to win the war. At no time during World War II did the American hope of victory turn to despair.

6. *Last resort.* Could the United States and the Allies have settled the differences between themselves and the Axis powers by any means short of war? Britain had tried peaceful negotiations with Germany in the middle 1930s, a process that became known contemptuously as "appeasement." In the Pacific, the United States and Japan had carried on a policy of action and reaction that led nowhere; meanwhile in Japan a war party successfully pressed for an armed attack on the United States. After the 1939 Nazi invasions in Europe and the Japanese attack on Pearl Harbor two years later, no other opportunities for peaceful settlements existed. For the United States to declare war in 1941 could properly be called a last resort.

7. *Proportionality.* The aim of this requirement of just-war theory has been described by James Turner Johnson of Rutgers University: "to ensure that the overall damage to human values that ensues from resort to force will be at least balanced by the degree to which human values are preserved or protected" ("What Guidance Can Just War Tradition Provide for Contemporary Moral Thought About War?" *New Catholic World*, March-April 1982, p. 84). Proportionality asks that two elements be weighed in the balance—damage done in the war and protection of human values achieved by the war. Unfortunately, there is no single gauge to measure these two elements; yet the comparison is forced upon a nation that is deciding whether engaging in a particular war will be moral. In World War II, the potential damage to human values at the hand of the Japanese and the Germans was truly gigantic; but what destruction would be inflicted by the United States to protect against that damage was not clearly known at the outset of the war. Potentially the destruction could be limited, but that limit depended on the ferocity with which Japan and Germany would prolong the war, especially if it went against them. As events worked out, the destruction visited upon Germany by means of strategic bombing and upon Japan by incendiary and finally atomic bombing was extensive. After the war most Americans believed that protection from the tyranny of Japan and Germany had been worth the price. Proportionality also requires that the particular means of warfare—the weapons— be justifiable by a balance between their destructiveness and their good effects. To many people today, counter-city obliteration bombing, including the bombing of Hiroshima and Nagasaki, seems to have violated this principle, but during World War II many believed the bombing was permissible.

Nuclear weapons created a new set of moral questions and, in the opinion of some moral philosophers and theologians, a challenge to the just-war theory itself. It may be argued that once the use of strategic nuclear weapons is contemplated, fulfillment of all of the seven just war conditions becomes impossible. But *tactical* nuclear weapons must also be considered; then the just-war criteria, though very difficult, are perhaps not impossible to fulfill.

In 1981 the Roman Catholic bishop of Cleveland, Anthony M. Pilla, applied traditional just-war criteria to the possibility of nuclear war. Tracing the theory to Augustine of Hippo, he summarized the just-war theory in six statements:

1. The decision for war must be made by a legitimate authority.
2. The war must be fought for a just cause.
3. War must be taken only as a last resort.
4. There must be a reasonable chance of "success."
5. The good to be achieved by the war must outweigh the evil that will result from it. (Proportionality)
6. The war must be waged with just means (in accordance with natural and international law). (Heyer, *Key Statements*, p. 145)

Bishop Pilla then brought these principles to bear on the possibility of nuclear war:

Nuclear weapons made possible the total destruction of entire innocent civilian populations in a very short amount of time. Not only was such annihilation against rules 5 and 6 of the just war doctrine, it far overstepped rule 4 by giving the aggressor overwhelming odds for success. Also, the simplicity and power of one atomic warhead made rule 1, assent of a legitimate authority, and rule 2, need for a just cause for aggression, easily bypassable by anyone in control of a bomb. Finally, the presence of nuclear technology led to the "first strike" philosophy and the arms race, thus negating rule 3. (Pp. 145-146)

Pilla concluded from his analysis: "So nuclear weapons clearly break all St. Augustine's standards for justice" (ibid.).

Evidently Bishop Pilla considered only strategic nuclear weapons—and thus only counter-city nuclear warfare—in his analysis; for tactical weapons and counter-force warfare would not totally destroy "entire innocent civilian populations." Moreover, what Pilla evidently understands by the requirements for lawful authorization of war and for a just cause for going to war seems not to fit the situation of a nation defending itself against aggression. Such hypothetical disagreements with Pilla's analysis illustrate that just-war theory is debatable when applied to nuclear war and nuclear weapons.

Yet other religious leaders have simply concluded that just-war criteria are inapplicable to nuclear warfare. Roman Catholic Archbishop John R. Quinn of San Francisco said in 1981: "If we apply each of [the] traditional principles of [just-war theory] to the current international arms race, we must conclude that a 'just' nuclear war is a contradiction in terms" (p. 161). Quinn singled out the criteria of proportionality and just means to underscore his point. He also appeared to have in mind strategic nuclear weapons and counter-city warfare. Yet the phrase "a contradiction in terms" seems to suggest that when nuclear weapons are considered, none of the just-war principles can possibly apply. This is another debatable point, since tactical weapons and counter-force warfare need to be included in the discussion.

The just-war theory remains a useful set of moral principles, however; it provides guidance today, even though the theory leads persons to differing conclusions. Some conclude that all forms of nuclear war would violate justice; but other thinkers conclude that some forms of nuclear war might be morally justifiable. This latter conclusion appears to have persuaded certain leaders in the Roman Catholic Church to doubt and criticize the just-war theory itself. Bishop Walter Sullivan of Richmond, Virginia, characterized the theory as "an excuse to go to war, mental gymnastics, casuistry of the worst sort" (*National Catholic Reporter*, 11 Dec . 1981). Although Bishop Sullivan may have had nuclear war in mind, his dismissal of the theory as such would seem to ban all conventional war also. Bishop Carroll Dozier of Memphis, Tennessee, in a speech to the 1982 national meeting of Pax Christi U.S.A., asserted that "the just-war theory should be put into a drawer along with the flat-earth theory."

The National Conference of Catholic Bishops reasserted the centrality of the just-war theory in Roman Catholic teaching in their pastoral letter, *The Challenge of Peace*. But they also acknowledged the "support for a pacifist option for individuals in the teaching of Vatican II and the reaffirmation that the popes have given to non-violent witness since the time of the council" (*Challenge*, p. 12). And although pacifism and the just-war ethic are incompatible in principle, the bishops believe that "the two perspectives support and complement one another, each preserving the other from distortion" (ibid.).

Of the just-war theory itself, the pastoral, says:

> Just war teaching has evolved. . . as an effort to prevent war; only if war cannot be rationally avoided does the teaching then seek to restrict and reduce its horrors. It does this by establishing a set of rigorous conditions which must be met if the decision to go to war is to be morally permissible. Such a decision, especially today, requires extraordinarily strong reasons for overriding the presumption *in favor of peace* and *against* war. . . . It is presumed that all sane people prefer peace, never *want* to initiate war and accept even the most justifiable defensive war only as a sad necessity. Only the most powerful reasons may be permitted to override such objection. (*Challenge*, p. 10)

According to the bishops, the just-war theory aims to prevent war by placing the burden of proof on any person or nation claiming that a particular war is morally acceptable. Individuals contemplating participating in a war would thus be required to reach a moral judgment beforehand rather than assuming that whatever one's country does is acceptable.

The bishops say that both pacifism and just-war principles seek to prevent war, and thus both positions morally condemn nuclear war: "As a people, we must refuse to legitimate the idea of nuclear war" (p. 13). This conclusion appears to derive, in part, from the argument that just-war principles make any form of nuclear war morally wrong under all circumstances.

The bishops reach two other conclusions with clarity and confidence:

Under no circumstances may nuclear weapons or other instruments of mass slaughter be used for the purpose of destroying population centers or other predominantly civilian targets. (Pp. 14-15)

We do not perceive any situation in which the deliberate initiation of nuclear warfare on however restricted a scale can be morally justified. (P. 15)

Both of these practical moral conclusions can be inferred from the just-war principles. A thread of just-war thinking runs through the pastoral letter, beginning with approval of the just-war theory and continuing through the moral outlawing of counter-city warfare and first nuclear strikes.

That the bishops and others run into difficulties with the idea of limited defensive nuclear war and with the more subtle issues of nuclear deterrence does not prove that the just-war theory is flawed nor that it must be abandoned, as Bishops Sullivan and Dozier would have it. It should be recognized that the . . . aspect of the just-war theory discussed here is limited to deciding whether a specific war would be morally acceptable. It does not address other moral problems associated with war—the risk of war caused by the buildup of armaments, for example, or the need for defensive capability in the face of aggressive neighboring nations, or the legitimacy of revolutionary violence. In the nuclear age, many of these moral problems, along with the decision of a nation to declare war against another nation, are nonetheless intense and badly in need of analysis.

Nuclear deterrence raises a very difficult moral problem that neither the just-war theory nor pacifism can solve. The U.S. deterrence force is intended to prevent nuclear aggression; thus it fulfills the goal of the just-war theory as understood by the American Roman Catholic bishops: to prevent war. But a nuclear deterrent runs grave risks: accidental discharge of missiles, for example, or provocation of potential enemies similarly armed, or overreaction when some defense of the United States less destructive than nuclear retaliation would satisfy. Whether these risks are acceptable morally is a vital question today, but the just-war theory cannot provide the answers. The most to be expected is that its application to such problems as deterrence will invite distinctions worthy of study and thought.

Questions

1. What are the seven conditions of the just-war theory?
2. How do strategic nuclear weapons differ in purpose from tactical nuclear weapons?
3. What does *The Challenge of Peace* say about the just-war theory? How does it support the theory?
4. Do you think war is ever justified? Why? Can nuclear war ever be justified?

The Christian and Total War

Paul A. Marshall

Paul A. Marshall is a senior member in political theory at the Institute of Christian Studies in Toronto. In this selection, Marshall argues that the means used to wage war must be as just as the war itself. A Calvinist view of God's Word requires that certain biblical principles guide the conduct of warfare. This is made more necessary with the presence today of nuclear, biological, chemical and other weapons of mass destruction. Marshall concludes that war fought with such weapons is never justified.

The appearance of techniques of mass destruction such as nuclear arms and chemical and biological weapons raises many new questions about warfare and the proper duty of governments. These weapons can lay waste to huge areas, perhaps even the earth itself, and invariably kill many noncombatants. Consequently, there must be grave doubts as to whether any war in which they are used could be legitimate. One nuclear bomb killed over one hundred thousand people at Hiroshima. The use of chlorine in the First World War and the use of chemical gases by Iraq against Iran and upon its own Kurdish population killed thousands of people in a matter of hours. The unfortunate victims had no chance to flee, or even to surrender. In the case of Hiroshima and the Kurds most of the dead were civilians who were owed protection under the international laws of war.

Certainly it is true that there has always been great bloodshed in war and that there have been wars of extermination in previous ages. Human sin always creates great evil. The Romans laid Jerusalem waste after its siege. The Mongols killed the inhabitants of cities that refused to surrender. Infectious diseases have been spread as a means of war. Even in the modern world the Nazis and the Khmer Rouge in Cambodia killed millions by much slower and more laborious means. The massacre of the innocent and the helpless is no new thing. In this sense the moral evil of the situation has not essentially changed in the modern age.

But one thing that has changed is modern science and technology. Our weapons are much more powerful and destructive, while at the same time much cheaper to acquire and easier to use than the weapons of former generations. At one time such destruction had to be carried out by many soldiers over months and years; but now it can be accomplished by a few people in a matter of hours. At one time it could be done only by the very powerful; but now even a small nation can acquire such means. The very power of such weapons hinders and even prevents a purely local attack on an enemy army; they necessarily kill and destroy more widely. This tremendous power also means that the progress of any nuclear war is unpredictable and probably uncontrollable. Most knowledgeable observers believe that there is little or no possibility of containing a nuclear war once it has begun. It will likely be played out to the destruction of all human and nonhuman life. It was this realization that led Secretary Gorbachev of the Soviet Union and President Reagan of the United States to declare jointly in their 1988 summit that "a nuclear war can never be won and must never be fought." Clearly these new weapons of mass destruction pose a new set of problems to which we as Christians must respond in addressing the question of war.

Judging the New Weapons

While there is much that is new in warfare we may still approach these problems in terms of the biblical view of war outlined in previous chapters. It was pointed out that Christians can and should engage only in wars that are just. For such a war to be legitimate it must be waged by a lawful government; it must be carried out only for the preservation of justice; it may be launched only if justice cannot otherwise be preserved; and it must be engaged in only as a last resort—if and when all other means, such as negotiation or arbitration or international law or peaceful sanctions, have failed.

But apart from the justifiability before God of the war itself, the actual *conduct* of the war must be proper. It is the *means* of fighting that the Calvinist must question. The law of God is never abrogated and must be followed even in conflict, difficult though this might seem. Enemies must be respected as human beings and not treated inhumanely. The means used to wage war must be in proportion to the goals of the war. The war itself must not do a greater harm in order to achieve a smaller good. We may not kill thousands in order to save the lives of ten. Prisoners must be treated humanely and noncombatants must be protected and shielded from attack. Existing laws and treaties, such as the Hague and Geneva Conventions on the rules of war, must be obeyed. The victory aimed at must not be the extermination of our enemies but their return to a proper place within the world. The earth itself must be safeguarded in war. In the Old Testament God called upon Israel not to destroy the trees but only to use those which they needed, asking "are the trees in the field men, that they should be besieged by thee?" (Deut. 20:19, 20).

In earlier ages it was possible to exterminate one's enemies even while using only very primitive weapons such as rifles or swords. But at least such weapons did not *have* to be used in such an atrocious way. It was possible also to use a rifle or sword in a more legitimate fashion. The problem with nuclear, chemical, and biological weapons is that they can only be used in an indiscriminate way, for they are inherently massive in their effects. Nerve gases blanket the landscape and kill or maim anybody who comes into contact with them—like the Kurdish villagers of Iraq in recent years. Nuclear weapons explode with the force of thousands of tons of TNT, and so their use necessarily levels a large area, killing—quickly or slowly—almost everyone and everything within that area. They cannot be used in a way that protects noncombatants.

They necessarily destroy the land of an enemy. Therefore, no war involving the use of nuclear weapons could meet the principles we have outlined for the proper conduct of belligerents in a legitimate war. No war which would annihilate humankind, or leave alive only a wretched fragment of it, could respect the lives of the innocent, honor existing laws of war, achieve a just peace with the enemy, or return an aggressor to its rightful place among the nations. Such weapons cannot be used in a just and legitimate way. If we submit ourselves to the Word of God, then we must resist the idea of fighting with nuclear, chemical, biological, or other weapons of mass destruction.

War in the Modern World

What we have said about the use of nuclear weapons does not mean that war itself is always wrong in this age. Rather it means that waging war with nuclear or other means of mass destruction is wrong. In fact there have been many wars during what we call the "nuclear age" which have not involved such weapons or the threat of their use. If the goal of the war is legitimate, the means are properly limited, and no other means are possible, then it may still be justifiable for a modern state to engage in war.

However, the presence of nuclear weapons still casts a long shadow even over those conflicts which do not involve their use and which may otherwise be just. This is especially true if one or more of the combatants possesses nuclear weapons, even though they do not use them and are committed to not using them. This is because the tension, fear, and pride present in any war increase the danger that someone will be tempted to use these weapons. In a world corrupted by sin we cannot ignore this possibility even though it would almost certainly be an act not only of destruction but of *self*-destruction. Such a temptation may be very strong for a country that is losing in a conventional conflict; it may face intense pressure to switch to nuclear combat.

For these reasons, while there may still be justifiable war in the nuclear age, all war now takes place in a more dangerous situation. The possibility of being drawn into a nuclear conflict makes it even more urgent that any war be avoided whenever and wherever possible.

The Christian's Duty

Given the dangers of modern means of mass destruction, it is our Christian duty to condemn the use of such weapons in war and to reaffirm God's requirements for the just conduct of war. We must also actively strive to prevent the outbreak of any war which could involve the use of nuclear weapons, and we must seek to end our dependence on them. We should not do these things because of any belief that the world is really a peace-loving place, that humankind can fundamentally transform itself, that nations will forsake self-interest, or that a utopia free from all war can be achieved. None of these things is true, and such perfection awaits the final reign of the Messiah. Our concern is not prompted by optimism or pacifism. Rather, the Calvinist's desire to limit the nuclear threat stems precisely from the recognition that all people are sinful and that, therefore, there is a real danger that nuclear arms will be used. We are motivated by our commitment to uphold the limits that God puts on war.

While an appeal for self-control can and should be made to the consciences of leaders, especially in countries that have been shaped by the Christian faith, we must also call for the formation of appropriate international law. We need to develop laws and treaties that limit the nuclear threat. Such treaties should limit the number, type, and location of weapons. In order to be effective they must also provide a means of detecting any violations, so there need to be inspection systems and safeguards. Another requirement is incentives or sanctions to guarantee adherence to the terms of the treaty. These should involve, at the mildest level, public opinion or peaceful sanctions such as trade embargoes. But by and large the major sanction and threat stem from the weapons themselves. Any country which uses nuclear weapons is liable to be destroyed itself and so each country shares an interest in limiting and removing such weapons. In a sense each country has become its own hostage.

It would be better if these treaties and safeguards could be properly administered by an international body such as the United Nations or the World Court. But at present such bodies do not have the resources for either administration or enforcement of such treaties. In addition the number of countries that possess nuclear weapons is relatively small, and the number seeking to limit and reduce them is even smaller. For this reason the most effective negotiations have involved only the nuclear powers. The usual format has been negotiations between the United States and the Soviet Union, or else between NATO and the Warsaw Pact countries. In the present situation Christians should strongly encourage and pray for such bilateral efforts. For this reason we commend efforts to establish treaties to limit antiballistic missiles and intermediate-range missiles. At this time we are particularly grateful to God for the major efforts underway to further reduce nuclear weaponry.

The Continuing Danger

It may be that by God's grace nuclear and other devastating weapons will be reduced to zero. But even then their threat will not have totally passed. It seems unlikely that we will forget how to build such weapons and so the possibility of their resurgence will always remain. Not only their possession but even their actual invention has fundamentally altered international relations. This is why treaties need to be safeguarded by rigorous inspection—to prevent people not only from concealing weapons but also from taking steps to rebuild them. Even then the threat will not totally disappear. Consequently, it is ever more urgent to leaven our international affairs with the gospel of the Prince of Peace. We will need continually to pray to God to preserve us from destruction, and we will need always to remember that our hope lies not in humankind's greatness but in God's promises and grace.

Questions

1. What reasons does Marshall give for insisting that weapons of mass destruction cannot be used in a legitimate way?

2. Of what value are international treaties to limit nuclear arms buildup? What specific goals can such treaties expect to achieve?

3. What is the Christian's duty in light of the arms situation today? What specifics does the author suggest?

The Way of Peace in a World at War

John H. Yoder

John H. Yoder teaches theology at a Mennonite seminary. This selection was originally presented as three lectures on the subject of peacemaking. Yoder says that Christians are to follow the example of Christ who was the Prince of Peace, who loved his enemies, and whose followers come from all nations on the earth. For the Christian, waging peace takes precedence over waging war.

I. Portraits of Christ

Following the example of Jesus himself, the first Christians and the writers of the New Testament were quick to see in the book of the prophet Isaiah a description of the innocent sufferings of Christ. They read there:

He was counted among evildoers . . .
For our welfare he was chastised . . .
Mistreated, he bore it humbly, without complaint,
silent as a sheep led to the slaughter,
silent as a ewe before the shearers . . .
They did away with him unjustly . . .
though he was guilty of no violence
and had not spoken one false word.

Isaiah 53:4-9

In all ages these words of the prophet concerning the one he called the "Servant of the Lord" have been beloved by Christians for the portrait they paint of our crucified Master. Yet when we find these same words echoing in the New Testament, it is not only because they are fitting or beautiful words to describe Christ and his sacrifice on behalf of sinful humanity; it is because they constitute a call to the Christian to do likewise. There we read

If you have done right and suffer for it
Your endurance is worthwhile in the sight of God;
To this you were called,
because Christ suffered on your behalf,
and left you an example;
it is for you to follow in his steps,
He committed no sin,
he was guilty of no falsehood;
when he suffered he uttered no threats.

1 Peter 2:20-22

The innocent, silently uncomplaining suffering of Christ is, in the teaching of Peter, whose letter I have just quoted, not only an act of Christ on our behalf from which we benefit; it is also an example of Christ for our instruction, which we are to follow. This portrait of Christ is to be painted again on the ordinary canvas of our lives. Did not Jesus himself say that those who would follow him must deny themselves and take up their cross? What then does it mean for the Christian to bear a cross?

What Is Our Cross?

We meet in this world some suffering that is our own fault; we bring accidents upon ourselves by our carelessness, or punishment by our own offenses. This is not "bearing a cross." As Peter wrote, there is no merit in taking punishment for having done wrong. "What credit is it," he asks, "if when you do wrong and are beaten for it, you take it patiently?"

We also sometimes suffer in ways we cannot understand, as from an unexpected or unexplained illness or catastrophe. Such suffering the Christian can bear, trusting in God's supporting presence and learning to depend more fully and more joyfully on him. Yet this is not what Jesus was talking about when he predicted suffering for his disciples.

The cross of Christ was the price of his obedience to God

amidst a rebellious world; it was suffering for having done right, for loving where others hated, for representing in the flesh the forgiveness and the righteousness of God among men both less forgiving and less righteous. The cross of Christ was God's method of overcoming evil with good.

The cross of the Christian is no different. It is the price of one's obedience to God's love toward all people in a world ruled by hate. Such unflinching love for friend and foe alike will mean hostility and suffering for us, as it did for him.

Jesus instructed his disciples, simply and clearly, not to resist evil.

Whoever slaps you on the right cheek, turn and offer him the left. If he sues you for your shirt, let him have your coat as well. . . . Love your enemies and pray for those who persecute you, only so can you be the children of your heavenly Father who sends his sun and rain to good and bad alike.

Matthew 5:39-45

In saying this, Jesus was not a foolish dreamer spinning out futile hopes for a better world, thinking that if only we keep smiling everything will turn out all right, with our opponents turned into friends and our sacrifices all repaid. He knew full well the cost of such unlimited love. He foresaw clearly the suffering it would mean, first for himself and then for his followers. But there was no other way for him to take, no other way worthy of God. Jesus' teaching here is not a collection of good human ideas; it is his divinely authoritative interpretation of the law of God.

Facing Our Conflicts

Over the years the world has not grown much more loving. The example of Cain, who killed his brother, still sets the basic pattern for dealing with conflicts, whether within the family or in the world of nations. Among nations it matters little whether they profess to be religious or not. The choice of weapons and the readiness to retaliate are similar. How few are they, how few even within the Christian churches, who in this embattled world seek to be conformed only to Christ, to find in the suffering servant of the Lord, and not in some honored king or warrior, the model for their lives!

"It is by this that we know what love is," says the apostle, "that Christ laid down his life for us. And we in turn are bound to lay down our lives for our brothers" (1 John 3:16, NEB).

Christians whose loyalty to the Prince of Peace puts them out of step with today's nationalistic world, because they are willing to love their nation's friends but not to hate their nation's enemies, are not unrealistic dreamers who think that by their objections they will end all wars. On the contrary, it is the soldiers who think they can put an end to wars by preparing for just one more. Nor do such Christians think that by virtue of their refusal to help with the organized destruction of life and property they are uninvolved in the complications and conflicts of modern life. Nor are they reacting in emotional fear to the fantastic awfulness of the weapons created by the demonic ingenuity of modern scientists.

They love their enemies not because they think they are wonderful people, not because they think their love is sure to conquer them, not because they fail to respect their native land or their rulers, not because they are unconcerned for the safety of their neighbors, not because they favor another political or economic system.

Christians love their enemies because God does so, and commands his followers to do so. That is the only reason, and that is enough. Our God, who has made himself known in Jesus Christ, is a reconciling, a forgiving, a suffering God. If, to paraphrase the apostle Paul, "it is no longer I who love, but Christ who loves in me" (Galatians 2:20), my life must bear the marks of that revelation.

We Have No Enemies

No one created in God's image and for whom Christ died can be for me an enemy, whose life I am willing to threaten or to take, unless I am more devoted to something else—to a political theory, to a nation, to the defense of certain privileges, or to my own personal welfare—than I am to God's cause: his loving invasion of this world in his prophets, his Son, and his church.

One of the most difficult things to understand in the history of the Christian church is the haste with which preachers and simple citizens have labeled the selfish interests of their own class, their own race, their own nation with the name of Christ, making a holy cause of the subjection, or even the destruction, of those whom Christ came to save and to give an abundant life.

In any kind of conflict, from the fist fight to the labor dispute, from the family quarrel to the threat of international communism, the Christian sees the world and its wars from the viewpoint of the cross. "When we were God's enemies, we were reconciled to him through the death of his Son" (Romans 5:10, NEB).

The Christian has no choice. If this was God's pattern, if his strategy for dealing with his enemies was to love them and give himself for them, it must be ours as well.

> From the top of the mountains I see him;
> From the hills I behold him
> Lo, a people dwelling alone
> and not reckoning itself among the nations.
>
> Numbers 23:9

> You are a chosen race,
> a royal priesthood,
> a holy nation,
> God's own people.
>
> 1 Peter 2:9

II. Nationality? Christian

It has always been true that people have many loyalties, many attachments to groups or causes for which they are willing to sacrifice. Such loyalty may be to a family or a school, a sporting club, or a business firm. Yet the overwhelming loyalty of most persons in our age is to the nation. Whether under the long-established governments of Europe and North America, or in those other parts of the world where national independence is a recent attainment or a goal still sought after, it is to the nation that young persons give their enthusiasm. For the nation young people will risk their lives. For the nation they will, if need be, kill and destroy in war.

What does Christ say about the Christian and national loyalty? For centuries, most professing Christians have believed that their faith made them not only more obedient citizens but also more courageous soldiers, that God helped them not only to love their neighbors but also to hate and destroy their enemies. Since the Roman emperor Constantine allied his government with the church, priests and preachers have been crowning kings, blessing armies, and praying for the defeat of their nation's enemies, all in the name of the Prince of Peace. Almost every theology and every denomination has explained how this had to be so. Today churchmen can be found who will argue that even the hydrogen bomb, even poison gas or germ warfare, can be used by Christians against their fellow-humans if only the nation so commands. But what does the gospel say?

"Out of Every Nation"

The Bible does not ignore the existence of nations. Once the missionary Paul, addressing a group of philosophers, spoke of how the Creator God had "made from one every nation of people to live on all the face of the earth, having determined allotted periods and the boundaries of their habitation" (Acts 17:26). But most often when we read in Scripture of "the nations," it is to say that *out* of every tribe and tongue and people and *nation* individuals have been redeemed to belong to God's people.

"You are a chosen race, a royal priesthood, a holy *nation*, God's own people," Peter wrote of the Christian church. The nation to which the Christian belongs *first* is "God's own people," the fellowship of the saints, the church of Jesus Christ. This "people for God's special possession" is united not by a common language or territory or government but by one and the same divine call and a common response. Reconciled to God, men and women belong to each other. The unity thus created breaches every wall and rends every curtain, whether of bamboo or of iron.

Then the apostle said that in Christ God had joined "Greek and Jew . . . barbarian, Scythian, whether slave or free" (Colossians 3:11). Today he would say, "white and black, Russian and American, labor and management."

This new nation, the people of God, is the Christian's first loyalty. No political nation, no geographical homeland to which one belongs by birth, can take precedence over the heavenly citizenship of a Christian in one's new birth.

These pious phrases—citizenship in heaven, new birth, people of God—are nothing new. They are in fact so familiar, so well worn, that it occurs to few Christians to stop and think what it would really mean to take them seriously. Well, what would it mean?

Brothers and Sisters in All Nations
First of all, God's call to put first loyalties first means that Christians of different nations, even of enemy nations, have more in common with each other, belong more closely to each other, should care more for each other's welfare than for that of their non-christian fellow citizens. Not for nothing do Christians call one another "brother" or "sister." How then can Christians, for the sake of their country's prestige or possessions, seek to take the lives of their spiritual brothers and sisters, when their sole offense is to have been born under another flag?

Today a great wave of concern for their dividedness is sweeping through the Christian churches. Differences of creed and denominational barriers are felt to be an offense against our Lord's will that his followers should be one as he and his Father are one. Church leaders labor over creeds and put forth considerable effort to be able to worship together. Yet is it not a yet more flagrant betrayal of Christian unity when children of the same Father, disciples of the same Lord, at a word from their secular rulers take up arms against one another?

To confess belief in the church universal means that we cannot grasp all of God's will by keeping our minds tidily fenced within our own borders. For instance, when the apostle Paul instructs his readers to be subject to the powers established over them (Romans 13:1), we cannot conclude, as do so many Christians, that this applies only to us and to our government. Paul wrote this about the rule of pagan Rome. He does not say that freedom-loving people shall be subject only to democratic governments, but that "every soul" shall be subject to the established rulers. If this is the Christian's duty in North America, it is as much the duty of Christians in China or France, in Poland or India.

Our governments may feel that they have reasons to refuse to recognize the existence of certain hostile powers, and even to seek their downfall. Some Christians make a virtue of advocating a more belligerent national policy than their government exercises. Some even consider it impossible that a Christian could live under a fascist or communist government without rebelling. Thereby they admit their lack of understanding of the universality of the church, which through most of history has thrived under unchristian, even tyrannical, governments, and has stagnated when it became the spiritual sponsor of a nation's aims.

Ultimate Values

Finally, the primacy of Christians' loyalty will show in our sense of ultimate values. In the minds of many serious people, what really matters about human history is the creation of institutions which will create and distribute material abundance, and will guarantee human rights. This is what we read about in the history books. These things do matter. And generally Christians do much to help achieve them. But what matters most, the real reason that God lets time go on, is his calling together of his own people through the witness of the gospel. Not building and protecting a bigger and better democracy, but building the church is God's purpose; not the defeat of communism, or of hunger, but the proclamation of his kingdom and the welding of all kinds of men and women into one new body is what we are here for. Kings and empires have come and gone in times past and shall continue to come and go until the day of Christ's appearing. For Christians to seek any government's interest—even the security and power of peaceable and freedom-loving democracy—at the cost of the lives and security of our brothers and sisters around the world, would be selfishness and idolatry, however much glorified by patriotic preachers and poets.

Not only in Abraham's time was it a testing of faith to be called by God to abandon all else out of loyalty to that "city whose builder and maker is God" (Hebrews 11:10). Even more today, when nationalism has become a religion for millions, will the true depth and reality of the Christian profession of church people be tested when they must choose between their earthly and their eternal loyalties.

What is our allegiance? It is to that people "elect from every nation, yet one o'er all the earth." Our nationality? Christian.

III. Disarmed by God

What causes conflicts and quarrels among you? Do they not spring from the aggressiveness of your bodily desires? You want something which you cannot have and so you are bent on murder; you are envious, and cannot attain your ambition, and so you quarrel and fight.

James 4:1-2, NEB

These words of the apostle James have not been worn out. When there is conflict, whether within small groups or between nations, we try to dignify the clash with lofty principles. We may speak of truth and honor, of democracy and of human rights, of great causes and of noble goals. Yet the apostle is not deceived: "What is the cause of conflicts among you?

... is it not your bodily desires? ... you are envious."

He has seen deeper than we care to admit. True enough, anyone—even groups of people, and perhaps, rarely, a nation—can seek sincerely some unselfish purpose, but only seldom and not for long. If great, noble, unselfish causes are constantly proclaimed as the guides of a group's actions, even the most gullible of us has learned to check a second time to see what the real reason is. In international affairs a nation may show great concern, as they usually say, to "liberate" some poor people from "tyranny." What they really care about, however, is the price of sugar or the use of some mine or port, or the aggrandizement of their political influence. In the dealings between labor and management, each side speaks of the good of the national economy. But the real desire is for an immediate one-sided gain, even at the cost of a rise in prices for everyone. In a neighborhood or family disagreement, we hastily announce that serious moral principles are at stake—honesty or decency—when in fact, it is our own pride that drives us.

Understanding the Cause

If we thus understand the true root of conflict, this explains a number of things. It explains, first of all, why the Christian is and must be a child of peace. The Christian is not primarily someone who has joined a church, or has accepted certain teachings, or has had certain feelings, or has promised to live up to certain moral standards, though all these things are part of the picture. The Christian is a person who has been, in the words of Jesus, "born anew," who has started life over, who by the power of God is a new person. Conflict was previously a normal, built-in part of one's nature, but now the person has been disarmed. The spring from which flowed enmity and strife has been clogged. The scrawny shrub of bitterness has been cut down to the stump. It may well spring up again, but the believer knows how to deal with it as with any other temptation—in repentance, confession, and spiritual victory.

The reason, therefore, for the Christian's being called to live above this world's battles is not that one of the Ten Commandments enjoins us not to kill, and not even that Jesus as a new lawgiver orders us to love our enemies. The Christian has been disarmed by God. No *orders* are needed to love one's neighbors, beginning in the smallest circle of daily relationships, or with one's enemies. The believer is driven to this by the love of Christ within.

The fact that selfish desire is the root of conflict explains why we cannot really expect whole nations and societies to build a peaceful world. Christian behavior flows from faith; we cannot impose it on entire nations. Many persons, when they hear of Christians whose conscience forbids their bearing arms, will argue against this position on the grounds that it is quite unrealistic to expect nations to follow this example. This is a strange argument. In our teachings about moral purity and holiness in any other realm, we do not wait for the world to be ready to follow us before we follow Christ. We know clearly that to be called by Christ means being different from the world.

How then should our living the disarmed life depend on whether nations are ready to lay down their weapons? Jesus predicted that there would continue to be wars as long as this world lasts, just as he predicted that people's faith would grow cold and their morals loose. But this cannot be a reason for Christians to follow this world's ways, anymore than the prevalence of theft or of waste is a model for Christians to follow.

Pray for Rulers

When we say that we do not expect nations to take the path of suffering and discipleship, this does not mean that it is wrong for Christians to desire and to work for peace among nations. The apostle Paul expressly instructs us to pray especially for rulers and for all those in authority, in order that we may lead a peaceful life. God's will is that we should be able to live quiet and godly lives. The duty of government before God is to permit this. We therefore can and should pray and testify concerning the folly of trusting in earthly arms, concerning the undermining of democratic government by peacetime military establishment, concerning the dangers of radioactive contamination and of "accidental war" which the great belligerent powers impose on the rest of the globe, and especially concerning the hideous immorality of the weapons now being devised.

It might even be that with more and more of our neighbors uneasy and disturbed about the menace of militarism, the example and refusal of a few resolute Christians could sound an alarm, a rallying cry for intelligent citizens who were waiting for someone with the courage to speak first and to suffer for it. But the Christian does not renounce war because one can expect intelligent citizens to rally around. They usually won't. The believer takes that stand because the defenseless death of the Messiah has for all time been revealed as the victory of faith that overcomes the world.

But wait a minute. Is this the whole picture? Is there not, after all, a moral difference between freedom and tyranny? Is it not our duty to care and even to sacrifice for the preservation of our civilization? Certainly not all such sacrifice can be accounted for as "selfish desires." Are we not socially responsible? The Christian who has been disarmed by God has several things to say at this point, but they may be gathered up into one question. Did not Jesus Christ face the same problem? Was not he, who was just as human as you and I, concerned for the victims of oppression? Was he not, with the thousands who gathered around to make him king, a man before whom the path to political responsibility was opening? Did he not believe that it was God's prophetically announced will to glorify himself by establishing righteousness among the nations and to make Zion the center from which justice would go out to all peoples?

The Supreme Example

And yet all of this did not swerve the Son of Man, in whom we see what God wants each of us to be, from his certainty that to seek and to save the lost his path must be one not of power but of humility—not of enforcing justice but of incarnating love. As Peter wrote, "He . . . committed his cause to the One who judges justly" (1 Peter 2:23, NEB). Yet has not the ministry of this one defenseless man—and of the line of dis-armed martyrs in his train across the years—done more to unseat tyrants and to defend basic human rights than all the belligerent zeal of those who were seeking to defend God's people against the godless with the weapons of war? Human wrath does not accomplish the justice of God.

When the apostle Paul says that "the weapons we wield are not merely human" or "not those of the world" (2 Corinthians 10:4, NEB), most of us, accustomed to thinking on the "merely human" level, would have expected him to say, "not human but spiritual," or, "not of this world but of the other world." But he says, "not merely human, but divinely potent." This is the "almighty meekness" of our reigning Lord. When the Christian whom God has disarmed lays aside carnal weapons it is not, in the last analysis, because those weapons are too strong, but because they are too weak. He directs his life toward the day when all creation will praise not kings and chancellors but the Lamb that was slain as worthy to receive blessing and honor and glory *and power* (Revelation 5:12-13).

Questions

1. How does Jesus serve as an example of the way of peace?
2. According to Yoder, is it ever right for a Christian to take up arms?
3. Why does his analysis of peacemaking not transfer from individuals to nations?

The Ways of Meeting Oppression

Martin Luther King, Jr.

Martin Luther King, Jr., (1929-1968) was an ordained Baptist minister who became the chief spokesperson and leader of the civil rights movement in the 1950s and 1960s. He was assassinated in Memphis, Tennessee, in April of 1968. In this selection, King outlines three possible ways oppressed people can react to their oppressors. He advocates only one— nonviolent resistance—a view which he learned from the life of India's Mahatma Gandhi.

Oppressed people deal with their oppression in three characteristic ways. One way is acquiescence: the oppressed resign themselves to their doom. They tacitly adjust themselves to oppression, and thereby become conditioned to it. In every movement toward freedom some of the oppressed prefer to remain oppressed. Almost 2800 years ago Moses set out to lead the children of Israel from the slavery of Egypt to the freedom of the promised land. He soon discovered that slaves do not always welcome their deliverers. They become accustomed to being slaves. They would rather bear those ills they have, as Shakespeare pointed out, than flee to others that they know not of. They prefer the "fleshpots of Egypt" to the ordeals of emancipation.

There is such a thing as the freedom of exhaustion. Some people are so worn down by the yoke of oppression that they give up. A few years ago in the slum areas of Atlanta, a Negro guitarist used to sing almost daily: "Ben down so long that down don't bother me." This is the type of negative freedom and resignation that often engulfs the life of the oppressed.

But this is not the way out. To accept passively an unjust

system is to cooperate with that system; thereby the oppressed become as evil as the oppressor. Noncooperation with evil is as much a moral obligation as is cooperation with good. The oppressed must never allow the conscience of the oppressor to slumber. Religion reminds every man that he is his brother's keeper. To accept injustice or segregation passively is to say to the oppressor that his actions are morally right. It is a way of allowing his conscience to fall asleep. At this moment the oppressed fails to be his brother's keeper. So acquiescence— while often the easier way—is not the moral way. It is the way of the coward. The Negro cannot win the respect of his oppressor by acquiescing; he merely increases the oppressor's arrogance and contempt. Acquiescence is interpreted as proof of the Negro's inferiority. The Negro cannot win the respect of the white people of the South or the peoples of the world if he is willing to sell the future of his children for his personal and immediate comfort and safety.

A second way that oppressed people sometimes deal with oppression is to resort to physical violence and corroding hatred. Violence often brings about momentary results. Nations have frequently won their independence in battle. But in spite of temporary victories, violence never brings permanent peace. It solves no social problem; it merely creates new and more complicated ones.

Violence as a way of achieving racial justice is both impractical and immoral. It is impractical because it is a descending spiral ending in destruction for all. The old law of an eye for an eye leaves everybody blind. It is immoral because it seeks to humiliate the opponent rather than win his understanding; it seeks to annihilate rather than to convert. Violence is immoral because it thrives on hatred rather than love. It destroys community and makes brotherhood impossible. It leaves society in monologue rather than dialogue. Violence ends by defeating itself. It creates bitterness in the survivors and brutality in the destroyers. A voice echoes through time saying to every potential Peter, "Put up your sword." History is cluttered with the wreckage of nations that failed to follow this command.

If the American Negro and other victims of oppression succumb to the temptation of using violence in the struggle for freedom, future generations will be the recipients of a desolate night of bitterness, and our chief legacy to them will be an endless reign of meaningless chaos. Violence is not the way.

The third way open to oppressed people in their quest for freedom is the way of nonviolent resistance. Like the synthesis in Hegelian philosophy, the principle of nonviolent resistance seeks to reconcile the truths of two opposites—the acquiescence and violence—while avoiding the extremes and immoralities of both. The nonviolent resister agrees with the person who acquiesces that one should not be physically aggressive toward his opponent; but he balances the equation by agreeing with the person of violence that evil must be resisted. He avoids the nonresistance of the former and the violent resistance of the latter. With nonviolent resistance, no individual or group need submit to any wrong, nor need anyone resort to violence in order to right a wrong.

It seems to me that this is the method that must guide the actions of the Negro in the present crisis in race relations. Through nonviolent resistance the Negro will be able to rise to the noble height of opposing the unjust system while loving the perpetrators of the system. The Negro must work passionately and unrelentingly for full stature as a citizen, but he must not use inferior methods to gain it. He must never come to terms with falsehood, malice, hate, or destruction.

Nonviolent resistance makes it possible for the Negro to remain in the South and struggle for his rights. The Negro's problem will not be solved by running away. He cannot listen to the glib suggestion of those who would urge him to migrate en masse to other sections of the country. By grasping his great opportunity in the South he can make a lasting contribution to the moral strength of the nation and set a sublime example of courage for generations yet unborn.

By nonviolent resistance, the Negro can also enlist all men of good will in his struggle for equality. The problem is not a purely racial one, with Negroes set against whites. In the end, it is not a struggle between people at all, but a tension between justice and injustice. Nonviolent resistance is not aimed against oppressors but against oppression. Under its banner consciences, not racial groups, are enlisted.

Questions

1. What are three ways oppressed people react to their oppressors?
2. King says that going along with oppression is a way of allowing your "conscience to fall asleep." What does he mean? Do you agree? Why or why not?
3. What legacy does violence in the face of oppression leave?
4. Why is love such an important component of nonviolent resistance? Is this a clue as to why nonviolent resistance is not a "natural" response for sinful human beings?

The Art of Reconciliation

Terry Dobson

Terry Dobson studied for eight years with Japan's Morihei Ueshiba, the founder of aikido, a strategy for settling conflicts similar to judo and jujitsu. In this selection, Dobson describes a scene on a Japanese commuter train where it seemed to him the application of aikido was clearly necessary. However, he learned that there are other, more effective ways to deal with conflict.

The train clanked and rattled through the suburbs of Tokyo on a drowsy spring afternoon. Our car was comparatively empty—a few housewives with their kids in tow, some old folks going shopping. I gazed absently at the drab houses and dusty hedgerows.

At one station the doors opened, and suddenly the afternoon quiet was shattered by a man bellowing violent, incomprehensible curses. The man staggered into our car. He wore laborer's clothing, and he was big, drunk, and dirty. Screaming, he swung at a woman holding a baby. The blow sent her spinning into the laps of an elderly couple. It was a miracle that the baby was unharmed.

Terrified, the couple jumped up and scrambled toward the other end of the car. The laborer aimed a kick at the retreating back of the old woman but missed as she scuttled to safety. This so enraged the drunk that he grabbed the metal pole in the center of the car and tried to wrench it out of its stanchion. I could see that one of his hands was cut and bleeding. The train lurched ahead, the passengers frozen with fear. I stood up.

I was young then, some 20 years ago, and in pretty good shape. I'd been putting in a solid eight hours of aikido training nearly every day for the past three years. I liked to throw and grapple. I thought I was tough. Trouble was my martial skill was untested in actual combat. As students of aikido, we were not allowed to fight.

"Aikido," my teacher had said again and again, "is the art of reconciliation. Whoever has the mind to fight has broken his connection with the universe. If you try to dominate people, you are already defeated. We study how to resolve conflict, not how to start it."

I had listened to his words. I had tried hard. I even went so far as to cross the street to avoid the *chimpira*, the pinball punks who lounged around the train stations. My forbearance exalted me. I felt both tough and holy. In my heart, however, I wanted an absolutely legitimate opportunity whereby I might save the innocent by destroying the guilty.

This is it! I said to myself as I got to my feet. *People are in danger. If I don't do something fast, somebody will probably get hurt.*

Seeing me stand up, the drunk recognized a chance to focus his rage. "Aha!" he roared. "A foreigner! You need a lesson in Japanese manners!"

I held on lightly to the commuter strap overhead and gave him a slow look of disgust and dismissal. I planned to take this turkey apart, but he had to make the first move. I wanted him mad, so I pursed my lips and blew him an insolent kiss.

"All right!" he hollered. "You're gonna get a lesson." He gathered himself for a rush at me.

A split second before he could move, someone shouted "Hey!" It was earsplitting. I remember the strangely joyous, lilting quality of it—as though you and a friend had been searching diligently for something, and he had suddenly stumbled upon it. "Hey!"

I wheeled to my left; the drunk spun to his right. We both stared down at a little old Japanese. He must have been well into his seventies, this tiny gentleman, sitting there immaculate in his kimono. He took no notice of me but beamed delightedly at the laborer, as though he had a most important, most welcome secret to share.

"C'mere," the old man said in an easy vernacular, beckoning to the drunk. "C'mere and talk with me." He waved his hand lightly.

The big man followed, as if on a string. He planted his feet belligerently in front of the old gentleman and roared above the clacking wheels, "Why the hell should I talk to you?" The drunk now had his back to me. If his elbow moved so much as a millimeter, I'd drop him in his socks.

The old man continued to beam at the laborer. "What'cha been drinkin'?" he asked, his eyes sparkling with interest.

"I been drinkin' sake," the laborer bellowed back, "and it's none of your business!" Flecks of spittle spattered the old man.

"Oh, that's wonderful," the old man said, "absolutely wonderful! You see, I love sake too. Every night, me and my wife (she's 76, you know), we warm up a little bottle of sake and take it out into the garden, and we sit on an old wooden bench. We watch the sun go down, and we look to see how our persimmon tree is doing. My great-grandfather planted that tree, and we worry about whether it will recover from those ice storms we had last winter. Our tree has done better than I expected, though, especially when you consider the poor quality of the soil. It is gratifying to watch when we take our sake and go out to enjoy the evening—even when it rains!" He looked up at the laborer, eyes twinkling.

As he struggled to follow the old man's conversation, the drunk's face began to soften. His fists slowly unclenched. "Yeah, I love persimmons too . . ." his voice trailed off.

"Yes," said the old man, smiling, "and I'm sure you have a wonderful wife."

"No," replied the laborer. "My wife died." Very gently, swaying with the motion of the train, the big man began to sob. "I don't got no *wife*, I don't got no *home*, I don't got no *job*. I'm so *ashamed* of myself." Tears rolled down his cheeks; a spasm of despair rippled through his body.

Now it was my turn. Standing there in my well-scrubbed youthful innocence, my make-this-world-safe-for-democracy righteousness, I suddenly felt dirtier than he was.

Then the train arrived at my stop. As the doors opened, I

heard the old man cluck sympathetically. "My, my," he said, "that is a difficult predicament indeed. Sit down here and tell me about it."

I turned my head for one last look. The laborer was sprawled on the seat, his head on the old man's lap. The old man was softly stroking the filthy, matted hair.

As the train pulled away, I sat down on a bench. What I had wanted to do with muscle had been accomplished with kind words. I had just seen aikido tried in combat, and the essence of it was love. I would have to practice the art with an entirely different spirit. It would be a long time before I could speak about the resolution of conflict.

Questions

1. Describe the scene on the train before and after the drunken man boarded.
2. What is aikido? Why do you think aikido is described as "the art of reconciliation"? Do you think it can successfully reconcile conflict?
3. How does Dobson's attitude toward the drunk conflict with the purpose of aikido? What was the basis for Dobson's decision to challenge the drunk? Was it successful?
4. What did the old Japanese man do to calm the drunk?
5. The title of this selection is "The Art of Reconciliation." Is this story about aikido or about something else?

Shalom

Gayle Boss-Koopman, Steven D. Hoogerwerf, Robert A. White

This selection presents a biblical view of shalom. More than just peace, shalom has to do with God's original purposes for his creation. It includes harmony, justice, and prosperity. Sin has ruined creation, but God's plan for the restoration of shalom continues to unfold. Our duty as Christians is to follow the leading of Christ and to do what we can to bring peace and social justice to our world.

Shalom: A Vision and a Task

SHALOM! Is this word familiar or new to you? Do you think of it as a term from a foreign tongue and tradition? Or do you, like many Christians, treasure shalom as a word of promise and hope? Shalom is an important word for our study because it is a key word in the Old Testament. It is usually translated "peace." The modern idea of peace often means little more than personal tranquility or the absence of war. Shalom is a richer word, much more inclusive and positive. *Shalom describes the wholeness, harmony, well-being, joy, and prosperity God wills for all creation.*

God created the world to live in this harmonious well-being called shalom. God is acting now to redeem the world according to his will for shalom. That is why we say that shalom is a vision. In this present world of hostility, conflict, and fear, shalom gives us a glimpse of the peaceful world that is sure to come. It is the promise of wholeness which God intends to fulfill in and for his divided creation. Walter Breuggemann, an Old Testament scholar, writes: "The central vision of world history in the Bible is that all of creation is one, every creature in community with every other creature."

God's Plan from the Beginning

In the beginning God spoke, and chaos became order and wholeness (Gen. 1:2). In the world as God created it, harmony is more basic than discord, goodness more original than sin, peace more natural than war. We need a rich word like shalom to describe that peaceable creation which God looked upon and called "very good." At the dawn of creation our world was one community in the Creator's loving presence. Its creatures lived in harmony with God, with each other, and with the earth.

The Bible tells us that this original shalom was soon shattered by sin. Peace was broken when God's human creatures rebelled. Man and woman rejected their role as creatures and their rightful place in the harmony of creation. Abusing their freedom, they tried to become "like God" (Gen. 3:4), and to set themselves up as the rulers of creation. Communion with God was replaced by competition. Man and woman came to know guilt and fear.

Their rebellion against the Creator destroyed the community of creation as well. The marriage relationship was strained by the pointing finger of blame (Gen. 3:12). Work became toil, and the lush garden was replaced by a field of thorns (Gen. 3:18). Jealousy infected family life, and Cain killed his brother in cold blood (Gen. 4:8). Humanity forged weapons of war and lived by a code of vengeance (Gen. 4:22-24). Soon the earth was filled with violence (Gen. 6:11), and the one language of community became the babble of many confusing tongues. The sinful human family was divided and scattered upon the earth (Gen. 11:9). Shalom was shattered.

But creation didn't lapse back into chaos. God did not abandon his world! Though we experience the brokenness of sin in and around us, shalom is still the purpose and promise of history. The Bible was written to tell the good news: God has a plan to fulfill the promise of peace. The Creator has become our Redeemer working patiently to accomplish his purpose as history unfolds. God will not fail! What's more, God wants to work through us to restore shalom to his world.

Isaiah's Vision of Peace

Of course, the shalom vision is not always clear to everyone. For Isaiah at first, and maybe for us, shalom seemed like an empty dream and a false hope. Idolatry, violence, and war had spread rubble over the land. Corrupt rulers lined their pockets with bribes while widows and orphans begged in the streets of Jerusalem. Isaiah was frustrated and fearful. Even the people chosen to be God's agents of blessing, even Israel mocked shalom by their wicked and violent ways. How could anyone hope for community and security in a world so constantly at war? How could anyone hope for wholeness in the midst of such brokenness and sin?

Then God opened Isaiah's eyes. He saw the shalom vision. The wholeness God willed at the dawn of creation will come to pass among the people and nations of this world (read again the full description of the vision in Is. 2:2-5):

> The Lord shall judge between the nations,
> and shall decide for many peoples;
> and they shall beat their swords into plowshares,
> and their spears into pruning hooks,
> nation shall not lift up sword against nation,
> neither shall they learn war anymore. (Isaiah 2:4)

Yes, the world Isaiah saw in the vision is a far cry from his own war-torn world and ours. But notice the crucial difference! In our world people and nations still fight for power and supremacy, lording it over one another. In the shalom vision the nations have surrendered their own self-centeredness and sovereignty as they bow to worship the Lord of all. The law of the Lord leads them in the paths of peace. The judgment of the Lord resolves the inequities of rich and poor, heals divisions, and provides a new foundation for unity. People of every nation and tongue walk together as sisters and brothers. Swords and spears are no longer needed for protection or attack. Weapons for fighting are reshaped into tools for feeding—plowshares and pruning hooks to cultivate a life of well-being and prosperity for all.

The shalom vision is God's gift to show us the direction in

which life and history are moving. The God who created order out of chaos in the beginning is acting now to heal the broken relationships that divide persons and families, set nations at odds, and cause humanity to abuse the rest of creation. It is not within our power to mend this fractured world. The shalom vision affirms that it is God who can and will establish peace in our midst. The work of shalom has already begun, for God has acted once and for all to heal the great division between humanity and himself. Isaiah envisioned the fulfillment of shalom in Zion. We have seen even more—God's peace revealed and accomplished by a person, Jesus Christ.

The Vision in Person: "Christ Is Our Peace"
In the fullness of time, God sent his Son, the Messiah, Jesus of Nazareth. In him God's peace plan entered a dramatic new stage. Shalom became visible in a person. . . .
Isaiah's vision has become a possibility here and now. Christ our peace "has made us both one." He has broken down the divisions of hostility, united warring factions in one body, and brought us back to God. Jew and Gentile, people of color and white, Russians and Americans, male and female, rich and poor—all can be united. This oneness is not achieved by human negotiation or compromise. It is accomplished by God through the reconciling cross.
Shalom envisions the future wholeness of God's kingdom. But with the coming of Christ, God's kingdom is no longer merely future. The kingdom is also present wherever God's people dare to cross boundaries and share the holy communion that Christ makes possible. The dividing walls are broken down. We are free to begin living out the peace God is building among us even now.

Living Toward Shalom
Shalom is both a vision and a task. It is something we wait for and something we are called to do while we wait.
The *vision* assures that God's peaceable kingdom will come. Knowing that shalom is the goal of *God's* activity in his-

tory, we have good reason for hope despite the evidence that the world is bent on destroying itself. This God who created harmony out of chaos in the beginning will reunite all things in Christ at the end. This vision of God's plan for the future strengthens us to be faithful here and now.

The *task* of shalom is to live the peace that God has already made possible. Isaiah did not sit idle waiting for the peaceable kingdom. He said, "Here am I! Send me" (Is. 6:8). Paul unfolded the mystery of God's peace plan and then urged the Ephesians: "I beg you to lead a life worthy of the calling to which you have been called" (Eph. 4:1). Shalom is an invitation to live toward the vision God has made known to us. The task is both demanding and challenging! Peacemakers demonstrate in their own lives the wholeness that will come to all.

We are called to live God's peaceable future now in very concrete ways—practicing forgiveness in personal relationships; working for justice in our society; using our voice and vote to shape national policy for peace; sharing the gospel of Christ's peace in word and deed; praying for our enemies, for our friends, and for the coming Kingdom. Shalom is both vision and task. Peacemakers need to keep this vital, biblical balance. When we are strengthened by the vision, our efforts for personal wholeness and peace in the world will not become frantic, fanatical or fatigued. When we are committed to the task, peace ceases to be a vague wish or pious platitude rarely practiced. In Christ our peace we see that shalom is both the goal of our journey and the way we are called to walk.

Peace With Justice: A Closer Look at Shalom

The Old Testament declares God's will for shalom, a world at peace. The New Testament proclaims that Christ has made peace possible by breaking down the walls of hostility that separate people from God and from each other. We are also involved because our Lord calls us to be peacemakers in our own time. Many people *wish* for peace. Some work to *keep* the peace. But what does it mean to *make* peace? A closer look at the shalom vision gives some specific directions for our peacemaking.

Peace Here and Now

Popular notions about peace tend to be vague and wishful. "Peace" is the absence of conflict, an inner serenity apart from the world's problems, or a perfect state of affairs which God will accomplish some day while we passively wait. The peace described in the Bible is much more practical and down to earth. Shalom is a life of wholeness lived in covenant relationship with God. This basic well-being is something for God's people to enjoy themselves and to share with others here and now!

A sampling of shalom passages shows the earthliness of shalom. For individuals shalom means long life and physical as well as spiritual health (Prov. 3:2); the blessing of children and grandchildren (Ps. 37:37); economic well-being (Ps. 147:14, Zech. 8:12); protection in danger (Ex. 4:18); adequate food and shelter (Judg. 19:20f); and even safe, restful sleep (Ps. 4:8). For families and nations a life of shalom brings prosperity (I Chrn. 4:40); national security (2 Ki. 20:19); the end of strife (Josh. 9:15); and harmony between human society and nature (Is. 11:6-9, Ezek. 34:25).

Our peacemaking task begins to take shape when we compare this vision of peace and security to the plight of many people in our world today. Robert McAfee Brown draws some important conclusions:

> Concern for shalom, or peacemaking, doesn't just involve keeping us out of war (though it obviously includes that); it also includes seeing to it that people have enough to eat; that they are not undernourished or malnourished; that they can go to bed at night without fear that someone will spirit them off to prison; that the society will be so planned that there is food enough to go around; that the politics of the country (and of the world) are so arranged that every body's basic needs are met . . . There's still plenty of work to keep peacemakers busy. (*Making Peace in the Global Village*, p. 14)

If shalom is well-being and security for the whole human family, then peacemaking is *any* activity that helps make the vision real for people today. Of course there are powerful factors and forces that deny shalom: world hunger, torture and denial of human rights, an escalating arms race, violence and crime in the streets, the growing gulf between rich and poor. Where do peacemakers begin when faced with such enormous obstacles? Pope John once offered advice both pointed and biblical: "If you want peace, work for justice."

The Path to Peace is Justice

Then justice will dwell in the wilderness,
*   and righteousness abide in the fruitful field*
And the effect of righteousness will be peace.
*   and the result of righteousness, quietness and trust forever.*
My people will abide in peaceful habitation,
*   in secure dwellings, and in quiet resting places.*
                                                    (Isaiah 32:16-18)

This passage and many other's teach that peace and justice are intimately related, like two sides of the same coin. Peace in the world will come when there is justice for all people of the world. The Hebrew words "justice" and "righteousness" are linked together many times in the Old Testament: "But let justice roll down like waters, and righteousness like an ever-flowing stream" (Am. 5:24). These two Hebrew words in one figure of speech mean social justice, an essential ingredient of shalom.

Biblical justice is more than law enforcement, social order, or the ruling of human courts which sometimes favor the powerful at the expense of the weak (Amos 5:10-15). Justice in the Bible means granting to every person their worth, dignity, and due as children of God and members of the human family. Justice also refers to God's zeal on behalf of people who have been denied this basic dignity.

In Justice and Violence

Peacemakers need to understand the many ways, often

subtle and hidden, that injustice disturbs and destroys the peace. War is a major threat but certainly not the only one. Shalom is shattered whenever people of power and privilege exploit the weak for their own personal, political, or economic gain. How can there be peace in a world where some live lavishly while many starve, in a nation where civil rights are trampled and citizens exploited, in personal relationships where one person or group dominates, uses, and abuses others? Such injustice breeds violence. As the Bible sees it, such injustice *is* violence because the humanity and God image of persons are violated by it.

Dom Helder Camara, a Brazilian church leader and defender of the poor, helps modern peacemakers understand this biblical connection between injustice and violence. He writes about "the spiral of violence" which traps both oppressors and the oppressed in a continuing cycle of conflict. Camara identifies *three* kinds of violence that fuel the vicious spiral.

The first is *injustice*. Land owned by peasant farmers is seized by their government and sold to a corporation which hires the same peasants to work the land at wages so low their families suffer malnutrition, disease, and death. Or racist policies force minority youth to endure poor housing, inferior schools, poverty, and high unemployment. Or security police seize innocent people and hold them without trial. This first form of violence is often called "invisible violence" because only the victims are aware of it. Physical conflict need not be involved. The violence is institutional. The unjust structures of a society violate the humanity and well-being of some people in it.

Because oppressed people seek the same freedoms we enjoy, injustice breeds a second form of violence—*revolt*. Peasant farmers form unions and strike for fair wages. Blacks in Watts or Soweto riot in angry protest over inhuman living conditions. Guerrilla groups take up arms to overthrow a government that enriches a few and impoverishes many.

The authorities usually respond to revolt with a third form of violence—*repression*. The army or the secret police move in to crush the labor union, arrest protesters, or do battle with revolutionaries. This violence attempts to restore "law and order" and return to the status quo. But repression usually involves even greater injustice which ignites further revolt. And the spiral whirls faster!

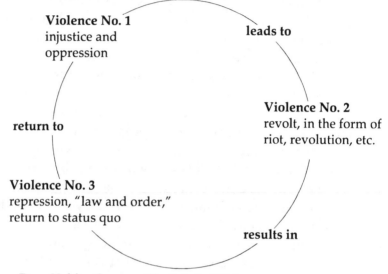

Violence No. 1
injustice and
oppression

leads to

Violence No. 2
revolt, in the form of
riot, revolution, etc.

return to

Violence No. 3
repression, "law and order,"
return to status quo

results in

from Dom Helder Camara, *The Spiral of Violence*

It is not enough to be concerned when violence becomes visible and physical in revolt. In fact, it is too late! The spiral begins when people are victimized by the invisible violence of injustice. Peacemakers know that the spiral is broken and peace becomes possible only when this first form of violence is overcome. We know because that is just how God works in history to bring about shalom.

Let My People Go!

Then the Lord said, "I have seen the affliction of my people in Egypt and have heard their cry because of their task masters; I know their sufferings, and I have come down to deliver them out of the hand of the Egyptians . . . "

(Exodus 3:7-8)

In the exodus God acted with power and love to free a band of helpless slaves. God revealed himself as the Lord "who executes justice for the oppressed," (Ps. 146:7). The exodus was no isolated event. This pattern was repeated many times in Israel's history: the people cried for help; the Lord heard their cry; the Lord delivered them . God's mighty deeds of liberation also set the pattern for his people's compassion toward the afflicted.

You shall not pervert the justice due the sojourner or to the fatherless, or take a widow's garment in pledge; but you shall remember that you were a slave in Egypt and the Lord your God redeemed you from there . . .

(Deuteronomy 24:18)

God's people themselves had been freed from bondage by a God who does justice in the earth. They had no right to oppress others. To do injustice is to break God's covenant, the only sure foundation for shalom.

How often the people of Israel forgot their liberating God and the justice and righteousness his covenant required! The oppressed soon became oppressors. Then the prophets proclaimed God's judgment on Israel and spoke out for the voiceless poor:

Woe to those who decree iniquitous decrees,
*   to turn aside the needy from justice*
*   and to rob the poor of my people of their right . . .*
What will you do in the day of punishment,
*   In the storm which will come from afar?*

(Isaiah 10:1-3)

God works justice for the oppressed even against his own people when necessary. But the promise of shalom is always present for those who join God on the side of the poor. "Did not your father eat, drink, and do righteousness? Then it was well with him. He judged the cause of the poor and needy. Is it not this to know me, says the Lord?" (Jer. 22:15-16) By struggling for the freedom and dignity of others, we come to know the

Lord better ourselves!

Jesus' Ministry of Justice and Peace

In Jesus we see the fullness of God's justice as well as God's love. Jesus came to save sinners. He also preached good news to those who are *sinned against*—the victims of human greed and exploitation. Early in his ministry Jesus proclaimed himself as the one the prophets promised, the Servant of the Lord sent to deliver the poor and oppressed:

The Spirit of the Lord is upon me,
because he has annointed me to preach good news to the poor,
He has sent me to proclaim release to the captives
and recovering of sight to the blind,
to set at liberty those who are oppressed . . .

(Luke 4:18)

In Jesus we see clearly the shalom of God working for human dignity and wholeness. He fed the hungry, healed the sick, and ministered to social outcasts. He dared to challenge the religious, economic, and political institutions that caused their pain. Jesus did more than minister to the victims of injustice. He identified with them. He put his own face on the faceless poor. Jesus calls his followers to serve him by serving them. "Truly, I say to you, as you did it to one of the least of these my bretheren you did it to me." (Mt. 25:31-46) Peacemakers should ponder this gospel mystery. Jesus is the Poor One among us today! We meet him in the poor and powerless people of our world. Their cry for justice is his cry for justice. The ministry of Jesus clearly defines a major peacemaking task: "to set at liberty those who are oppressed."

The Task of Peace and Justice Today

God gives his people power to break the spiral of violence in our world. We do so by doing justice. This peacemaking task demands a great deal from us. First, we must try to *listen* to the cry of millions of poor and oppressed peoples. This listening is not easy for many of us, because the comforts and privileges we enjoy keep us far removed from their pain. Second, we must be willing to *hear* the message of powerless people. They tell us they are hurting, but also that affluent Americans and others benefit from the systems that cause their suffering. Food exports like sugar, bananas and coffee on our tables often come at the expense of poor peasants denied land to grow food for themselves. Racist attitudes and policies deny minority people their dignity and rightful share in society's benefits. American taxes sometimes support military regimes that maintain power through torture and repression. Wealthy nations spend billions of dollars on weapons while millions of people in our world suffer hunger, poverty and disease. Peacemakers pray earnestly and often, "Lord, give us ears to hear."'

Once we have listened and heard, peacemakers *act* by God's power to do justice. By practicing a simple lifestyle resources are freed for sharing with the poor. By involvement in the political process politicians can be held accountable for just national policies. Many Christians multiply their influence by joining organizations that work for peace and justice. . . .

Jesus Christ is God's salvation for sinners and for those who are sinned against. He has broken down the barriers of race, class, sex, wealth, and geography. Because Christ has broken down these "walls of hostility" (Eph. 2:14), the church must live as a sign of this shalom in the world community.

Questions

1. What does *shalom* mean? How is shalom a vision? A task?
2. The authors say that shalom is "practical and down to earth." Describe ways that this is so.
3. Describe Dom Helder Camara's "spiral of violence." How can the spiral be broken?
4. What are the tasks of peace and justice today?

Prayers for a
Social Awakening

Allen Verhey

*Allen Verhey is a teacher of religion at Hope College. This
selection is from his book* Living the Heidelberg. *Verhey
examines the Lord's Prayer using the Heidelberg Catechism
(questions and answers 115-117) as a springboard. He calls
for honesty and sincerity in our praying and asks that our
prayers carry a genuine social concern as we engage the
world each day.*

Q. *No one in this life*
can obey the Ten Commandments perfectly:
Why then does God want them
preached so pointedly?

A. *First, so that the longer we live*
the more we may come to know our sinfulness
and the more eagerly look to Christ
for forgiveness of sins and righteousness.

Second, so that,
while praying to God for the grace of the Holy Spirit,
we may never stop striving
to be renewed more and more after God's image,
until after this life we reach our goal: perfection.
—Heidelberg Catechism Q & A 115

Q. *Why do Christians need to pray?*

A. *Because prayer is the most important part*
of the thankfulness God requires of us.

And also because God gives his grace and Holy Spirit
only to those who pray continually and groan inwardly,
asking God for these gifts and thanking him for them.
                              —Heidelberg Catechism Q & A 116

Q. *How does God want us to pray*
   so that he will listen to us?

A. *First, we must pray from the heart*
   to no other than the one true God,
   who has revealed himself in his Word,
   asking for everything he has commanded us to ask for.

   Second, we must acknowledge our need and misery,
   hiding nothing,
   and humble ourselves in his majestic presence.

   Third, we must rest on this unshakable foundation:
   even though we do not deserve it,
   God will surely listen to our prayer
   because of Christ our Lord;
   That is what he promised us in his Word.
                              —Heidelberg Catechism Q & A 117

Lord, teach us to pray.
                              —Luke 11:1

You invoke as Father him who judges each one impartially.
                              —1 Peter 1:17

A mighty fortress is our God,
A bulwark never failing;
Our helper he, amid the flood
of mortal ills prevailing.
For still our ancient foe
Doth seek to work us woe;
His craft and power are great,

And armed with cruel hate,
On earth is not his equal.

Did we in our own strength confide,
Our striving would be losing;
Were not the right Man on our side,
The Man of God's own choosing.
Dost ask who that may be?
Christ Jesus, it is he;
Lord Sabaoth his name,
From age to age the same,
And He must win the battle.
                        —*"A Mighty Fortress Is Our God," Martin Luther.*

It remains for us to seek in him, and in prayers to ask of him,
what we have learned to be in him.

                        —*Calvin,* Institutes, 3, xx, 1

The heart of the Christian ethos is that those who are freed and
summoned to pray "Thy kingdom come" are also freed and sum-
moned to use their freedom to obey the command that is given
therewith and to live for their part with a view to the coming
kingdom.

                        —*Karl Barth,* The Christian Life

The closing section of the catechism comments on the Lord's
Prayer. Nowhere is the Heidelberg's reputation for devotional
quality more deserved: each answer is itself a beautiful short
prayer. And nowhere is the catechism's social interest more fit-
tingly expressed: each beautiful little prayer for the reign of
God's grace nurtures certain social intentions and dispositions.

The catechism turns to prayer after dealing with the law.
Acknowledging that even the holiest make only a small beginning in the obedience God permits and requires, the Heidelberg insists that the commandments, nevertheless, are to be
preached pointedly. Such preaching is important "so that,
while praying to God for the grace of the Holy Spirit, we may

never stop striving to be renewed more and more after God's image" (Q & A 115).

Prayer and "striving to be renewed more and more after God's image" are inseparable. The intention of prayer is not to get things out of God but rather to get ourselves formed and reformed by the mind of God in Jesus Christ. Prayer is thus part of our gratitude (Q & A 116). Prayer does not evade life with its problems and ambiguities and perplexities; it embraces life—that life which God gives and claims—and asks God for the grace and power to live it as he permits. Prayer does not negate this world and this history in some spiritual flight to God; it affirms God's creative power and providential care in this world and this history and asks God to establish his cosmic reign against the powers of evil and injustice which still threaten and frustrate God's purpose. Prayer does not blind us to this world; it asks God for eyes to see it in the light of God's righteousness in Christ.

The life that is permitted and required of us—which includes our social, political, economic life—drives us to prayer, to look to God in Christ, the author and perfecter of our life; and prayer drives us back to life when it renews our faith and our reliance on the righteousness of Christ. Prayer is not some pious duty that stands apart and separated from the other duties of our Christian life; it is an utter necessity *because* of our other duties and the most important resource for the comfort and courage to live as God permits in all our living. Perhaps Calvin said it best: "It remains for us to seek in him, and in prayers to ask of him, what we have learned to be in him" (III, xx, 1).

Toward Honesty in Prayer

It is little wonder, then, that Calvin and the catechism both maintain that prayer must be "from the heart" (Q & A 117). It may not be merely a pious ritual; it may not be merely a mechanical exercise; it may and must be "from the heart." Simply to mouth the words of confession is not to pray; we must honestly "humble ourselves in his majestic presence" (Q

& A 117). Simply to let petitions for renewal trip over our lips is not to pray; we must honestly "rest on this unshakable foundation" of God's grace which also claims us. To pray "from the heart," to pray honestly, to feel the hurting sting of our need and misery, and to see the humbling and joyous vision of the life the Lord promises and permits—that is what prayer must be (cf. Q & A 117).

Honesty in prayer has social implications. To pray for the death of the racial lie that plagues ourselves and our society and then continue in our apathy and indifference to the racial situation is not to have prayed "from the heart." To pray regularly and piously for the hungry or the poor and then go on our way unconcerned about the poor in our world and in our communities is not to have prayed "from the heart." Such prayers are more like blasphemy than prayer. And God said, "Even though you make many prayers, I will not listen; your hands are full of blood" (Isa. 1:15). But that exactly is the tragedy of so much Christian prayer—that Christian men and women so seldom bridge the chasm between prayer and practice. It is a kind of schizophrenia that leaves us tragically divided against ourselves.

Not so for the catechism. Prayer is tied to "striving to be renewed more and more after God's image" (Q & A 115). And not so for our faithful Savior, Jesus Christ. When he prayed, "Father, forgive them," he laid down his life for God's fulfillment of that prayer.

When the church of which I am a member first declared a day of prayer for racial reconciliation, they recognized that connection between prayer and work, *ora et labora:* "Members of the Christian Reformed Church, through persevering prayer and the diligent use of their Spirit-given talents, ought to labor unceasingly to cause the light of the gospel of reconciliation to shine upon all men so that the hate engendered in the present racial crisis by the prince of darkness may be speedily dissipated."

Persevering prayer and unceasing labor—that is what praying "from the heart" comes to. The "comfortable" mouthing of phrases of confession (even confession of our social sins) and of petitions for renewal (even the renewal of society) has little to do with the costly comfort of the catechism. Our comfort permits and demands a life of prayer; it gives us the courage for a life of active prayer and prayerful activity—even socially and politically and economically.

In its exposition of the Lord's Prayer, it is worth observing, the catechism adds very little new material. The themes have all been stated before. For example, Qs & As 120 and 121 are closely related to Qs & As 26-28; Qs & As 122-124 are closely related to the material on Christian obedience. Q & A 125 is close to Q & A 27; Q & A 126, to Qs & As 56-60; Q & A 127, to Q & A 114. What is new in this section is that the knowledge worked through earlier is turned to petition.

The Christian faith exists as hope and prayer. The norm for belief is the norm for prayer *(lex credendi lex orandi)*. The catechism would reject any antithesis between doctrine and piety. And it has been the single point of this book that it would also reject any antithesis between piety or doctrine and engagement in the social and political problems of our life together. Christian faith exists as hope and prayer and as obedience. It is "active in love." The norm for belief is the norm for prayer is the norm for action *(lex credendi lex orandi lex agendi)*.

The Social Meaning of the Lord's Prayer

The Lord's Prayer took shape as a protest against the empty phrases and vain repetition with which people try to flatter God and themselves (Matt. 6:7-8). And, indeed, its simplicity and sincerity crystallized the shape of faith as prayer. But its very greatness has made it so familiar that we need to remind ourselves not simply to let the words trip over our tongues. The prayer is committed to memory so easily that we need to will the pause that commits our lives in such prayer. For prayer, too, is not simply a matter of tongue but of life.

When Jesus asked us to say "Our Father," he reminded us of our unity and solidarity. He did not teach us to pray "My Father," as though each of us stood alone. Before God no one stands alone. Before God each person stands related to those near and far, those whom he likes and dislikes, those whom she serves or oppresses. And we "invoke as Father him who judges each one impartially" (1 Pet. 1:17).

Before him we stand with our neighbors in unity and also in equality, for he is no respecter of persons. The master comes to God as one with and equal to the slave when he says "Our Father." The male comes as one with and equal to the female. The white comes as one with and equal to the black. The American comes as one with and equal to the citizen of the Third World. We all clasp hands and approach God together through the Christ in whom there is neither master nor slave, neither male nor female, neither American nor Third-World citizen.

"The childlike awe and trust that God through Christ has become our Father" is "basic to our prayer" (Q & A 120), and it includes our duty to love our brothers and sisters. It is, as Calvin said (3, xx, 38), "For if one father is common to us all, and every good thing that can fall to our lot comes from him, there ought not to be anything separate among us that we are not prepared gladly and wholeheartedly to share with one another." Then "what we ask in faith" (Q & A 120) and what we "expect . . . for body and soul from his almighty power" (Q & A 121) may not be individualistic either, may not be inattentive to the needs of all our neighbors. To quote Calvin again, "All prayers ought . . . to look to that community which our Lord has established in his kingdom and his household" (3, xx, 38). Since that kingdom is a cosmic kingdom, through prayer the believer embraces as brothers and sisters in Christ "not only those whom he at present sees and recognizes as such but all men who dwell on earth" (3, xx, 38).

The petitions that follow the invocation of God as "our Father" express our hope and desire that his future reign will be established soon and already take effect in our lives. Jesus came announcing that kingdom and, in his works and words, made its power felt; and he now sits at God's right hand. Therefore, the petitions "Hallowed be thy name; Thy kingdom come, Thy will be done, on earth as it is in heaven" are said in gratitude for the decisive victory God has won in Jesus Christ even while we "groan inwardly" (Q & A 116) together with the whole creation (Rom. 8:22, 23) for the final unveiling of God's cosmic triumph.

Such petitions nurture lives of humility and confidence and hope (Q & A 117)—lives lived under the sign of the cross, out of the power of the resurrection, and toward the new age of God's peaceable kingdom. Such petitions put us at the disposal of God's name, his "power, wisdom, kindness, justice, mercy, and truth" in "all our living" (Q & A 122). They enlist us against the forces of evil in this world, including injustice and enmity and greed and deceit, until all submit to his rule (Q & A 123). They commit us to obedience, to the costly comfort that receives the permission and command of God with gratitude and "without any back talk" (Q & A 124).

These requests are not otherworldly or individualistic. We are not asking to be rescued from our world or from our communities. Rather, we are asking confidently, hopefully, and humbly that God will reign in our world and in our communities.

Honesty in such a prayer will have significant social effects. If, with these petitions, we yearn for the final consummation of God's victory in Christ, the final destruction of the devil's work, the complete surrender of those principalities and powers that alienate people from God's permissions and from each other, then we must live in yearning too. We must be "straining forward to what lies ahead" (Phil. 3:13), a peaceable kingdom. If we pray in gratitude and in hope for God's victory, then in the interim between resurrection and consummation we must fight the good fight, we must enlist in the battle against human suffering, against hunger and sickness, against war and poverty, against human injustice, against economic inequities and political tyrannies, against racial prejudice and international exploitation. The battle must be joined against "every force" (Q & A 123) which helplessly and hopelessly continues the revolt against God and his intentions with the creation.

That is why the catechism includes the petition "Keep your church strong, and add to it" (Q & A 123). The church serves the kingdom. It yearns for it, and its yearning is its striving against the devil and all his works. Of course, the church knows "His craft and power are great, and armed with cruel hate." It knows "Did we in our own strength confide, our striving would be losing." And therefore it prays. The church knows it cannot itself usher in the new heaven and the new earth; it can only pray for it. But it also knows that Christ has won the victory and "more and more" (Q & A 123) submits to him. It knows there are some things it can and may do which, although they will not themselves usher in the new age, may at least relieve the bitterness of someone's tears, may at least lessen the load of suffering someone carries, may at least make some social relation relatively more just, and which may indeed bring abundant joy and justice to our neighbors. Every member of the church may know that such is "the work he is called to" (Q & A 124).

The next petitions deal with our needs, but without forgetting either God's glory or our neighbor's good. Indeed, they are the bold requests that already, even now in this sad world, God's future and Christ's righteousness may be known and lived, that the heavenly banquet may be already experienced in common bread, that the eschatological joy of forgiveness may be already known in forgiving and being forgiven, and that God's final triumph may strengthen and protect us even now against temptation and evil.

Among these the prayer for daily bread takes first place. In the Bible "bread" is used in two senses—as that which is necessary for life and as an earthly symbol of God's eternal grace. The petition asks God already now for a foretaste of the future manna, of the banquet of his kingdom, but it also asks him to satisfy our physical needs now. Jesus never exalted the soul at the expense of the body. He exalted the whole person. And while the whole person does not live by bread alone, Jesus never belittled the elemental physical needs of people. Neither may we. To pray for a foretaste of the heavenly banquet is to pray for food and nourishment—not just for me, but for *us*, for all those with whom we stand in this petition, with all God's children. Together, in solidarity, we ask for our daily bread. We gather at a common table. There before God shall we habitually take more than our share and leave others hungry?

The catechism reminds us that God is "the only source of everything good" (Q & A 125, cf. Q & A 27) and that nothing God made is god (Q & A 125). The Heidelberg knows that the God who will reign is the creator and provider, and that his care is the world's constant companion. And it reminds us that these affirmations and this petition can only be made in spite of and in the spite of hunger and poverty.

The remaining petitions recognize that "in this life even the holiest have only a small beginning of this obedience" (Q & A 114). They ask boldly for the forgiveness of our pasts and deliverance in our futures; and again the petitions are in and for a community. In pleading for our forgiveness, we commit ourselves to forgive our neighbors (Q & A 126). God's permissions do not include being pious toward him while we are merciless toward our neighbors (cf. Matt. 18:21-35). Rather, his permission and our petition are to shape our lives to his forgiveness and righteousness.

The realism of the last petition recognizes that "our striving would be losing" were it not for the power of the one to whom we pray and on whom we rely (Q & A 127). But it is not a request for leave; it is a battle cry. This petition enlists us in just such a world as this one; it enlists us to resist the resistance to God's intentions, to fight the skirmishes, confident that in Christ we "do begin to live according to all, not only some, of God's commandments" (Q & A 114), confident indeed that in Christ we will "finally win the complete victory" (Q & A 127).

We are not honest to God if we pray the Lord's Prayer content to pass through an evil world in safety and "comfort," leaving the world's evil unchallenged. The Lord's Prayer commits us to live in God's costly comfort, loving our neighbor while we are realistic about sin; responsible to God the creator, judge, and redeemer; confessing that God is creator and provider and that Jesus Christ is Lord; sharing in Christ and all his costly benefits; gratefully receiving all God's permissions to live a truly human life.

Prayers for a Social Awakening.

Ordinarily at this point in the chapter we have tried to see the social implications of the catechism with some more specificity. We have tried to follow the catechism's lead into our social lives. In this section the catechism leads to prayer. Its commentaries on the petitions of the Lord's Prayer are themselves prayers. And it seems fitting that we should end our discussion of the catechism, like the catechism itself, in prayers.

Our Father who art in heaven.

We are bold to address you as your son, Christ our Lord, himself has taught us. In our homes we learned to rely on the strength and goodness of our parents. We know how they loved and cared. We know how they suffered to give good things to their children (Q & A 120, Matt. 7:9-11). And your Son has taught us that we may rely still more confidently on your strength and goodness. So we come to you with "child-like awe and trust." It is from you that we "expect everything for body and soul" (Q & A 121, cf. Qs & As 26-28). We know that all things are from you and through you. Help us to treat all of your creation as good and nothing of your creation as god. Help us to live all our life in the certainty of your constant care and in spite of evil.

We come to you, together with all your children, united to them by the grace of your creation and redemption. We thank you for the wonderful variety of races and cultures in your world. Show us your presence even in those most alien to us, until our knowledge of your fatherly love is completed in our love for all our brothers and sisters. Remind us that we invoke as Father him who judges impartially (1 Pet. 1:17). Remind us that we come to you as Father only through Christ, your Son, in whom there is neither rich nor poor, neither male nor female, neither black nor white. And help us strive to be a community "renewed more and more after God's image" (Q & A 115).

Hallowed be thy name.

"Help us to really know you, to bless, worship, and praise

you for all your works and for all that shines forth from them: your almighty power, wisdom, kindness, justice, mercy, and truth" (Q & A 122). Help us to live in ways which acknowledge your name, your power and work in our history. Help us to keep free from the blasphemy of piously praying for social, racial, political, economic justice without being willing to make the patient effort necessary to fight injustice. "Help us to direct all our living"— including our living together, "what we think, say, and do"; including our social, racial, political, economic thoughts, words, and deeds—"so that your name will never be blasphemed because of us but always honored and praised" (Q & A 122). Forgive us that some think of you as the rich people's god or the white race's god or the western world's god. Renew us and our social life so that we find and honor your name in our neighbor's good and so that your power, wisdom, kindness, justice, mercy, and truth shine forth from our life together and from our presence in the world. Enlist us in your cause. Refuse our attempts to enlist you in ours. Help us to serve you. Destroy our presumption when we would have you serve us.

Thy kingdom come.
"Rule us by your Word and Spirit in such a way that more and more we submit to you" (Q & A 123). Help us to celebrate your kingship established in Christ and coming in completeness. And even now rule us as a "lover of justice" (Ps. 99:4); even now "judge the world with righteousness, and the peoples with equity" (Ps. 98:9); even now let justice and peace kiss each other and embrace the world (Ps. 85:10). Enable us to celebrate your kingship in the way you permit and require, by submission and obedience to that justice. Enable us under your kingship to be the humble kings who "defend the cause of the poor of the people, give deliverance to the needy, and crush the oppressor" (Ps. 72:4). We give you thanks for the company that acknowledges your kingship and strives for your cause. "Keep your church strong, and add to it" (Q & A 123). Enable her to be the servant of your kingdom, not her own. Through her may

your wise kingship "now be made known to the principalities and powers" (Eph. 3:10). Help her to discern your will amid the ambiguities of our social order and help her then to do your will, as the very image of her Lord.

"Destroy the devil's work" (Q & A 123). Destroy the terrible powers of institutionalized oppression and covetousness. Destroy racism and injustice. Destroy corruption and inequity. And permit us to be your instruments of righteousness, your tools of justice. Where there is hatred, make us tools of your love. Where there is injury, make us tools of your healing. Where there is division, make us tools of your unity. Where there is a racial lie, make us tools of your truth. Where there is oppression, make us tools of your deliverance. Wherever there is social evil, make us tools of your righteousness. "Do this until your kingdom is so complete and perfect that in it you are all in all" (Q & A 123).

Thy will be done, on earth as it is in heaven.

"Help us and all men to reject our own wills and to obey your will without any back talk" (Q & A 124). Our only comfort is that we are not our own but belong—body and soul, in life and in death, Sunday and Monday, at worship and at work, politically and economically—to our faithful Savior. Command us and give us the courage of our comfort. Comfort us and give us the grace of your command. "Your will alone is good." Save us from all unwillingness to learn your will, from clinging to our own plans and desires, from trying to limit the scope of your purposes. Save us from cowardice in following your lead, from allowing our ambitions to blur the vision of your will for us, from trying to receive your comfort without the cost. Save us from ignoring the responsibility of our place in your world. "Help everyone carry out the work he is called to as willingly and faithfully as the angels in heaven" (Q & A 124).

We pray that your will may be done in the marketplace, whether the marketplace be international trade or the corner grocery. We pray that your will may be done in assemblies, whether the assembly be the United Nations, the Senate, the City Council, or the Consistory.

Give us this day our daily bread.

Our Father, we stand together in this petition too. We thank you for all your good gifts and for the knowledge that we are all your children. Together then, as if at a common table, we ask for our daily bread. There we confess that some of us habitually take more than our share and leave others hungry. But we dare to pray that you will graciously behold your family and continue to be the provider of every good thing. Save us from misusing your gifts by our greed and self-ishness. Save us from indifference to the needs of all your chil-dren. Save us from acquiescence in their suffering and hunger. And permit us to glorify you in the stewardship that uses all your gifts for our neighbors' good.

So may we know "that you are the only source of every-thing good, and that neither our work and worry nor your gifts can do us any good without your blessing" (Q & A 125). Bless us then with food and with your costly blessing so that our participation in Christ may be acknowledged as participa-tion in the one who did not send the hungry multitudes away.

And forgive us our debts, as we also
have forgiven our debtors.

"Because of Christ's blood, do not hold against us, poor sinners that we are, any of the sins we do" (Q & A 126). For-give our sins and help us not to shrink from confession. We would not hide our sins from you, for we believe that you know us as we are and yet you love us. Teach us to respect ourselves for your sake. And permit us so to accept and wel-come, to respect and love, to forgive all our neighbors "as evi-dence of your grace in us" (Q & A 126).

Forgive as well "the evil that constantly clings to us" (Q & A 126), the unrest of the world to which we contribute and in which we share. Forgive the inequities which mark and mar our world but with which we are often aligned and to which we are often indifferent. Forgive the preoccupation with material stan-dards, the discrimination against persons of different color, the indifference to the poor "that constantly clings to us." And forgive us Christians for being so unsure of your comfort that we are unwilling to announce it and to live it and to bear its cost. Forgive us and renew us. Raise us from the paralysis of guilt into "the wholehearted joy in God through Christ" so that we "delight to do every kind of good" (Q & A 90).

And lead us not into temptation,
but deliver us from evil.

Father, "by ourselves we are too weak to hold our own even for a moment" (Q & A 127). We do not ask for release from the struggle; we ask for your gracious and demanding presence with us. You have won the victory over the devil, the world, our flesh, the principalities and powers. We pray that we may participate in your victory by your demanding grace. We pray that we may not be tempted to avoid the cost, the cross. Help us to take up his passion, his patient love, and to follow him. Show us the way of the cross. Show us the reality which may shape and reform our social intentions and actions. Show us the reality which may criticize and redefine our political and economic vocations. Show us the reality that enlists us against the pride of power and the sloth of worldly comfort. Show us the power and the comfort of the cross. So "uphold us and make us strong with the strength of your Holy Spirit, so that we may not go down to defeat in this spiritual struggle, but may firmly resist our enemies until we finally win the complete victory" (Q & A 127).

For thine is the kingdom, and the power,
and the glory, forever.

"We have made all these requests of you because, as our all-powerful king, you not only want to, but are able to give us all that is good" (Q & A 128). Few of us, Father, are people of very great influence and we wonder sometimes how our prayers can affect society and business and politics. But we know that hunger and oppression and poverty and racism are not the conditions you will for your children. And so we pray to you as the all-powerful king to end them. Father, there are too many children whose lives are handicapped by pain or prejudice, by hatred or boredom, by luxury or poverty, by malnutrition or racism. We know and love some of these. We believe you know and love them all. Take them into the care and skill, the kindness and severity, the love and justice, of your own hands. And help us to be your own hands.

"Your holy name, and not we ourselves. should receive all the praise, forever" (Q & A 128).

Amen.
"This is sure to be! It is even more sure that God listens to my prayer, than that I really desire what I pray for" (Q & A 129). That's the focus of prayer: to say "Amen" to God's intentions, including his social intentions. That's the focus of the catechism: the costly comfort which says "Amen" to God's intentions. May that be the focus of our social life: to say "Amen" to God's intentions.

This book has not tried to say "the last word" about either the catechism or the social message entrusted to the church. It has only intended to be a helpful word, to encourage the churches to think, talk, and pray about their social responsibilities in the light of their confession. But if there must be a last word, then let it be "Amen"—"Amen" to God's intentions for his creation's flourishing.

Questions

1. Calvin's comment is worth remembering: "It remains for us to seek in him, and in prayers to ask of him, what we have learned to be in him." State this in your own words.
2. In what ways should Christians say "Amen" to God's intentions in the earth?

Acknowledgments

Defining Morality

"The Three Parts of Morality" from *Mere Christianity* by C.S. Lewis. Reprinted by permission of HarperCollins Publishers - London.

"Commands for Fiddlers" from *Mere Morality: What God Expects from Ordinary People* by Lewis B. Smedes. Copyright © 1983. Reprinted by permission of Wm. B. Eerdmans Publishing Co.

"Sin" by Philip Yancey from *Christianity Today*, March 6, 1987, 30-34. Reprinted by permission.

"Hardness and Freedom" from *Fearfully and Wonderfully Made* by Paul W. Brand and Philip Yancey. Copyright © 1980 by Paul Brand and Philip Yancey. Used by permission of Zondervan Publishing House.

"Law and Morality" from *Wishful Thinking* by Frederick Buechner. Copyright © 1973 by Frederick Buechner. Reprinted by permission of Harper-Collins Publishers.

Making Moral Choices

"38 Who Saw Murder Didn't Call the Police" by Martin Gansberg from The New York Times, March 16, 1964. Copyright © 1964 by The New York Times Company. Reprinted by permission.

"Conformity: A Way Out" from *The Human Connection: How People Change People* by Martin Bolt. Reprinted by permission of InterVarsity Press.

"Shooting an Elephant" from *Shooting an Elephant And Other Essays* by George Orwell. Copyright © 1950 by Sonia Brownell Orwell and renewed 1978 by Sonia Pitt-Rivers. Reprinted by persmission of Harcourt Brace Jovanovich, Inc.

"The Reuben Option" from *Walking on Thorns, The Call to Christian Obedience* by Allan Boesak. Copyright © 1984. World Council of Churches, Geneva, American edition by Wm. B. Eerdmans Publishing Co. Used by permission.

"A Chicken Sexer's Tough Choices" by George K. Brushaber from *Christianity Today*, April 7, 1989. Reprinted by permission.

"Prayers of Steel" from *Cornhuskers* by Carl Sandburg. Copyright © 1918 by Holt, Rinehart and Winston, Inc. and renewed 1946 by Carl Sandburg. Reprinted by permission of Harcourt Brace Jovanovich, Inc.

Exploring Issues

Work

"Working People's Voices" from *Working* by Studs Terkel. Copyright © 1972, 1974 by Studs Terkel. Reprinted by permission of Pantheon Books, Inc., a division of Random House, Inc.

Racism/Bigotry

Medical Ethics

Peace